ABOLITION

Praise for **ANGELA DAVIS: AN AUTOBIOGRAPHY**

"Riveting; as fresh and relevant today as it was almost 50 years ago. The words fire off the page with humour, anger and eloquence." —*The Guardian*

"*Angela Davis: An Autobiography* continues to fulfill that goal as the rare book that even almost 50 years later feels timely and relevant. Maybe too relevant, considering how little has changed in the interim." —*Los Angeles Times*

"This new edition of the autobiography is meant to bring Davis and her story to a new generation of readers, who can still identify with her experiences. Still a key work in the areas of prison abolition and feminism, this reissue of a classic autobiography deserves a place of honor in any collection." —*Library Journal*

"A landmark text of left-wing Black politics." —Keeanga-Yamahtta Taylor, *New York Review of Books*

Praise for **FREEDOM IS A CONSTANT STRUGGLE**

"This is vintage Angela: insightful, curious, observant, and brilliant, asking and answering questions about events in this new century that look surprisingly similar to the last century." —Mumia Abu-Jamal

"Angela Davis once again offers us an incisive, urgent, and comprehensive understanding of systematic racism, the grounds for intersectional analysis and solidarity, and the importance of working together as equals to unmask and depose systems of injustice. . . . Angela Davis gathers in her lucid words our luminous history and the most promising future of freedom." —Judith Butler

Angela Y. Davis

ABOLITION

Politics, Practices, Promises

VOLUME I

Haymarket Books
Chicago, Illinois

Published in 2024 by
Haymarket Books
P.O. Box 180165
Chicago, IL 60618
773-583-7884
www.haymarketbooks.org
info@haymarketbooks.org

ISBN: 978-1-64259-964-0

Distributed to the trade in the US through Consortium Book Sales and Distribution (www.cbsd.com) and internationally through Ingram Publisher Services International (www.ingramcontent.com).

This book was published with the generous support of Lannan Foundation, Wallace Action Fund, and Marguerite Casey Foundation.

Special discounts are available for bulk purchases by organizations and institutions. Please email info@haymarketbooks.org for more information.

Cover and interior design by Rachel Cohen.

Printed in Canada by union labor.

Library of Congress Cataloging-in-Publication data is available.

10 9 8 7 6 5 4 3 2 1

Contents

Preface

These writings, which revolve around the prison, the prison industrial complex, and their abolition, represent collective and, given their relationship to developing movement practices, tentative efforts to comprehend processes responsible for ongoing and systematic forms of devastation in our society. Even as the institution of the prison has always revealed its inadequacies both as a guarantor of public safety and as rehabilitation for those subject to incarceration, it has nevertheless always advanced its own permanence.

Given that these essays were written during a historical moment that is quite different from the present one, I hope that there may be some contemporary value in the insights I share. More specifically, I hope that these writings may assist current movement participants and scholar-activists to appreciate the fact that, even though there may be no straightforward correlation between the changes we try to generate through radical movement practices and the actual consequences of those practices, these consequences can themselves potentially make a vast difference and may reveal changes that we might otherwise never have known we needed. Every essay in this collection represents thoroughly collaborative insights and practices, and, even though I may be listed as the author of the majority of the writings, I would never attempt to claim sole responsibility for the ideas they explore. I revisit them today for the purpose of apprehending the historical, intellectual, and practical progressions (and regressions) they enabled. And it is in this spirit that I offer them to a broader readership.

Over the last years—and especially since the uprisings of 2020 in response to the police murders of George Floyd, Breonna Taylor, and too many others—we have witnessed the emergence of a new collective awareness of the pervasiveness of carceral institutions and of our severely stunted capacity to imagine other ways of assuring public health and safety. Although regressive political forces are still in the process of attempting to expunge evidence of this surging consciousness, the political possibilities announced by abolitionist (as opposed to reform) strategies are increasingly recognized—sometimes even within mainstream public discourse.

This, of course, is not to argue that we are actually moving toward the abolition of prison and policing structures, but rather that public conversations about immigrant detention, the family policing system, policing more broadly, and incarceration as the major form of punishment cannot now proceed along with its previously unavoidable partner "reform" without acknowledging abolition as a possible strategy for more habitable futures.

At the same time this is not to imply that because abolition has been barred from mainstream discourse for so many decades, we are now satisfied with its mere acknowledgement. The acknowledgement of abolition as a possible strategy of addressing contemporary imprisonment practices allows us to proceed more confidently with our radical critiques of carcerality that reveal the persisting influences of ideologies linked to what are assumed to be defunct institutions. This moment of abolition—and of abolition feminism—helps us to create new points of departure for our ongoing efforts to reveal how repressive systems and structures that thrive on racism, heteropatriarchy, and class hierarchies hold us captive to the past, tether us to capitalism in so many ways, and prevent us from collectively envisioning socialist futures.

A good number of the articles collected in these two volumes (a second volume is forthcoming) reveal early attempts to think through some of the entanglements of what are generally considered to be acceptable modes of surveillance and punishment with elements of the institution of slavery. Many southern prisons—but not only prisons in the South—still bear the imprint of slavery and the convict lease system. At the end of the last century, as we were developing our analysis of the connection between slavery and the prison, we recognized that pursuing the path of examining that relationship as analogical—that is, imprisonment strategies bear a similarity to slavery—would be far less fruitful that postulating a different framework for the relationship, one that is genealogical rather than analogical. Indeed, there may be elements of similarity between the two institutions, but we can benefit much more from examining the history of ideas, ideologies, and institutions that reveal historical connections between slavery and the prison.

These essays attempt to reveal how we might think critically about institutions that constitute themselves as the very preconditions of our lives. For example, democracy—represented in public discourse as the institutional guarantee of civil rights and liberties—can also be thought of as the foundational condition of possibility for the prison, which, in turn, would have to be seen as a quintessentially democratic institution. Imprisonment as punishment consists of the revocation of democratic rights and liberties, thus philosophically their constitutive negation.

Why is it helpful to engage in such critical interrogations of the prison? Precisely because it assists us to overturn prevailing assumptions regarding the permanence—the ahistorical character—of the prison. If prisons as structures of state punishment are produced through history and are, in fact, closely associated with the rise of capitalism and its political expressions in bourgeois democracy—democracy for a rising class, but not for other sectors of society—then they can be expected to lose their historical relevance as history itself is transformed. And this process can be helped along, and hopefully accelerated, by mass movements and other kinds of radical political action. Such abolitionist engagement with our planet's carceral institutions pushes us to recognize that we cannot stop with the call to abolish prisons, jails, immigrant detention, policing structures, and other carceral institutions. In fact, as we do the work of imagining and developing strategies for new ways of generating safety and security in our societies, we can never accomplish this if we do not think and imagine beyond the carceral institutions we want to abolish.

As long as racial capitalism dictates exploitative economic scenarios around the world, the very conditions that gave rise to and enforced retributive modes of legality will continue to assert the permanence of racist-inspired carceral structures. It is thus entirely contradictory to call for the abolition of prisons (and police), and to engage in practices that leave capitalist democracy and indeed capitalism itself intact. Abolition is a mandate to create new social, economic, and political conditions that will render carceral punishment obsolete. It is a mandate for revolution.

Precisely because abolition is a mandate for revolution, these essays also attempt to demonstrate why gender is a central analytical category, overlapping and crosshatched with class and race as it helps to consolidate the ideological work of carceral institutions. Since these essays were originally published, we have developed more complex ways of theorizing gender.[1] Importantly, the emergence of a radical and influential trans movement has deepened our awareness of how such institutions function to routinely produce and reproduce norms that are putatively situated beyond the realm of critical interrogation. These essays were written in the period that predated the rise of a broad awareness of the way challenges to the gender binary can upend institutions and ideologies.

The radical and transformative work of LGBTQ leadership of abolitionist movements has resonated broadly, even in the absence of a specific awareness of how this leadership has accelerated deeper analyses and more powerful demands. It is not accidental that prior to the mass uprisings in the summer of 2020, one of the most recent political campaigns in the epicenter of the upsurge, Minneapolis, Minnesota, was the site of struggle to free CeCe McDonald, a Black trans woman who was sentenced to a men's prison for defending herself when a white man who did not believe that he should have to cohabit space with a trans person chose to use force and violence to convey this message. Thanks to the collective work of Minneapolis activists and their allies in the United States and beyond, CeCe was released after nineteen months. I highlight this particular campaign because an uprising that was simplistically represented by the media as a purely spontaneous response to the police lynching of George Floyd owed a great deal to this and many other movement campaigns. In fact, the massive protests in the summer of 2020 would be better understood as the culmination of years, even decades, of organizing work generated by activists representing a broad range of intersecting movements.

There are many lacunae in this collection, but perhaps the most important theme missing here is the major and transformative role played by the Free Palestine movement. I especially regret that the centrality of Palestine to the theory and practice of abolition is not represented in these essays because at this very moment the Israeli war against Gaza and the continued military occupation of Palestine by Israel has become the central focus of the world's attention. All of the writings in this volume were originally published before my own trip to Palestine in 2011 with a delegation of women-of-color and Indigenous feminist scholar-activists.[2] Over the course of our visit we had many discussions with individuals and organizations about the Israeli government's prison practices and about the carceral structures of quotidian life in the West Bank, where we spent most of our time. The period when we began to publicly emphasize close ties between antiracist struggles in the United States and beyond and the struggles against Israeli settler colonialism followed the 2014 protests against the police killing of Michael Brown in Ferguson, Missouri. Palestinian resisters in Palestine contacted Ferguson activists (including Palestinian Americans) in order to convey to them, as many people still remember, that the same brand of tear gas cannisters was being used both in Palestine and in Ferguson. Moreover, Palestinian resisters conveyed important advice to their Ferguson counterparts on how to reduce the deleterious effect of the gas. As a result of this and many other important exchanges, Palestine has become a touchstone of the Black Lives Matter era. This affiliation is reinforced by the immense numbers of young Black people participating at this moment in daily solidarity protests all over the United States and the world, reinforcing what Nelson Mandela said in 1997: "In extending our hands across the miles to the people of Palestine, we do so in the full knowledge that we are part of a humanity that is at one."[3]

As I try to frame the writings included in this volume, I am attending an international conference in Brisbane, Australia (November 8–10, 2023), called by the abolitionist organization Sisters Inside. Founded in 1999, the organization provides a range of services for women who are either incarcerated or formerly incarcerated as it simultaneously advocates for an end to imprisonment for women, girls, and people of all genders. As is currently happening in many gatherings, in many sites, in many countries, the conference has foregrounded the crucial effort to end the war in Gaza and to express solidarity with the struggle for justice in Palestine. Throughout the conference sessions, papers and other presentations are highlighting settler colonialism and the kinship among the struggles of Indigenous and Torres Strait Islanders' struggles in Australia, Māori struggles in Aotearoa, and the Palestinian resistance against an especially repressive form of settler colonialism that attempts to extend its geographic reach and its political control well into the twenty-first century. On display on the conference stage and illustrating that kinship were the closely positioned Aboriginal, Māori, and Palestinian flags.

Readers of this book should be aware of the vast number of important writings on abolition that have been published in the last two decades. I am fortunate to have been able to learn from all of them that I have had the occasion to read. I offer this collection as a small part of the history of the ideas that helped to generate this rapidly expanding literature on abolition.

I should note that I have not attempted to alter the sometimes outmoded expressions that remain as evidence of the era during which the pieces were written. For example, I tend to use "Native American," when today we are more likely to use "Indigenous" to emphasize that their presence predates by many thousands of years the imposition of the identity "American" on this part of the world. Instead of "Latinx," a still contested designation of people of Latin American descent, I use "Latino/a." Moreover, I had not yet learned how to indicate gender inclusivity more broadly by acknowledging gender identity beyond the controlling binary that has fortunately begun to lose its power. Moreover, we have learned how not to imprison human identities within concepts we unwisely thought of as neutral descriptors. All of these shifts bear witness to the fact that our struggles for freedom extend to the very language we use to represent them. Thus, as we have learned not to imprison human beings within the designation "slave," referring instead to "enslaved person," so we apply the same logic to "prisoner," "convict," and other terms that try to enact the very forms of repression they designate. Other changes reflect political and economic shifts, such as the shift from "Third Word" to the Global South (in part because the "second world" has disassociated from the socialism that rendered it a perceivable threat to the capitalist "First World").

While I cannot hope to offer a comprehensive list of what would be expressed differently had I updated my language (which would not have been possible without also updating both the descriptive and analytical context, which, in turn, would have meant writing entirely new essays), I also want to acknowledge my failure to recognize the extent to which ableist metaphors have become so pervasively attached to our modes of expression. Only with the aid of persistent, collective intellectual labor will we manage over time to expunge them from our vocabularies. And I do want to emphasize again how gratifying it has been to live long enough to witness changes that have only occurred because so many activists, organizers, and indeed also scholar-activists have labored painstakingly over years and lifetimes—not for the honor they may or may not receive, but for the knowledge that they have collectively contributed to the project of expanding the reach of freedom in the world.

—Angela Y. Davis
Brisbane, Australia
November 2023

PART I

Capitalism, Democracy, and the Prison

CHAPTER 1

The Prisoner Exchange

The Underside of Civil Rights*

Thinking recently about the meaning of the phrase "the prison industrial complex" led me to Derrick Bell's short story "The Space Traders," which opens with a description of the arrival on January 1, 2000, of a thousand spacecraft from a distant planet, whose mission is to exchange an immense supply of material resources for Black bodies:

> Those mammoth vessels carried within their holds treasure of which the United States was in most desperate need: gold, to bail out the almost bankrupt federal, state, and local governments; special chemicals capable of unpolluting the environment, which was becoming daily more toxic, and restoring it to the pristine state it had been before Western explorers set foot on it; and a totally safe nuclear engine fuel, to relieve the nation's all-but-depleted supply of fossil fuel. In return, the visitors wanted only one thing—and that was to take back to their home star all the African Americans who lived in the United States.[1]

Within the story, however—and for my purposes, this is a crucial point—it is rumored that US negotiators attempt to make a deal with the Space Traders that involves accepting the idea of the trade for all those in prison or in walled-off inner-urban environments

* First published in *Not for Sale: In Defense of Public Goods*, eds. Anatole Anton, Milton Fisk, Nancy Holmstrom (Westview Press, 2000), 131–44.

but allowing other, more affluent Black people to remain on Earth. The modern-day slave traders hold instead to a strict legal basis for inclusion, shunning almost all other category differentiation (save age and disability), and are set to deport all individuals whose birth certificates list them as "Black," regardless of economic status and of their social or political prestige. The exchange takes place on January 17, 2000, Martin Luther King Day, which, given the correlation of racial identity, interest, and historical memory that the story enacts, effectively eradicates the need for such a celebration:

> The dawn of the last Martin Luther King holiday that the nation would ever observe illuminated an extraordinary sight. In the night, the Space Traders had drawn their strange ships right up to the beaches and discharged their cargoes of gold, minerals, and machinery, leaving vast empty holds. Crowded on the beaches were the inductees, some twenty million silent men, women and children, including babes in arms. As the sun rose, the Space Traders directed them, first, to strip off all but a single undergarment; then to line up; and finally, to enter those holds which yawned in the morning light like Milton's "darkness visible." The inductees looked fearfully behind them. But, on the dunes above the beaches, guns at the ready, stood U.S. guards. There was no escape, no alternative. Heads bowed, arms now linked by slender chains, Black people left the New World as their forebears had arrived.[2]

Bell's parable about the "permanence of racism"—the subtitle of the collection in which the story was published—raises important and disturbing issues regarding the material, ideological, and psychic structures of racism and specifically about the nation's willingness to pursue a strategy "in which the sacrifice of the most basic rights of Blacks would result in the accrual of substantial benefits to all whites."[3] Predictably, this story has occasioned controversies, especially among scholars reluctant to criticize liberal ideas regarding the history of progress in US "race relations," and who consequently criticize Bell for overly pessimistic and historically obsolete narratives of racism. There is another way, however, to critically examine the version of racism presented in Bell's parable, while also taking seriously his insistence on the permanence—or at least, the persistence—of racism and on the role of the law in achieving this permanence through the institutionalization of racist ideologies.

I should note that we might raise serious questions, as does Michael Olivas, about the relationship between the historical frame of Bell's story and the histories of Native American, Latino, and other non-Black populations of color that might also "mark them as candidates for the Space Traders' evil exchange."[4] In his response to Bell's "Space Traders," Olivas considers the Cherokee Removal and Chinese Exclusion laws as well as the Bracero program and Operation Wetback. He concludes with the argument that these abiding historical patterns of expulsion can also be discovered in 1990s US immigration policy, which has created a scenario that ironically resonates with the parable of the Space Traders. Olivas points out that

> *The Chronicle of the Space Traders* is not . . . too fantastic or unlikely to occur, but rather the opposite: This scenario has occurred, and more than once in our nation's history. Not only have Blacks been enslaved, as the *Chronicle* sorrowfully notes, but other racial groups have been conquered and removed, imported for their labor and not allowed to participate in the society they built, or expelled when their labor was no longer considered necessary.[5]

By expanding Bell's ideas to include Latino, Native American, and Asian American populations in the scenario, as well as the class and gender axes that cut across the racial order, we can discover significant contemporary examples that increasingly involve the removal of substantial numbers of people from civil society.

If we focus specifically, nonetheless, on US Black history, even there we must ask if it is necessary for middle-class and politically conservative African Americans to be caught in the same web of racism as impoverished and working peoples for us to confirm the persistence of anti-Black racism in the United States. I want to suggest that although the racial sacrifice all African Americans are compelled to make in Bell's story may help us to understand conventional historical features of US racism, if we look further to note the exceptions to the mass transplantation and the rumored substitute proposal for the expatriation of prisoners and inner-urban dwellers, we find insights about the contemporary relationship between race and criminalization. Moreover, the Space Traders' plan confirms some of the most stereotypical thinking about labor and the capacity to work. The masculinized zones of the prison and inner city provide sites of raw potential profit but alone are insufficient to reproduce themselves. The feminization of the elderly and disabled condemns them to the zone of apparently benign neglect. The elderly and disabled, along with the 1,000 detainees delegated to hold Black property in trust—in case the group is ever returned—are the only Black people allowed to remain on Earth, useless to the Space Traders' purposes. In its division of the Black population, Bell's story exposes the insidious conjunction of capitalism with what is ostensibly the realm of justice, as the Space Traders' logic is in fact ironically coincident with prison practice in its acknowledgment that prisoners and the un- and underemployed (who will soon be subject to arrest) are already an ideal laboring population. This contravenes media portrayals of lazy prisoners who receive free room and board and who apparently prefer the constant surveillance of police to substantial employment in legalized economies. The compassionate release of prisoners who are elderly or ill (and thus can no longer have their labor effectively extracted), though hard-won, is surely one of the great ironies of prison activism, since the victory must always be measured against the system that no longer finds the released prisoner cost-effective.

passes 70 percent to 30 percent.[7] It may be enough to pause here to ask, taking Lani Guinier's suggestions a bit further,[8] how this constitutes democracy, given that those who would be sacrificed could not even be said to constitute the dissenting 30 percent, and that the individualist framework of "one man/one vote" (which in its current antifeminist register already betrays its own insufficiency) does not and cannot account for group interests. But how are we to understand those structures of racism that do not require legislation or that cannot be contested through a deployment of the abstract juridical subject who putatively remains the same across class, gender, and other axes of social power? If racism can only be confirmed in legal terms, the most salient examples of which are those segregation-era laws that the civil rights movement succeeded in eliminating, and if we can assume that laws targeting Black, Latino, or other subjects of color are not likely to reemerge, then it would be quite reasonable to accept the prevailing liberal discourse about the withering away of the racial order.

In Bell's parable, the fictional referendum for a new constitutional amendment requiring the conscription of all African Americans incites protests and engenders organizing efforts supporting the Black community. On the other hand, real forcible removal of more than a million people of color, presently incarcerated in a proliferating network of prisons and jails, has failed to incite widespread opposition and protest. Can this absence of activism be explained by the fact that no special legal procedures designating racial exclusion have been required to justify this "new segregation"?[9] The March 1999 Bureau of Justice Statistics report on "Prison and Jail Inmates at Midyear 1998" revealed that more than 1.8 million people are incarcerated in the country's prisons and jails.[10] The incarceration rate is 668 per 100,000—more than twice the rate in 1985 (313 per 100,000). One in every 150 US residents is in prison or jail. These figures are alarming on their face, but when one considers that approximately 70 percent of these 1.8 million prisoners are people of color,[11] one might meditate on the unacknowledged role of the law. Simultaneously enabling the racialization of punishment and rendering invisible its devastating impact on populations of color, the law constructs individual "criminals" about whom it can justly decide the question of guilt or innocence. The subject of the law is the abstract rights-bearing citizen and, indeed, the civil rights movement made great strides in deracializing the law and in extending its putative neutrality. However, the condition for the legal assimilation of racially marginalized communities is their conceptualization as aggregations of rights-bearing individuals who must appear separately before a law that will only consider their culpability and not its own. It has become increasingly difficult to identify the profound and egregious impact of racism, in and outside the law, on these communities. No racially explicit laws have facilitated the shifting of vast Black and Latino populations from the free world to the universe of the imprisoned. Still, one wonders how the civil rights community might have responded thirty-five years ago had it been informed that by the year 2000 there would probably be (according to policy analyst Jerome Miller) 1 million Black men and growing numbers of Black women behind bars.[12] Ironically, it is their relatively new status as equal rights-bearing subjects that prepares them to be deprived of such rights in the arena of punishment and profit, for such an equality implies equal responsibility. This recapitulates, as I will later explain, the historical origins of the prison.

In another article, "Racial Realism," Bell proposes the following evaluation of the limitations of civil rights strategies:

> As a veteran of a civil rights era that is now over, I regret the need to explain what went wrong. Clearly, we need to examine what it was about our reliance on racial remedies that may have prevented us from recognizing that these legal rights could do little more than bring about the cessation of one form of discriminatory conduct, which soon appeared in a more subtle though no less discriminatory form. The

> question is whether this examination requires us to redefine goals of racial equality and opportunity to which Blacks have adhered for more than a century. The answer must be a resounding yes.[13]

The emphasis in mainstream civil rights discourse on abstract equality and color blindness (these principles have been abundantly analyzed by critical race theorists[14]) has rendered it extremely difficult to develop a popular understanding of the way—as Bell suggests we should move beyond the civil rights paradigm—imprisonment practices recapitulate and deepen practices of social segregation. Because it cannot be demonstrated that the people of color who have been herded into the country's prisons and jails have been convicted and sentenced under laws that explicitly identify them in racial terms, the vastly disproportionate numbers of Black, Latino, Native American, and increasingly Asian American prisoners cannot be offered as material evidence of racism. The limitations of civil rights strategies of the past for considering the socioeconomic underpinnings of racism become even more clear when viewed in light of their contemporary deployment by opponents of affirmative action.

It may be more than a mere coincidence that the first state to abolish affirmative action in public education and employment has the largest prison population in the country.[15] The language used in the 1996 ballot measure known as the California Civil Rights Initiative (CCRI) was specifically designed to link this anti–affirmative action strategy to the civil rights movement of the 1950s and 1960s. Its advocates argued that by ending racial and gender preferences, quotas, and set-asides, it will be possible—evoking the oratory of Dr. Martin Luther King—to "realize the dream of a color-blind society."[16] Yet, in California, a Black man is five times more likely to be found in a prison cell than in a classroom at a public university.[17] Texas, which has the second largest prison population, has also abolished affirmative action. And at this writing, Florida, which has the fourth-largest prison population (New York has the third), has been identified by Ward Connerly, the Black regent of the University of California who chairs the CCRI, as the next state for the passage of a similar proposition eliminating affirmative action.* The concurrence of anti–affirmative action efforts and the rising prison populations in California, Texas, and Florida would not appear accidental if we were willing to understand the historical link between the assertion of democratic rights for some and their guarantee by the deprivation of rights for others. In the debate around affirmative action, we should therefore examine the general failure, even by those who are genuinely interested in the extension of civil rights, to account for those who are clandestinely deprived of their rights (albeit legally) by the prison industrial complex.

The main clause of the CCRI contains the following language: "The state shall not discriminate against, or grant preferential treatment to, any individual or group on the basis of race, sex, color, ethnicity, or national origin in the operation of public employment, public education, or public contracting."[18] As implied here, a fundamental supposition of anti–affirmative action advocacy is that civil rights are now equally distributed among the citizenry (*any individual or group*) without regard to race. To account for the obviously inferior social and economic status of those who are putatively equal before the law, opponents of affirmative action tend to use an explanatory framework of social and cultural dysfunctionality. For example, Nicholas Capaldi's argument against affirmative action, which does not seriously consider its impact on any groups other than African Americans, is based on his assertion that as a set of policies, it cannot effectively deal with the problem it is designed to solve, namely, "the failure of African Americans to participate fully in American life."[19]

> What is meant by participating fully? To participate fully in our society means to be an autonomous and responsible individual—to be law-abiding, self-supporting, self-defining, and constructively active in one or more institutions. Any

---

* Connerly retired from the Board of Regents in March 2005.

> statistical survey will confirm that with regard to unemployment, welfare, crime, family breakdown, and other social problems, African Americans are "overrepresented" remarkably out of proportion to their percentage in the population. What these statistics show is that not only are African Americans as a group not participating fully but far too many of them are socially dysfunctional.[20]

Thus, pursuing the logic of Capaldi's argument, political figures like Ward Connerly dismiss the "overrepresentation" of people of color in the country's prisons and on the welfare rolls as an outcome of this dysfunctionality. Such logic, in turn, misapprehends the relationship between the structural equality of law on its face and the predictable and racialized outcomes it masks. In this instance, the narrow interpretation of civil rights principles is thus effectively deployed to exclude consideration of forms of discrimination and marginalization that disappear behind legal equality and spatial segregation in the prison. Precisely because mainstream civil rights discourse—with its conventional Black/white framework—is predicated on such a narrow construction of citizenship, it fails to register not only the situation of prisoners but also those, like undocumented immigrants, who share similar status and often the same physical space in the prison. The Immigration and Naturalization Service* in fact constitutes an important sector of the prison industrial complex, with the largest numbers of armed federal agents and an expanding network of detention centers, and detainees overflowing into the nation's jails and prisons. The irony of the shared status of the prisoner and the immigrant is not only in their racialized criminalization but in the fact that the pattern of their criminalization demonstrates a fundamental failure of the law: it cannot apprehend their individuality except on its own behalf. The paradigmatic immigrant and prisoner (read nonwhite) are

* In 2003, Immigration and Naturalization Service (INS) was replaced by Immigration and Customs Enforcemenrt (ICE) and two other agencies.

marked in advance of appearing before the law as members of criminalized groups. The assertion of individual rights is only respected in the negative—the assumption of responsibility for illegality.

That prisoners might even possess civil rights is a relatively new notion. In 1871, several decades after the establishment of incarceration as the dominant mode of punishment in the United States, the Supreme Court of Virginia ruled that the convict had "not only forfeited his liberty but also his personal rights, except those which the law in its humanity affords him." In other words, the prisoner was "for the time being, the slave of the state."[21] Although various court decisions have reversed the ruling in *Ruffin v. Commonwealth of Virginia,* which stated that prisoners possessed no rights except those expressly extended to them by the state, in the United States and in those countries that have regarded the US criminal justice system as a model, democratic rights continue to have little meaning for those behind bars.

Citizens convicted of crimes are divested of rights on a constitutional basis. That these citizens are disproportionately citizens of color is attributed not to their racial targeting but rather to individual and community dysfunctions. The historical stage was set for this ideological masking of the racialization of imprisonment with the passage of the Thirteenth Amendment to the Constitution, which, in abolishing the generalized slavery of Black Americans, preserved the status of slaves for those "duly convicted of a crime."[22] That racist structures lurk within and behind the processes deployed to "duly convict" some "citizens" of crimes, leaving others relatively immune, cannot be uncovered by a narrow interpretation of *legal* discourse. It becomes impossible to argue that race is responsible for the fact that some citizens are charged, "duly convicted," sentenced, and imprisoned with greater facility than others, even as the disproportions become more and more grotesque.

Racial differentials in sentencing practices have been a perennial feature of the criminal justice system at least since the end of the Civil War. But they have rarely been taken up by antiracist activists. Not even Frederick Douglass, who spoke out so eloquently against lynching, developed a critique of the convict lease system, which radically transformed the southern prison systems in the aftermath of the Civil War.[23] During the era of the civil rights movement, there were rare references to Black people whom imprisonment had deprived of full citizenship. Even as the civil rights movement focused its energies on extending the right to vote to the Black population, the disenfranchisement of prisoners was not assumed to present a serious problem. These misconceptions return us to Bell's assessment of the failure of civil rights activists and their reliance on legal principles and demonstrate the imperative of challenging such a limited view today.

Current prison activism has produced abundant evidence of the magnitude of the problem of the disfranchisement of prisoners. A 1998 report by the Sentencing Project and Human Rights Watch reveals that a total of 3.9 million people are currently or permanently disenfranchised by virtue of being felons or ex-felons.[24] As a result of state laws, 1.4 million Black men—13 percent of all adult Black men—have lost the right to vote. In the states of Alabama and Florida, 31 percent of all Black men have been permanently divested of their right to participate in the electoral process.[25] It is a not entirely unpredictable irony that as prison populations expand under the conditions of an emergent prison industrial complex, civil rights principles have been appropriated by conservative ideologists and have become unavailable for use in what might otherwise be a massive voting rights campaign.

This raises some larger questions about the evolution of democracy under conditions of capitalism. In what sense can we say that the measure of citizenship (or of rights available) has always been linked to the denial of rights to some? A brief discussion of prison history may be helpful here, particularly if we focus on the implications of the simultaneous emergence of imprisonment as the reigning mode of punishment and industrial capitalism, with its attendant discourses of individual rights within civil society. Just as the young United States of America furnished a model of political democracy to the Western world, it also provided a new model of punishment—imprisonment in penitentiaries. As an alternative to corporal punishment, the penitentiary was the supreme expression of bourgeois democracy as it negatively affirmed the citizen's status as a rights-bearing subject—criminalizing poverty, segmenting the population, and burdening the individual (read male) with the moral responsibility for social welfare, thereby liberating the state.

Based on their visits to numerous US prisons in 1831, Alexis de Tocqueville and Gustave de Beaumont conceded:

> The penitentiary system in America is severe. While society in the United States gives the example of the most extended liberty, the prisons of the same country offer the spectacle of the most complete despotism. The citizens subject to the law are protected by it; they only cease to be free when they become wicked.[26]

This observation, which was made in the coauthored work *On the Penitentiary System in the United States and Its Application in France*,[27] was based on research conducted during the same voyage to the United States that furnished Tocqueville with the material for *Democracy in America*. It is significant that discussion on imprisonment as a reverse image of democracy, and thus as a peculiarly "undemocratic" institution inextricably linked to the democratic process, is lacking in *Democracy in America*. The only reference Tocqueville makes to prisons in that work is in the chapter on "The Unlimited Power of the Majority," where he refers to mobilization of public opinion for the reform of criminals. There he is critical of the power of the majority for having supported the new penitentiaries designed to reform and neglecting the old institutions "so that in the immediate neighborhood of a prison that bore witness to the mild and enlightened spirit of our times, dungeons existed that reminded one of the barbarism of the Middle Ages."[28]

But Tocqueville was impressed enough by the new American penitentiary to become a pivotal figure in the parliamentary debate on the reform of French prisons. He contended that American prisons—even the worst ones—were vastly superior to their French counterparts: "Our prisons are so inferior to American prisons, even to those they declared harmful to health, and mental balance, that to try to compare them is to abuse reason."[29] During the parliamentary debate, Tocqueville argued in support of the Pennsylvania system—devised by Quaker prison reformers—of absolute separation and silence, which, he claimed, would prevent prisoners from further corrupting one another and thus result in the moral reformation of the individual convict.[30]

This reformation, however, could only be achieved through the most absolute repression of civil society. A democratic society in which freedom of assembly and free speech were the hallmarks could only be preserved by relegating its outlaws to solitude and silence—not only by banishing them from civil society but by preventing them from engaging in any manner of social relations. Of course, Charles Dickens, another European who visited US prisons, found the Pennsylvania system to be entirely incompatible with democracy. In an often quoted passage of his *American Notes* Dickens prefaced a description of his 1842 visit to Eastern State Penitentiary with the observation that "the system here is rigid, strict, and hopeless solitary confinement. I believe it, in its effects, to be cruel and wrong."

> In its intention I am well convinced that it is kind, humane, and meant for reformation; but I am persuaded that those who devised this system of Prison Discipline, and those benevolent gentlemen who carry it into execution, do not know what it is that they are doing. I believe that very few men are capable of estimating the immense amount of torture and agony that this dreadful punishment, prolonged for years, inflicts upon the sufferers . . . I am only the more convinced that there is a depth of terrible endurance in it which none but the sufferers themselves can fathom, and which no man has a right to inflict upon his fellow-creature. I hold this slow and daily tampering with the mysteries of

> the brain, to be immeasurably worse than any torture of the body . . . because its wounds are not upon the surface, and it extorts few cries that human ears can hear; therefore I the more denounce it, as a secret punishment which slumbering humanity is not roused up to stay.[31]

Unlike Tocqueville, who believed that such punishment would result in moral renewal and thus mold convicts into better citizens, Dickens was of the opinion that "those who have undergone this punishment MUST pass into society again morally unhealthy and diseased."[32]

The Pennsylvania system incorporated the English concept of "civil death," to which outlaws (and to which married women, who had no legal standing except through their husbands) were relegated. However, the prisoner banished from civil society was expected to reemerge phoenixlike through his own meditative exertions as a new citizen-subject. Yet, as Dickens predicted, insanity was the more likely consequence of years of isolation and silence. The notion of the prisoner's "civil death" had obvious and intentional resonances with slavery, for slaves and their freed descendants were legally divested of a range of rights, including the right to vote. As slaves and their descendants were exempted from constitutional protection, so have imprisoned individuals found themselves beyond the pale of the Constitution. Although prisoners have periodically succeeded in winning certain rights (such as the right to proceed in federal courts under a writ of habeas corpus for the purpose of bringing Eighth or Fourteenth Amendment suits), these rights were drastically curtailed by the Reagan-Bush Supreme Court. In California and other states, prisoners have recently lost the right to be interviewed by the media. Since the majority of imprisoned individuals are people of color, the communities historically targeted by racism are the same communities whose members continue to be disproportionately treated as second-class citizens, and thus whose abilities to speak for themselves in legal and public arenas have been severely restricted.

On the one hand, the racialization of imprisonment is taken for granted. Since the abolition of slavery, Black people have been incarcerated in discernibly excessive numbers. Today 49 percent of all state and federal prisoners are Black and 17 percent are Latino.[33] Categories of Blackness and criminality have mutually informed each other within dominant popular and scholarly discourses. In regions of the country with substantial Latino and Native American populations, criminality is also racialized accordingly. Not only are undocumented immigrants from Central America and Asia continually subject to arrest and deportation, but Latinos and Asian Americans who are US citizens as well. On other hand, legal discourses—especially in the post–civil rights era—rely on racially neutral categories to explain the process of punishment. Thus, the historical divestment of rights of people of color has merged with the historical treatment of criminals.

With these brief evocations of the historical connection between the rise of imprisonment as punishment and the rise of industrial capitalism, and of the attendant discourses of individual rights associated with bourgeois democracy, I want to allude to the complexities of developing persuasive arguments against the prison industrial complex and against the systematic and racist use of confinement in prisons and jails as the solution to what are perceived as social dysfunctions associated with racialized communities. Just as a historical analysis of the emergence of the prison system necessitates a critique of early capitalism, an analysis of the prison industrial complex today must be linked to a radical critique of the structures and values of global capitalism, including the strategic significance of racism and patriarchy. (In an earlier article,[34] I tried to suggest theoretical strategies for avoiding a masculinist approach to the prison industrial complex in light of the overwhelmingly male population of prisons by locating women's punishment on a continuum that includes both public and private circuits of power.) I have intended here to suggest the radical potential of theorizing and organizing against the prison

CHAPTER 2

Prison: A Sign of US Democracy?*

Not long ago I was going through old family papers and happened upon a term paper written by my younger brother during his first year of college. His paper not only tried to make a case for the abolition of prisons, relying largely on the available literature by convicts and ex-convicts, but it also argued that the project of revolutionary democratic transformation could not be accomplished without the participation and leadership of prisoners. My initial surprise gave way to a troubling moment of nostalgia as I tried to ward off the feeling that prison abolitionists are condemned, like Sisyphus, to endless rehearsals of all the compelling reasons—many of which were initially proposed at the moment of the prison's first appearance as a technology of punishment—why prisons simply do not work, why they are anathema to "democracy," and why they should thus be removed from the social arena.

Are we now simply repeating the arguments that achieved some measure of acceptance during the sixties and seventies but failed to stand up to the law-and-order discourse associated with the Reagan-Bush era? After the Attica Rebellion in 1971, prison abolition was widely acknowledged in popular, scholarly, and legal circles—and not only in young Black and radical communities—as a legitimate topic of discussion. As I questioned why my younger brother's term paper seemed to be a strange artifact of a bygone era, I thought

* First delivered as a speech at the Cultural Studies Symposium, University of California, Santa Cruz, November 28, 2007.

about the way my own reaction recapitulated the current assumption that prison abolition has no history—and that it can only be envisioned either as a wild and unrealizable utopian fantasy or as a forever delayed future project.

Prominent legal scholar Michael Tonry begins his preface to the 2004 tribute to Norval Morris, *The Future of Imprisonment,* with this observation:

> Not so long ago, serious people thought the prison's days were numbered. "The days of imprisonment as a method of mass treatment of lawbreakers," wrote Norval Morris's mentor Hermann Mannheim, in 1943, "are largely over." In a 1965 festschrift for Mannheim, Morris wrote that the prison's origins were makeshift, its operation is unsatisfactory, and its future lacks promise," and "confidently predicted" that "before the end of this century," the prison, as Mannheim and Morris knew it, would "become extinct."[1]

However, even though Tonry is in agreement with the critiques proposed over sixty years ago by Mannheim and over forty years ago by Morris, he concludes that while the prison is indisputably iatrogenic—its putative cure creates more disorders—it still has a future—at least for the lifetimes of those who are now adults. He even goes so far as to suggest that just as imprisonment was proposed two centuries ago as a humane alternative to capital and corporal punishment, it might now be conceived as a humane alternative to the possible use of psychotropic drugs to control the impulses of lawbreakers, who might be introduced in a zombie-like state into the free world. Such drugs, he believes, would violate the autonomy of human beings even more than imprisonment.

While Tonry does not explicitly relegate abolitionism to the ultraradical fringes of prison activism, he seems reluctant to ask how the demise of the prison might be accelerated, instead of assuming that the institution itself can only fall as a result of its own internal contradictions. What he proposes are mandates for the proper functioning of the prison during the remainder of its life.

In this sense, he reenacts the two-hundred-year-old drama, to which Foucault turned our attention, of proposing the prison as the only solution to the problems that have never managed to be solved—indeed they have been consistently exacerbated—by the prison. Bigger and better prisons have always produced more crises, the solutions for which are always even better prisons, which, in turn, produce more crises.

The state of California's prison system, under threat of federal receivership because of such crises, is about to enter another period of major expansion, if the governor has his way. When governor Arnold Schwarzenegger was recently faced with the very real possibility of releasing a substantial number of women prisoners, he chose instead to propose a new "gender responsive" network of prisons for women. Schwarzenegger's contribution to the two-hundred-year-old drama has been to accentuate the historical amnesia it furthers by adding the term "rehabilitation" to the name of the agency controlling the prisons, so that the former Department of Corrections is now the California Department of Corrections and Rehabilitation. Now we are back to the early days of the penitentiary.

In the United States, the project of instituting imprisonment as the dominant mode of punishment was historically linked to the postrevolutionary metamorphosis of government and society during the late 1700s and early 1800s. The rise of the penitentiary in the new United States of America was viewed simultaneously as dramatic evidence of democratization and as symptom of the unacknowledged racial, gender, and class inequalities embedded in the very structure of the new democracy. Imprisonment as punishment meant, on the one hand, that the denial of liberty provided negative proof of the emergence of liberty as the social standard. The denial of liberty was, so to speak, the exception that proved the rule. On the other hand, there were those who argued that (I am quoting scholar

Adam J. Hirsch) "liberty was too precious a treasure to confiscate for minor (or even major) criminal infractions."[2] Hirsch's study of the rapid spread of the penitentiary in postrevolutionary America also points out that during the debates regarding the new punishment, there were radicals who called for the abolition of all punishments, "a viewpoint that, had it prevailed, would not have led Americans toward the penitentiary."[3]

But, alas, this viewpoint did not prevail and, although an important, albeit subjugated, element of the intellectual history of the prison is precisely the persistence of arguments for its abolition (almost always overshadowed by calls for prison reform) the prison has obstinately established itself as a permanent and hegemonic institution in US democracy. Ironically, it still presents itself both as evidence of democracy, thus necessary exception, and as irreconcilable contradiction. The question I want to ask is whether a deeper consideration of the relationship between imprisonment and democracy might establish a more productive framework for arguments against the hegemony of the prison and thus for prison abolition today.

Before I proceed, I need to share with you the more immediate reasons for these reflections. For the last decade, I have worked with an organization and movement that works under the rubric "Critical Resistance: Beyond the Prison Industrial Complex." This movement, which is largely responsible for the introduction of the term "prison industrial complex," has now embarked on an intensified campaign to popularize the notion of prison abolition. We are currently organizing an international conference, which will celebrate the tenth anniversary of the founding of Critical Resistance.

Therefore to pose such questions as what is responsible for the phenomenal resilience of carceral punishment; why has the institution of the prison managed to attach itself to the very idea of democracy, at least in its US manifestation; to what extent is imprisonment a racialization process that insinuates racial, gender, and sexual inequality into the heart of liberal democracy—to pose these questions is also to interrogate the prospects for a viable twenty-first-century abolition campaign.

In other words, it is not enough now—as it has never been enough—simply to propose evidence of the prison's failure and hope that these indisputable facts will initiate the prison's decline. As naturalized as it may be, the prison will definitely not die a natural death.

Previous campaigns for the abolition of various modes of punishment, the prison included, have largely relied on the assumption that certain kinds of punishments are morally and politically incompatible with liberal democratic ideals. Despite the huge archive of legal cases relying on the Eighth Amendment to the Constitution, which prohibits "cruel and unusual punishment" (along with excessive bail and fines), the Supreme Court not yet been persuaded to abolish the death penalty, and certainly not even the most extreme forms of incarceration—the indefinite solitary confinement and sensory deprivation characteristic of the most recent reinvention of the US prison, the super-maximum security prison. It has been frequently observed that "few constitutional guarantees of individual liberty have so often been relied upon, to so little avail, as has the eighth amendment."[4]

In her study of the Eighth Amendment, Colin Dayan argues that the bizarre juxtaposition of legal affirmations of cruel punishments alongside their prohibition in the Eighth Amendment can be traced to the history of slavery and the ideological efforts to justify racialized subjugation within a social order based on democracy.

> If the methods of punishment used in the United States today—the death penalty, prolonged solitary confinement, extreme force, and psychological torture—seem barbaric by our standards and by those of the rest of the so-called civilized world, this can be traced to the colonial history of the legal stigmatization and deprivation of a group considered less than human.
>
> The Supreme Court's most recent Eighth Amendment decisions, the ones underlying the torture memos, summon

> in new places and under new guises the genealogy of slavery and civil incapacitation.[5]

Dayan traces the history of the Eighth Amendment as she attempts to understand the current legal justifications for the treatment of prisoners of the US global war on terror, which she links to legitimized practices within domestic prisons, which, in turn, are historically anchored in the practices of slavery.

It is significant, for my purposes, to take note of the fact that the institution of the prison has played a pivotal role in the US-initiated global war on terror, which George W. Bush has frequently characterized as an "ideological struggle in defense of democracy." The articulation of carceral institutions with neoliberal democratic ideologies poised against the threat of terror recapitulates the early history of US democracy as it executed the project of extending rights and liberties to some, while denying them to others—denying them most consistently to Black slaves.

This raises the question: what if imprisonment is so philosophically anchored to liberal conceptions of democracy, inflected with and infected by racial exclusion, that we cannot unthink it—much less disestablish its institutions—without reconceptualizing democracy? This requires us to pay serious attention to the complicated interdependencies of racism and capitalism that are responsible for the peculiar institutions of democracy in the US.

Considerations of punishment and democracy are expected to make an obligatory nod to Alexis de Tocqueville's research for his book *Democracy in America*, which was occasioned by a commission he and his colleague Gustave de Beaumont received from the French government to study the new American penitentiary in light of its applicability to France. Explanations for the silence regarding this new form of "democratic punishment" in *Democracy in America* usually assume that he was not really interested in prisons (even though he visited every major prison in the US and interviewed almost all the prisoners held in the new Eastern State Penitentiary in Pennsylvania.)

Ten years ago, in celebration of the "Tocqueville revival," C-SPAN sponsored a nine-month school bus tour exploring democracy in America. They retraced Tocqueville and Beaumont's trip, stopping in the communities visited by the two researchers for discussions on topics such as "religion and politics, the impact and power of the press and the changing role of government." The goal of the trip was to discover "what democracy means today."

This series—on C-SPAN 3, used largely in high school and community college classrooms—coincided with a renewed public awareness of the prison crisis. While the series did include some discussions about specific prison sites—such as Sing Sing and Eastern State, they do not appear to have had any organic relationship to the discussion of democracy. I wonder how this tour might have turned out had they visited as many prisons and talked to as many prisoners (and wardens and guards) as Tocqueville did.

In this sense the C-SPAN tour was consistent with the historical tendency to secret the prison behind the shadows of democracy. Following the example of Tocqueville, and the reception of Tocqueville, the punishment of imprisonment—even though it simultaneously relied on and negatively constituted individual rights and liberties—was expelled beyond the margins of democracy. In a very real sense, it was the negation that liberal democracy required as evidence of its existence. It was and remains the constitutive negation of liberal democracy. Carceral punishment, i.e., punishment that consists in the deprivation of rights and liberties, only makes sense within a society that putatively respects individual rights and liberties.

The liberal democratic subject knows he is free precisely because he is not imprisoned (and I use the masculine gender intentionally here). But this constitutive negation is a necessary negation that demonstrates the value of freedom. In this sense it is structurally similar to slavery. I know I am free because I am not a slave. I know I am free because I am not a prisoner.

How else can we explain the persisting fascination with the prison? In the nineteenth century, prisons were major tourist destinations (10,000 people visited Eastern State Penitentiary in 1858, for example) and the historical prisons continue to hold this fascination for tourists. Over 68,000 visitors walked through the cellblocks of Eastern State in 2002.

It is interesting that with all the secondary literature on Tocqueville's *Democracy in America*, there is very little attention to the fact that his intimate engagement with the American penitentiary may have influenced his analysis of democracy. How might the silences regarding the prison be read—including and beyond Roger Boesche's speculation that the prison may well have been Tocqueville's model for despotism?

There are now more people in and out of prison during the course of a year than there were in the entire population of the US at the time of Tocqueville's visit. In 1831, there were approximately 13 million people in the country. Today, 13.5 million people spend time in jail or prison over the course of a year. The figure we usually hear is 2.2 million, which reflects the number of people in jail or prison on any given day of the year. The lives of 7 million people are directly supervised by prison guards, probation officers, and parole officers. $60 billion dollars annually.[6]

I could continue this litany of statistics—relying on the Bureau of Justice Statistics, which publishes an annual prison census entitled "Prisons and Jails at Midyear." The latest census taken on June 30, 2006, highlights the fact that 4.8 percent of all Black men were in prison or jail—11 percent of Black men between the ages of 25 to 34 (1.9 percent of Hispanic men and 0.7 percent of white men).

I quote the BJS knowing full well that the enormity of the numbers has little impact on how the public responds to the knowledge that the US now holds more people behind bars—both absolutely and proportionately—than any other country. But I cannot restrain myself, and despite the abstractness of numbers—and more than anything else conventional ways of knowing the prison relies on numbers—I do want you to think about the quantitative impact of imprisonment on Black communities.

I have referred to the clandestine ideological role the prison has played and continues to play in affirming individual rights and liberties in liberal democracy. Now I want to dwell for a moment on the way these rights and liberties operate within the trajectory that leads to imprisonment. What is peculiar to the United States is the entanglement of slavery in the historical emergence of the prison. Already during slavery—as Saidiya Hartman has pointed out—Black people were acknowledged as individuals with legal personality only through their culpability. That is to say, there was one significant sense in which slaves could not be said to be property—property cannot be found guilty of a crime.

The legal trajectory that concludes with a prison sentence recognizes the individual as a juridical subject with a range of rights—to confront one's accuser, to due process, to a trial by a jury of one's peers, etc. Thus, the prisoner—and as we have seen, in the current prison population, there are more Black people than white, and a significant number of Latino people (in California, they constitute the majority)—experiences his/her rights and liberties precisely through the process of their denial.

Even within the confines of the prison, such rights are supposed to be respected. Some years ago, I had the opportunity to sit in on a classification hearing at a maximum-security men's prison in California. The hearing was to decide whether the prisoner would be classified as a Level IV inmate to be housed in a 180-degree facility or as a Level III inmate to be housed in a 270-degree facility. What was most emphasized was the right to due process he possessed. In other words, he could not be indiscriminately classified to whatever level. The administration had to follow due process in deciding whether he was so dangerous as to merit housing consisting of cells that were always in the line of vision of the guard tower.

From its advent, the prison has been a quintessentially democratic institution—it demonstrates through the process of negation the centrality of individual rights and liberties. Civil life is negated and the prisoner is relegated to the status of civil death. Following Claude Meillassoux and Orlando Patterson, Colin (Joan) Dayan and other scholars have compared the social death of slavery to the civil death of imprisonment, particularly given the landmark legal case *Ruffin v. Commonwealth,* which in 1871 declared the prisoner to be "the slave of the state."

> A convicted felon . . . has, as a consequence of his crime, not only forfeited his liberty, but all his personal rights except those which the law in its humanity accords to him. He is for the time being a slave of the State. He is *civiliter mortuus;* and his estate, if he has any is administered like that of a dead man.

Although prisoners' state of civil death has now mutated so that they are no longer the living dead, as Dayan characterized them—that is to say, their residual rights have been slightly augmented—there remains a range of deprivations that situate the prisoner, and indeed also the ex-prisoner, beyond the boundaries of liberal democracy.

I want to look at one such deprivation—the loss of the right to vote—and would like to think about the impact of felon disenfranchisement on the workings of contemporary US democracy. The majority of the imprisoned population loses the franchise either temporarily or permanently. Felon disenfranchisement emerged as a key factor in the disputed 2000 presidential elections. Interestingly, it was not identified as a central issue in the 2004 elections although few changes had occurred in the law.

5.3 million people have lost their right to vote—either permanently or temporarily. Among Black men, the figures are even more dramatic—almost 2 million Black men, or 13 percent of the total population of Black adult men. In some states one out of every four Black men are barred from voting.

Felon disenfranchisement has a long history, but during its early appearance in the US—in fact when the first law prohibiting ex-felons from voting was passed by Virginia in 1776—voting itself was a rare practice, largely because a very small minority of the population (as low as 6 percent of the population) had the right to vote.[7] This was clearly democracy for the few—those who were white, propertied, and male.

The historical period that witnessed a significant expansion of felon disenfranchisement laws was the post–Civil War era—in other words after the passage of the Fourteenth and Fifteenth Amendments. In fact, just as the Thirteenth Amendment, which legally (and only legally) ended slavery, designated convicts as exception, the Fourteenth Amendment, which guaranteed all persons equal protection of the law, also contained an exception—section 2 permitted states to withdraw suffrage rights from those who were engaged in "rebellion or other crimes."[8]

According to Elizabeth Hull, southern constitutional conventions during the period following the overthrow of Radical Reconstruction—to use Du Bois's periodization—developed strategies of criminalization precisely to divest former slaves and their descendants of the right to vote. Many southern states passed laws that linked those crimes that were specifically associated with Black people to disenfranchisement, while those associated with white people did not result in withdrawal of the right to vote. In states such as Mississippi, there was the ironic situation that if you were convicted of murder you retained your voting rights, but if convicted of miscegenation you lost your right to vote.[9]

I do not have time to develop an extended analysis of the historical development of the current practices of felony disenfranchisement, so I will point to sociologists Jeff Manza and Christopher Uggen's findings that between 1850 and 2002, states with larger proportions of people of color in their prison populations were more likely to pass laws restricting their right to vote, which leads them to conclude that there is a direct connection between racial politics and felon disenfranchisement. "When we ask the question of how we got to the point where American practice can be so out of line with the rest of the world," they write, "the most plausible answer we can supply is that of race."[10]

I conclude by reminding us all that it can be confidently argued that the Bush presidency was precisely enabled by the relegation of a large, majority Black population of "free" individuals to the status of civil death. Most of you know the story of the Florida elections, and you are aware of the fact that not only were former prisoners removed from the voting rolls, but also suspected felons as well.

What would the world look like today—what would be the prospects for democracy—if ex-prisoners had been able to vote in the 2000 elections? As I reflect back on the meaning of my baby brother's college term paper in which he predicted that revolutionary democratic transformation would have to involve the participation of prisoners, it sheds its anachronistic aura. As Congressman John Conyers has pointed out, the fact that 600,000 ex-felons were denied participation in the elections in the state of Florida alone "may have literally changed the history of this nation."[11]

PART II

Slavery and the US Prison

Genealogical Connections

CHAPTER 3

From the Prison of Slavery to the Slavery of Prison

Frederick Douglass and the Convict Lease System*

"Slavery in the United States," wrote Frederick Douglass in 1846, "is the granting of that power by which one man exercises and enforces a right of property in the body and soul of another." Throughout his career as an abolitionist, his writings and speeches probed the contradictions of the legal definition of the slave as "a piece of property—a marketable commodity."[1] He used this definition of the slave as property, for example, as the basis for his analysis of theft by slaves as an everyday practice of resistance to slavery. The slave "can own nothing, possess nothing, acquire nothing, but what must belong to another. To eat the fruit of his own toil, to clothe his person with the work of his own hands, is considered stealing."[2] Because the slave "was born into a society organized to defraud him of the results of his labor . . . he naturally enough thought it no robbery to obtain by stealth—the only way open to him—a part of what was forced from him under the hard conditions of the lash."[3] When Douglass himself escaped from slavery, he also stole property that belonged, in the eyes of the law, to his master. As a fugitive slave, both state and federal law constructed him as a criminal—a thief who absconded with his own body.

* First published in *Frederick Douglass: A Critical Reader*, eds. Bill E. Lawson and Frank M. Kirkland (Malden, Mass.: Blackwell, 1999), 339–62.

Throughout his life, Douglass periodically referred to the criminalization of the Black population as a by-product of slavery. In 1877 President Rutherford Hayes appointed him US marshal in the District of Columbia (over much criticism by both Blacks and whites), which he said brought him into direct contact with Black individuals stigmatized as criminals.[4] While he invariably contested the prevailing presumption of ex-slaves' natural proclivities toward crime, he nevertheless agreed that "they furnish a larger proportion of petty thieves than any other class,"[5] attributing this "thieving propensity" to holdovers from slavery. A central component in Douglass's philosophy of history was the assumption that over time, as the Black population became increasingly removed from the era of slavery, these criminal propensities would recede accordingly:

> It is sad to think of the multitude who only dropped out of slavery to drop into prisons and chain-gangs, for the crimes for which they are punished seldom rise higher than the stealing of a pig or a pair of shoes; but it is consoling to think that the fact is not due to liberty, but to slavery, and that the evil will disappear as these people recede from the system in which they were born.[6]

More than a century after Douglass expressed his confidence that over time the Black population would be transformed by material progress and spiritual enlightenment and would thus cease to be treated as a criminalized class, Blackness is ideologically linked to criminality in ways that are more complicated and pernicious than Douglass ever could have imagined. The overwhelming numbers and percentages of imprisoned Black men and women tend to define the Black population as one that is subject a priori to incarceration and surveillance. In 1997, there were 1.8 million people in the country's jails and prisons, approximately half of whom were Black. Almost one-third of all young Black males were either incarcerated or directly under criminal justice surveillance.[7] Although women constitute a statistically small percentage of the overall prison population (7.4 percent), the rate of increase in the incarceration of Black women surpasses that of their male counterparts.[8] Whereas the prison system established its authority as a major institution of discipline and control for Black communities during the last two decades of the nineteenth century, at the close of the twentieth century, carceral regulation of Black communities has reached crisis proportions.

Considering the central role race has played in the emergence of a contemporary prison industrial complex and the attendant expansion of incarcerated populations, an examination of Douglass's historical views on the criminalization of Black communities and the racialization of crime may yield important insights. In this essay, I am especially interested in Douglass's silence regarding the post–Civil War system of convict lease, which transferred symbolically significant numbers of Black people from the prison of slavery to the slavery of prison. Through this transference, ideological and institutional carryovers from slavery began to fortify the equation of Blackness and criminality in US society.

When the Thirteenth Amendment was passed in 1865, thus legally abolishing the slave economy, it also contained a provision that was universally celebrated as a declaration of the unconstitutionality of peonage. "Neither slavery nor involuntary servitude, *except as a punishment for crime,* whereof the party shall have been duly convicted, shall exist within the United States, or anyplace subject to their jurisdiction" (my emphasis). The exception would render penal servitude constitutional—from 1865 to the present day. That Black human beings might continue to be enslaved under the auspices of southern systems of justice (and that this might set a precedent for imprisonment outside the South) seems not to have occurred to Douglass and other abolitionist leaders. It certainly is understandable that this loophole might be overlooked amid the general jubilation with which emancipation initially was greeted. However, the southern states' rapid passage of Black Codes—which criminalized such behavior as vagrancy, breach of job contracts, absence from work, the possession of firearms, and insulting gestures or acts[9]—should have stimulated critical reconsideration of the dangerous potential of the amendment's loophole. Replacing the Slave Codes of the previous era, the Black Codes simultaneously acknowledged and nullified Black people's new juridical status as US citizens. The racialization of specific crimes meant that, according to state law, there were crimes for which only Black people could be "duly convicted." The Mississippi Black Codes, for example, which were adopted soon after the close of the Civil War, declared vagrant "anyone who was guilty of theft, had run away [from a job, apparently], was drunk, was wanton in conduct or speech, had neglected job or family, handled money carelessly, and . . . all other idle and disorderly persons."[10] Thus vagrancy was coded as a Black crime, one punishable by incarceration and forced labor.

Considering the importance Douglass accorded the institution of slavery as an explanatory factor in relation to the vast numbers of "free" Black people who were identified as criminal, it is surprising that he did not directly criticize the expansion of the convict lease system and the related system of peonage. As the premier Black public intellectual of his time, he seems to have established a pattern of relative silence vis-à-vis convict leasing, peonage, and the penitentiary system, all of which clearly were institutional descendants of slavery. Douglass's most explicit denunciation of peonage did not occur until 1888, after a trip he made to South Carolina during which, according to Philip Foner, he "realized how little he had known about the true conditions of his people in the South."[11] In a speech on the occasion of the twenty-sixth anniversary of emancipation in the District of Columbia, Douglass said that the landlord and tenant laws in the South sounded like "the grating hinges of a slave prison" and kept Black people "firmly bound in a strong, remorseless, and deadly grasp, a grasp from which only death can free [them]."[12] However, by the time he made this observation, tenant farming, peonage, and convict leasing had been in place for over two decades in some states. The Hayes-Tilden Compromise of 1877 led to the expansion and strengthening of these systems throughout the South. Precisely at the time Frederick Douglass's voice was most needed to trouble the rise of this new form of slavery—experienced directly by thousands of Black people and symbolically by millions—his political loyalties to the Republican Party and his absolute faith in principles of Enlightenment seemed to blind him to the role the federal government was playing in the development of convict leasing and peonage. In fact, just as President Rutherford Hayes prepared to withdraw federal troops from the South (one of the stipulations of the Compromise), he also decided to appoint Frederick Douglass as US marshal of the District of Columbia.

According to Milfred Fierce, who has authored one of the earliest extended studies of the convict lease system within the field of African-American studies, little is known about Douglass's views on convict leasing or those of other Black leaders of his era.[13] Later, Booker T. Washington did occasionally speak out against convict leasing, and he integrated into his own project of industrial education some efforts to assist individuals caught up in the system of debt peonage. But he never developed an explicit strategy to abolish convict leasing. W. E. B. Du Bois published an essay in 1901 entitled "The Spawn of Slavery: The Convict Lease System of the South" in a now-obscure missionary periodical, and while it proposed a radical analysis, it seems that it was not widely read or discussed.[14] Du Bois argued that not only was crime a "symptom of wrong social conditions," but that the entrenchment of convict leasing "linked crime and slavery indissolubly in [Black people's] minds."[15] In 1907, Mary Church Terrell published an essay in *The Nineteenth Century* entitled "Peonage in the United States: The Convict Lease System and the Chain Gangs."[16]

Fierce explains the relative silence on the part of leaders like Frederick Douglass in part as a result of their limited knowledge of the atrocities connected with this system. However, it is difficult to believe that Douglass was unaware of the development of the lease system in the aftermath of emancipation or of its expansion at the close of Radical Reconstruction. While his speeches and writings suggest that he did not consider this an issue important enough to deserve a place on his agenda for Black liberation, recurring references to presumptions of Black criminality and evocations, albeit abstract, of chain gangs persuade me that Douglass must have been aware of the atrocities committed in the name of justice. I therefore tend to think that Fierce is more accurate when he contends that

> in addition, Black leaders fell victim to the notion that "criminals" were getting what they deserved and, despite the cruelty of convict leasing, a crusade on behalf of prisoners was not seen as more important than fighting the lynching bee, opposing voting restrictions, or protesting the acts of racial bigotry that abounded. Those who accepted this analysis failed to fully appreciate how many of the convicts were kidnapped, held beyond their sentences, or actually innocent of the crimes, for which they were incarcerated, the total number of which will never be known.[17]

They also failed to recognize that Black children were not exempt from the convict labor system. David Oshinsky, author of *Worse Than Slavery,* refers to a pardon petition for a six-year-old girl named Mary Gay, who was sentenced to thirty days "plus court costs" on charges of stealing a hat.[18]

The general impact of the convict leasing system was even more far-reaching than the horrors it brought to individual Black lives. According to Oshinsky:

> From its beginnings in Mississippi in the late 1860s until its abolition in Alabama in the late 1920s, convict leasing would serve to undermine legal equality, harden racial stereotypes, spur industrial development, intimidate free workers, and breed open contempt for the law. It would turn a few men into millionaires and crush thousands of ordinary lives.[19]

By the time the National Committee on Prison Labor convened in 1911, a number of southern states had already abolished convict labor, and the abolitionist campaign had been rendered legitimate by the rising influence of the penal reform movement. The general secretary of the National Committee on Prison Labor entitled his book on the committee's findings *Penal Servitude* and introduced it with the following observation:

> The State has a property right in the labor of the prisoner. The Thirteenth Amendment of the Constitution of the United States provides that neither slavery nor involuntary servitude shall exist, yet by inference allows its continuance as punishment for crime, after due process of law. This property right the state may lease or retain for its own use, the manner being set forth in state constitutions and acts of legislature.[20]

Although the loophole in the Thirteenth Amendment was apparently missed by most at the time of its passage, in retrospect it is easy to see how the very limitation of "slavery" and "involuntary servitude" to "criminals" could facilitate the further criminalization of former slaves.

Throughout his post–Civil War writings and speeches, Frederick Douglass argued that vast numbers of Black people discovered that crimes were imputed to them that carried no prison sentence for whites. Had he decided to examine this attribution of criminality to Black people more thoroughly, he might have discovered a link between the leasing system and other institutions for the control of Black labor. The Thirteenth Amendment putatively freed Black labor from the total control to which it was subject during slavery. In actuality, new forms of quasi-total *control* developed—sharecropping, tenant farming, the scrip system, and the most dramatic evidence of the persistence of slavery, the convict lease system. Although Alabama and Louisiana had begun to use the lease system before the Civil War, it was only with the emancipation of the slaves that they and the other southern states began to use convict leasing on a relatively large scale. During the post–Civil War period, the percentages of Black convicts in relation to white was often higher than 90 percent. In Alabama, the prison population tripled between 1874 and 1877—and the increase consisted almost entirely of Blacks.[21]

Radical Reconstruction did not abruptly end with the withdrawal of federal troops in 1877. However, as the first Black recipient of a federal appointment that required Senate confirmation, Douglass failed to use his position to forcefully challenge the Republican Party's complicity with the repressive process of reestablishing control over southern Black labor. "It was clear by inauguration day," Philip Foner contends, "that Hayes' agreement to remove the last remaining federal troops from the South had rendered meaningless his pledge to uphold the rights of the colored people. At this crucial moment, Douglass voiced no opposition to Hayes' policy."[22] Instead, Douglass continued to define freedom as access to political rights, thus prioritizing political progress over economic freedom. His argument that "slavery is not abolished until the Black man has the ballot"[23] was transformed into intransigent—although not always uncritical—support for the Republican Party, which was combined with an Enlightenment philosophy of history that emphasized inevitable future progress for the former slaves. Throughout his campaign for the Fifteenth Amendment and for the legislation necessary to enforce it, Douglass represented the ballot as the engine of progress for African Americans—even if these political rights were explicitly gendered as male and proscribed by the criminalization process to which all Black people were vulnerable. However, after the fall of Radical Reconstruction and the solidification of the move toward disfranchisement, Douglass developed other arguments that revealed the Hegelian character of his unswerving belief in Enlightenment and historical progress.

In an 1879 paper opposing the Exoduster movement, Douglass contended that Black people were the only hope for progress in the South. He argued that "whatever prosperity, beauty, and civilization are now possessed by the South" could be attributed to the labor of

Black slaves. This dependence of the South on Black people was no less the case in the aftermath of slavery: "[The Negro] is the arbiter of her destiny."[24] In addition, Douglass asserted:

> The Exodus has revealed to southern men the humiliating fact that the prosperity and civilization of the South are at the mercy of the despised and hated Negro. That it is for him, more than for any other, to say what shall be the future of the late Confederate States; that within their ample borders, he alone can stand between the contending powers of savage and civilized life; that the giving or withholding of his labor will bless or blast their beautiful country.[25]

That Douglass could represent Black workers as already having achieved the status accorded white workers—that is, they were free to sell or withhold their labor to southern employers—revealed his astounding failure to engage with the actual position of Black labor in the South:

> The Negro . . . has labor, the South wants it, and must have it or perish. Since he is free he can now give it, or withhold it; use it where he is, or take it elsewhere, as he pleases. His labor made him a slave, and his labor can, if he will, make him free, comfortable and independent. It is more to him than either fire, sword, ballot boxes, or bayonet. It touches the heart of the South through its pocket.[26]

Ironically, Douglass's argument here foreshadows in starkly literal terms Booker T. Washington's admonition to "cast down your bucket where you are." If Black labor was free at all, it was only in the formal sense that the economic system of slavery had been declared unconstitutional. Tenant farming, sharecropping, peonage, the practice of paying wages in scrip—and, for a vastly disproportionate number of Black people, convict labor—militated against any assertion *of* economic freedom on the part of the masses of former slaves. Although a relatively small number of people were directly affected by the convict labor system, its symbolic importance resided in its demonstration to all Black workers that incarceration and penal servitude were their possible fate. Convict leasing was a totalitarian effort to control Black labor in the postemancipation era, and it served as a symbolic reminder to Black people that slavery had not been fully disestablished.[27] That Black women could be housed, worked, and physically and sexually abused by inmates and guards in camps that were largely male constituted a message that there was a fate even worse than slavery awaiting them. D. E. Tobias, one of the few Black intellectuals at the turn of the century to prioritize the campaign against convict leasing, referred to the "immorality" abounding in the convict camps because of the cocorrectional housing policies and because women were whipped nude in the presence of male convicts.[28] As long as it was possible to arrest and imprison Black people (not only on serious charges, but also on petty charges that would never land a white person in jail) and lease out their labor under oppressive conditions that often surpassed those of slavery, Black labor could not be said to be free.

In *Black Reconstruction,* W. E. B. Du Bois would later argue that because there was no historical precedent for a Black presence in southern prisons and because white convicts were released during the war to join the Confederate armies, the role of southern penitentiary systems was reconceptualized after the outbreak of the Civil War. "The whole criminal system," wrote Du Bois, "came to be used as a method of keeping Negroes at work and intimidating them. Consequently there began to be a demand for jails and penitentiaries beyond the natural demand due to the rise of crime."[29] After the initiation of the convict lease system, one Black member of the legislature presented a bill for the abolition of the penitentiary system.[30]

Douglass's argument against the Exoduster movement was thus based on a highly abstract construction of "free labor" that bore no relationship to Black economic realities in the South and, in this context, served as a surrogate for the failed notion that the ballot promised full freedom and equality for the former slaves. However, to do Douglass's argument justice, it should be pointed out that he did not deploy it against emigration per se, but rather he focused his opposition on the organized Exoduster movement and its demands for federal financing. In light of the horrendous situation in the South, he suggested that "voluntary, spontaneous, self-sustained emigration on the part of the freedmen may or may not be commendable. It is a matter with which they alone have to do."[31] As long as emigration remained a private and individual matter, Douglass had no objections. However, when it was raised publicly and politically as a strategy for liberation, he strongly opposed it.

In summarizing the arguments in favor of emigration, Douglass refers to Senate testimony by the emigrants themselves. He points to their contention "that a crime for which a white man goes free, a Black man is severely punished" and "that the law is the refuge of crime rather than of innocence; that even the old slave driver's whip has reappeared, and the inhuman and disgusting spectacle of the chain-gang is beginning to be seen."[32] Douglass did not contest the truth of this testimony—in fact, he had and would continue to rely on the fact that the criminal justice system had become a sanctuary for racism of the cruelest sort—but he nonetheless chose to respond to it by maintaining that Black labor was "free" and held a far greater promise than emigration.

But even though the violent racism that was at the core of restructured criminal justice systems in the South did not, in Douglass's opinion, furnish compelling arguments for a political strategy of exodus from the South, his speeches and writings for the rest of his life powerfully evoked ways in which crime was racialized and race criminalized. In an essay for *North American Review* in 1881, challenging essentialist constructions of race prejudice, he wrote that "the colored man is the Jean Valjean of American society. He has escaped from the galleys, and hence all presumptions are against him."[33] Although Douglass's contention that the social conditions of slavery and the persistence of racism during the post-slavery era were entirely responsible for the criminalization of Black people led him to challenge these presumptions of criminality, they also steered him toward an analytical impasse. If slavery produced criminals, then Black people had to be acknowledged as criminals. However, he argued against the imputation of guilt where none was present:

> If a crime is committed, and the criminal is not positively known, a suspicious-looking colored man is sure to have been seen in the neighborhood. If an unarmed colored man is shot down and dies in his tracks, a jury, under the influence of this spirit, does not hesitate to find the murdered man the real criminal, and the murderer innocent.[34]

As indicated above, Douglass often alluded to the fact that Black people were punished for minor offenses as if they were hardened criminals, that "the crimes for which they are punished seldom rise higher than the stealing of a pig or a pair of shoes." In fact, the Mississippi legislature passed its notorious "Pig Law" in 1876, classifying the theft of any cattle or swine as grand larceny and carrying up to five years in the penitentiary. This law was in part responsible for a vast increase in the penitentiary population in that state.[35] In 1875, the Democratic legislature in Arkansas passed a similar law classifying the theft of property worth two dollars as a felony punishable by one to five years.[36] Several weeks after the Mississippi Pig Law was passed, the legislature legalized the leasing of convict labor to private companies. Prisoners, according to this act, would be permitted to "work outside the penitentiary in building railroads, levees or in any private labor or employment."[37] As David Oshinsky observes, "throughout the South, thousands of ex-slaves were being arrested, tried, and convicted for acts that in the past had been dealt with by the master alone. . . . An offense against [the master] had become an offense against the state."[38] In 1875 Governor John Brown of Tennessee expressed his opinion that to imprison a Black man who had stolen a pig with a white murderer was a gross injustice—to the white man.[39]

Because Black people were more likely to be imprisoned for minor offenses than white people, in states like Florida, large numbers of Black people convicted on charges of stealing were incarcerated alongside white men who had often committed appalling crimes. The author of an account on forced labor in the Florida turpentine camps pointed out that it was possible "to send a negro to prison on almost any pretext but difficult to get a white there, unless he committed a very heinous crime."[40]

Douglass was certainly conscious of the degree to which crime was racialized, of the South's tendency to "impute crime to color."[41] With his usual eloquence, he said that "justice is often painted with bandaged eyes . . . but a mask of iron, however thick, *could* never blind American justice, when a Black man happens to be on trial."[42] Not only was guilt assigned to Black communities, regardless of the race of the perpetrator of a crime, white men, Douglass claimed, sometimes sought to escape punishment by disguising themselves as Black:

> In certain parts of our country, when any white man wishes to commit a heinous offence, he wisely resorts to burnt cork and blackens his face and goes forth under the similitude of a Negro. When the deed is done, a little soap and water destroys his identity and he goes unwhipt of justice. Some Negro is at once suspected and brought before the victim of wrong for identification, and there is never much trouble here, for as in the eyes of many white people, all Negroes look alike, and as the man arrested and who sits in the dock in irons is Black, he is undoubtedly the criminal.[43]

Douglass made these comments during an 1883 speech in celebration of the twenty-first anniversary of emancipation in the District of Columbia. Three years later on the same occasion, he referred to his previous remarks and produced a recent example of a white man in Tennessee who had been killed while committing a crime in Blackface:

> Only a few days ago a Mr. J. H. Justice, an eminent citizen of Granger County, Tennessee, attempted under this disguise to commit a cunningly devised robbery and have his offense fixed upon a Negro. All worked well till a bullet brought him to the ground and a little soap and water was applied to his face, when he was found to be no Negro at all, but a very respectable white citizen.[44]

Cheryl Harris argues that a property interest in whiteness emerged from the conditions of slavery and that "owning white identity as property affirmed the self-identity and liberty of whites and, conversely, denied the self-identity of Blacks."[45] Douglass's comments indicate how this property interest in whiteness was easily reversed in schemes to deny Black people their rights to due process. Interestingly, cases similar to the ones Douglass discussed have emerged during the 1990s—the case of Charles Stuart, who killed his wife in Boston and attempted to place the blame on an anonymous Black murderer, and Susan Smith, who killed her children in Union, South Carolina, and claimed they had been abducted by a Black carjacker.

The last period of Frederick Douglass's life coincided with the consolidation of Jim Crow segregation in the South. Within the penitentiaries and convict labor camps, the criminality imputed to Blackness gave rise to ideologies of separation that, in comparison to those of the "free" world, were magnified and exaggerated. In the "free" world, school systems, transportation systems, hospitals, and neighborhoods were being subjected to strict laws of segregation. In some states there was the practice of incarcerating white convicts in penitentiaries and sending Black convicts to labor camps.[46] While the prisons and labor camps were establishing lines of racial demarcation, Black convicts who were incarcerated on charges of petty larceny were often treated as a danger to white convicts, even those in prison for murder. During the 1880s, meetings of the National Prison Association (NPA) were replete with racist defenses of convict leasing, including arguments that the camps were a notch above Black people's living conditions in freedom and that prison simply denied them "liberty, liquor and lust." White convicts, however, endured a much more trying ordeal, largely because they were compelled to live among Black people.[47] It was claimed that the law "lays on the Caucasian a dreadful grief, which the African does not feel. . . . The fact remains, and will remain, that there is a psychological repulsion between races, horrible to one but not the other."[48] Southerners speaking before the NPA meetings called up such exaggerated comparisons as that between incarcerated whites with Blacks and "the 'ancient torture' of tying up murderers with 'decaying corpses,' resulting in death to the living murderer."[49]

In light of Frederick Douglass's reticence regarding penal servitude, an analysis of his response to the prevailing discourses on race—which rendered criminality an obligatory ideological companion of Blackness—might yield insights into the relative silence regarding penal servitude in Black intellectual circles today. Douglass was quite outspoken on the issue of lynching, and, in his many speeches and essays devoted to this subject, he was certainly required to address the criminalizing ideology of racism. But why speak out against lynching and remain silent on leasing? Lynching was outside the *pale* of the law. It could be opposed on the basis of its unlawfulness, of its seemingly chaotic and aberrant quality. The issue, as Douglass formulated it, was not so much the guilt or innocence of lynch victims but rather that they were divested of their right to confront their accusers in an arena structured by law. To take on convict leasing would have required Douglass to relinquish some of his major Enlightenment principles—and his vision of Black liberation was too solidly anchored in the promise of legislated justice to permit him to ponder the possibility of the profound complicity of legal institutions in the continuation of this microcosmic slave system.

Consider this description of lynching from his well-known essay, "Why Is the Negro Lynched?":

> It [mob-law] laughs at legal processes, courts and juries, and its red-handed murderers range abroad unchecked and unchallenged by law or by public opinion. If the mob is in pursuit of Negroes who happen to be accused of crime, innocent or guilty, prison walls and iron bars afford no protection. Jail doors are battered down in the presence of unresisting jailers, and the accused, awaiting trial in the courts of law, are dragged out and hanged, shot, stabbed or burned to death, as the blind and irresponsible mob may elect.[50]

What Douglass failed to recognize is that the very iron bars that he looked to for security were as much a weapon of terror as the mob itself. "In a perverse way," according to Oshinsky, "emancipation had made the Black population more vulnerable than before. It now faced threats from two directions: white mobs and white courts. Like the Ku Klux Klan, the criminal justice system would become a dragnet for the Negro."[51]

Perhaps Douglass's confidence in the law blinded him to ways in which Black people were constructed, precisely through law, as only fit for slavery. This was the symbolic meaning of the convict lease system. By 1911, the National Prison Association openly acknowledged the links between the prison system and slavery:

> The *status of the convict* is that of one in *penal servitude*—the last surviving vestige of the old slave system. With its sanction in the common law, its regulation in the acts of legislatures, and its implied recognition in the Constitution of the United States, it continues unchallenged and without question, as a basic institution, supposedly necessary to the continued stability of our social structure.[52]

When Douglass wrote in 1894 about "the determination of slavery to perpetuate itself, if not under one form, then under another,"[53] he referred to the landlord tenant system as well as the practice of paying Black laborers with store orders (instead of with money) as ways of perpetuating slavery. "The landowners of the South want the labor of the Negro on the hardest terms possible. They once had it for nothing. They now want it for next to nothing."[54] Interestingly, he suggested that landowners employed three strategies, yet he only mentioned two (tenant farming and payment in scrip). Perhaps he originally meant to include convict leasing and/or peonage, but, on second thought, decided to remove references to these systems because they involved direct intervention or implicit sanction by the state.

Convict leasing and the accompanying laws permitting the criminal prosecution of people who did not fulfill their job contract were even more closely linked to slavery than the systems explicitly mentioned by Douglass. At the same time, all these legal and economic systems—leasing, peonage, tenant farming, sharecropping, and payment in scrip—mutually informed each other, all overdetermined by slavery in their techniques of controlling Black labor. With respect to the fact that most people subject to these systems were Black, Milfred Fierce points out that "for them, the distinction between antebellum de jure slavery and postbellum de facto slavery was close to being much ado about nothing."[55] Moreover, according to Fierce:

> Southern Blacks were trapped in [a] penal quagmire in excessive numbers and percentages of the total prison population of each southern state. For the victims, many of whom were ex-slaves, this predicament represented nothing short of a revisit to slavery. Those Blacks who were former slaves, and became victims of the convict lease system—especially those convicted and incarcerated on trumped up charges, or otherwise innocent of crimes for which they were imprisoned—must have imagined themselves in a time warp.[56]

Fierce argues—as indicated by the title of his study, *Slavery Revisited*—that the lease system established conditions that were tantamount to slavery, permitting plantation owners and industrialists to rent crews of mostly Black convicts, using the same methods of coercion to guarantee their labor that had been practiced during slavery.

While Douglass may not have addressed the convict lease system because of its legal character and its elaboration under the auspices of criminal justice systems, had he examined this system more closely, he might have discovered that the authority of the state was not directly exercised through the lease system—rather the state served to mediate the privatization of convict labor. Alabama had already set a precedent for the privatization of convict labor before the abolition of slavery, which further affirms the historical link between slavery and leasing. The first penitentiary was constructed in Alabama in 1840, and by 1845 it was so much in debt the entire prison was leased for a period of six years to a J. G. Graham. Graham simply became warden and took the profits from the convicts' *labor.*[57]

When all the southern states established the system of convict leasing, it made overwhelmingly Black convict labor forces available to planters and capitalists under conditions modeled along the lines of slavery, conditions that, in many ways, proved worse than the slave system. Matthew Mancini, author of *One Dies, Get Another,* proposes an analysis of the lease system that complicates the obvious connection with slavery. He persuasively argues that given the indisputable similarities and continuities, it is the differences and discontinuities that provide the most interesting perspective on convict leasing. He points out that the rate of economic exploitation—defined in Marxian terms as the value of unpaid labor (and thus also the rate of profit)—was actually greater with the lease system than with slavery. Slaveholders were responsible not only for the maintenance of the laboring subjects, but were expected to guarantee the maintenance of the entire slave community—including children and elders who were not able to work.[58] Lessees, however, were only responsible for individual convicts, each of which represented a labor unit. Moreover, lessees purchased the labor of entire crews of convicts, not of individuals. According to Mancini:

> The individual convict as such did not represent a significant investment, and his death or release was, therefore, not a loss. When considered as a source of labor, then, slaves received a "wage" best thought of as aggregated, convicts one that was individual; as a form of capital, by contrast, slaves were individually significant, convicts collectively so. This does turn out to be a relevant distinction rather than a metaphysical exercise, for the consequence was an economic incentive to abuse prisoners. These two economic factors—the subsistence or lower-than-subsistence "wage" the convicts received and their status as aggregated capital—served to reinforce one another and to make leasing, from the point of view of the economic definition, "worse" than slavery.[59]

A small but significant number of Black men and women were condemned to live out the worst nightmares of what slavery might have been had the cost of purchasing slaves been low enough to justify conditions of genocide, i.e., no man, woman, or child unable to work would be supported by the slave owners. Under these conditions (which were not entirely unheard of during slavery), it also would have been profitable to literally work slaves to death, because the cost of purchasing new ones would not have interfered with profits. Precisely because of this, Mancini decided to entitle his study of convict leasing *One Dies, Get Another.* We can only speculate as to how Frederick Douglass might have responded to the convict lease system had he extricated himself from his faith in formal legalities and examined more closely this symbolic and malignant reincarceration of slavery. We can also only speculate about the impact his engagement with the lease system might have had on future agendas for Black liberation and on the future relationship between Black intellectuals and social movements against the US prison system.

Although Frederick Douglass did not enlist his communicative powers in an examination of convict leasing, three of his intellectual descendants did see fit to write about this issue.[60] D. E. Tobias, a self-taught researcher and organic intellectual in the Gramscian sense, published an essay in 1899, a significant portion of which was devoted to leasing. In 1901, W. E. B. Du Bois published a relatively obscure article on convict leasing, and in 1907, Mary Church Terrell wrote about the subject in the same journal that had published Tobias's piece.

In his article, "A Negro on the Position of the Negro in America," D. E. Tobias described himself as a twenty-nine-year-old Black man, son of slaves, who was studying the prison system in the US.[61] Unfortunately, this seems to be Tobias's only published writing. Interestingly, he positioned the campaign against convict leasing at the very top of his agenda for Black liberation. In this sense, he directly contested the philosophical tradition initiated by Frederick Douglass—and later taken up by Du Bois in his debate with Washington—according to which Black political rights were the sine qua non of Black liberation. Tobias did not deny the importance of the ballot. But he argued, in effect, that as long as convict leasing continued to exist, Black people could never fully enjoy the franchise. Moreover, he suggested that the imprisonment of such large numbers of Black people was tantamount to robbing them forever of their rights as citizens. "Once a Negro voter is sent to prison, he is forever thereafter disfranchised, and for this reason alone the whites have made thousands of negro convicts for the purpose of depriving them of their votes."[62] The use of incarceration as an explicit scheme to erode the potential political power of the Black population reflected, in Tobias's view, what Frederick Douglass had referred to as "the determination of slavery to perpetuate itself." "The sole purpose of the South in going to war with the Nation," Tobias wrote,

> was to keep the Black race as chattels, and having been defeated in that, ex-slaveholders were determined that the negroes should be held in bondage to serve them. Accordingly, the remarkable ingenious scheme of making the negroes prisoners was soon devised, and at once scores and thousands of ex-slaves were arrested and convicted on any sort of flimsy charges, and farmed out to the highest bidders for human flesh. By reason of this new form of slavery, hundreds and thousands of Black men and women have never known that they were emancipated.[63]

Tobias points out that southern authorities justified the institution of the convict lease system by evoking the Civil War destruction of most of the South's prison structures and thus by representing the lease plan as a "makeshift and an experiment until other means of caring for the large negro criminal population could be found."[64] However, after more than three decades, the lease system had become a critical component of southern criminal justice.

W. E. B. Du Bois's 1901 article, "The Spawn of Slavery: The Convict-Lease System in the South," examines the lease system as a structural inheritance of slavery wherein Black people accused of committing crimes were disciplined by the private imposition of labor, using "the slave theory of punishment—pain and intimidation."[65] He defined this system as "the slavery in private hands of persons convicted of crimes and misdemeanors in the courts."[66] This method of controlling Black labor, Du Bois argued, emerged alongside a juridical construction of Black criminality in the chaos that followed emancipation when punishment was no longer the private purview of slavemasters, when Black slaves were legally recognized as the property of their masters. "Consequently, so far as the state was concerned, there was no crime of any consequence among Negroes. The system of criminal jurisprudence had to do, therefore, with whites almost exclusively."[67] Although the Freedmen's Bureau attempted to create innovative methods of mediating legal relationships, these new strategies failed and the state courts reestablished their authority:

> As the regular state courts gradually regained power, it was necessary for them to fix by their decisions the new status of the freedmen. It was perhaps as natural as it was unfortunate that amid this chaos the courts sought to do by judicial decisions what the legislatures had formerly sought to do by specific law—namely, reduce the freedmen to serfdom. As a result, the small peccadilloes of a careless, untrained class were made the excuse for severe sentences. The courts and jails became filled with the careless and ignorant, with those who sought to emphasize their newfound freedom, and too often with innocent victims of oppression. The testimony of a Negro counted for little or nothing in court, while the accusation of white witnesses was usually decisive. The result of this was a sudden large increase in the apparent criminal population of the Southern states—an increase so large that there was no way for the state to house it or watch it even had the state wished to. And the state did not wish to. Throughout the South laws were immediately passed authorizing public officials to lease the labor of convicts to the highest bidder. The lessee then took charge of the convicts—worked them as he wished under the nominal control of the state. Thus a new slavery and slave trade was established.[68]

I quote this long passage because it is such an insightful summary of the way the convict lease system served as a decisive lever for the transition from a bifurcated system of criminal justice—privatized punishment for Blacks and public punishment for whites—to a system in which the state concentrated on the punishment of Blacks and functioned as a mediator for punishment through privatized labor. In other words, "the state became a dealer in crime, profited by it so as to derive a net annual income for her prisoners."[69] Du Bois would later write in *Black Reconstruction,* "In no part of the modern world has there been so open and conscious a traffic in crime for deliberate social degradation and private profit as in the South since slavery."[70] Du Bois's analysis of the convict lease system implicitly contested Douglass's construction of Black labor as "free." Du Bois made the astute observation that so-called free Black labor was, in a very concrete sense, chained to Black convict labor, for in many industries in which Black people sought employment—such as brickmaking, mining, roadbuilding—wages were severely depressed by the fact that convicts could be leased from the state at costs as low as $3 a month.[71] Moreover, Du Bois pointed out that the very theory of work embodied in convict leasing would have to be radically transformed in order to establish a criminal justice system free of racial bias. Instead of convict labor serving as a scheme for both private and state profit, it would have to be reconstructed as a means of correction and reformation of the convict him/herself. With the abolition of the profit motive, Du Bois seemed to imply, a powerful incentive for the racism at the core of the system would cease to exist.

Unfortunately, Du Bois's contemporaries did not take up this insightful and radical analysis of the convict lease system. The relative obscurity to which it was relegated may be attributed to the fact that the essay appeared in a Protestant periodical devoted to writings on missionary projects, *The Missionary Review of the World.* As a result, its audience probably consisted largely of theologians and missionaries. Today, it is probably only read by students of religious studies and scholars researching convict leasing. However, Du Bois did refer to convict leasing and peonage in his monumental study—*Black Reconstruction.*

Twelve years after Douglass's death, Mary Church Terrell remarked that "it is surprising how few there are among even intelligent people in this country who seem to have anything but a hazy idea of what the convict lease system means."[72] Her essay on convict leasing was published in the prestigious review *The Nineteenth Century*, and although it is difficult to document how the essay was received, Milfred Fierce asserts that it "influenced many others, both Black and White."[73] Terrell, like Douglass in the preceding generation, was one of the major figures in the anti-lynching crusade. However, she wrote as passionately against the convict lease system as she had against lynching, meticulously documenting her allegations of untold cruelty with references to comments by southern legal authorities and official reports. "It is no exaggeration," Terrell wrote:

> to say that in some respects the convict lease system, as it is operated in certain southern States, is less humane than was the bondage endured by slaves fifty years ago. For, under the old regime, it was to the master's interest to clothe and shelter and feed his slaves properly, even if he were not moved to do so by considerations of mercy and humanity, because the death of a slave meant an actual loss in dollars and cents, whereas the death of a convict today involves no loss whatsoever either to the lessee or to the State.[74]

There are several references in the article to the way women were integrated into the convict lease system with little regard to their gender—they worked and were housed together with men. Focusing her examination on the state of Georgia, she quotes extensively from a report issued several years before by Colonel Alton Byrd, who had been appointed a special investigator into the conditions of Georgia's convict camps. In one passage he described a young Black woman:

> Lizzie Boatwright, a nineteen-year-old negress sent up from Thomas, Georgia, for larceny. She was clad in women's clothing, was working side by side with male convicts under a guard, cutting a ditch through a meadow. This girl was small of stature and pleasant of address, and her life in this camp must have been one of long drawn-out agony,

> horror, and suffering. She told me she had been whipped twice, each time by the brutal white guard who had beaten McRay (an elderly Black convict at the camp) to death, and who prostituted his legal rights to whip into a most revolting and disgusting outrage. This girl and another woman were stripped and beaten unmercifully in plain view of the men convicts, because they stopped on the side of the road to bind a rag about their sore feet.[75]

It is probably the case that Terrell devoted her most extensive discussion of women in the labor camps to white women, because she assumed that the brutal treatment of white women would provoke more widespread expressions of outrage than would that of Black women. Although she did not indicate the source of her information, she wrote that in the preceding year, news was released about "one thousand white girls . . . [who] wear men's clothing and work side by side with coloured men who are held in slavery as well as the girls. . . . In the black depths of [Florida] pinewoods, living in huts never seen by civilised white men other than the bosses of the turpentine camps, girls are said to have grown old in servitude."[76] Terrell concluded this section with the observation that "not only does peonage still rage violently in the Southern states and in a variety of forms, but that while it formerly affected only coloured people, it now attacks white men and women as well."[77] In this sense Terrell was probably influenced by the discourse of prison reform, which tended to equate the cruelty of peonage and convict leasing with its allegedly increasing impact on white people. For example, Richard Barry's 1907 article in *Cosmopolitan Magazine* emphasized the fact that employers in Florida had come under investigation because of the "monumental error" they made "in going beyond the Black man with their slavery. Had they stuck to the racial division they might have escaped castigation, as they have for a decade. But, insatiate, and not finding enough Blacks to satisfy their ambitious wants, they reached out and took in white men."[78]

Consequently, the movements to abolish convict leasing tended to reinforce notions of Black criminality even as they emphasized the brutality of the leasing system. This abolitionist movement coincided with the increasing influence of discourses on eugenics and scientific racism. Although Black leaders attempted to refute essentialist theories of innate criminality by emphasizing the historical conditions under which Black criminality emerged, they did not openly examine the structural role of the expanding network of penitentiaries and convict labor camps in constructing and affirming these ideologies. Philosophically, this represented an engagement with the presumption of criminality, but not with the institutions that concretely structured this ideology of criminality.

If Douglass was consistently silent on the issue of convict leasing, then Terrell did not integrate her insights on leasing into her anti-lynching work and thus could not effectively challenge a criminal justice system that perpetuated notions of Black criminality that still persist during the contemporary era. The same observation may be made of Du Bois. This is particularly important in light of the popular historical memory of lynching that remains a critical component of African American identity. If convict leasing and the accompanying disproportionality with which Black people were made to inhabit jails and prisons during the postemancipation period had been taken up with the same intensity and seriousness as—and in connection with—the campaign against lynching, then the contemporary radical call for prison abolition might not sound so implausible today.

Of course it is not fair to blame Douglass for over a century of failure to take on the pivotal role of the prison system in constructing and preserving ideological equations of Blackness and criminality. And it certainly is not fair to hold him responsible for the "commonsense" acceptance of the inevitability of prisons. However—and this is the conclusion of my examination of Douglass's silence vis-à-vis the convict lease system—scholars who rightfully criticize Douglass for the tenacity with which he embraced Enlightenment principles

CHAPTER 4

From the Convict Lease System to the Super-Max Prison*

Albert Wright Jr., is a fifty-year-old African American man who is serving a forty-year term in the Western Illinois Correctional Center. In this prison of 2,000 men, of whom some 66 percent are Black, he wrote in an impassioned plea to readers of *Emerge*, a Black monthly magazine: "[T]here is seldom a positive response to the cries for help in combating the inhuman treatment that we are subjected to daily. Few of you know what the treatment is like. What prison administrators tell you is not anything near the truth." Wright makes it very clear that he is not asking for financial support or material goods. "I am talking about genuine interest in what is happening to your people. We are still people. We just happen to be in prison."[1] But like many of the hundreds of thousands of Black men currently trapped in a political web of state and privately run prisons, Wright's humanity—and that of the imprisoned youth on whose behalf he made his appeal—goes unrecognized by a penal system that has abandoned the goals of individual rehabilitation and social reintegration in favor of increasingly harsh forms of punishment and retribution. Because the racist-informed discourse on criminality goes largely unchallenged, Black male bodies are treated as dispensable by communities in the "free world" that have all but forsaken those who are marked as criminal. Albert Wright obviously was concerned that middle-class Black communities are among those

* First published in *States of Confinement: Policing, Detention, and Prisons*, ed. Joy James (New York: St. Martin's Press, 2000), 60–74.

guilty of distancing themselves from the plight of prisoners; by submitting his piece to *Emerge*, he was simultaneously criticizing and reaching out to these communities.

Black men are now the primary targets of what prison reform advocate Jerome Miller calls the "search and destroy"[2] mission of a criminal justice system that, we must remember, also trains its sights on Black women and other men and women of color as well as on poor white people. African American males, who comprise less than 7 percent of the US population, constitute nearly half of the people in jail and prison.[3]

I do not intend to suggest that most imprisoned people have not committed a crime of some sort. In fact, studies repeatedly have found that a vast majority of most populations have engaged at one point in their lives in some type of behavior that is proscribed by law. However, only a small percentage of these acts is ever examined within the context of the criminal justice system.[4] Considering the fact that in the late 1990s, approximately one-third of all young Black men are either in prison or directly under the control of a correctional system, it is not entirely far-fetched to argue that one has a greater chance of going to jail or prison if one is a young Black man than if one actually has committed a crime. While most imprisoned young Black men also may have broken a law, it is more the fact of their race and gender than of their guilt or innocence that tends to bring them into contact with the criminal justice system.

The staggering numbers of imprisoned Black men should not, however, eclipse the fact that Black women—a majority of whom are arrested for drug-related offenses—constitute the most rapidly expanding of all imprisoned populations.[5] This phenomenon is attributable to the fact that poor Black women are increasingly targets of police surveillance for similar reasons as their male counterparts as well as for reasons related directly to their gender. The dismantling of welfare, for example, and the attendant demonization of single Black mothers—who are represented as procreators of crime and poverty—contribute to a problem that is leading large numbers of poor Black women into prison. Moreover, differential criminalization of drug use means that those unfortunate enough to become addicted to crack cocaine can be arrested and thrown in jail, while their middle-class counterparts who have access to legal drugs like Valium or Prozac are free to indulge their drug habits.

In fact, the current rise in the numbers of imprisoned Black men and women can hardly be justified by any recent increase in the crime rate among Black people. Human rights attorney Steven Donziger points out that "there are so many more African Americans than whites in our prisons that the difference cannot be explained by higher crime among African Americans—racial discrimination is also at work, and it penalizes African Americans at almost every juncture in the criminal justice system."[6] Yet Black people and people of color in general are increasingly the main human raw material being used for the expansion of the US penal system. I believe that the peculiarly racialized and gendered history of punishment in the United States has, in part, facilitated the structural and ideological transformation of the penal system into a prison industrial complex that imprisons, dehumanizes, and exploits ever-increasing numbers of people, the vast majority of whom are poor and Black.

It is not a coincidence that rehabilitation, the historical goal of the prison, has receded theoretically and practically as US prisons have come to house spiraling numbers of Black men. The current notion that the "criminals" with which prisons are overcrowded are largely beyond the pale of rehabilitation—that "nothing works"—is very much connected with the fact that in the contemporary era, the terms "Black" and "male," when combined, have become virtually synonymous with "criminal" in the popular imagination. This is not to ignore the complex historical evolution of the rehabilitative ideal, from a moral and religious to a medicalized framework, or the problematic category of recidivism, which has figured prominently in measurements of the success of rehabilitation.[7] However, narratives of rehabilitation have been so informed by the racial assumptions that have shaped moral and religious frameworks on one hand and medical frameworks on the other that an examination of these relationships may yield insights about the current construction of imprisonment as the inevitable destiny of young Black men. It also may assist us in understanding why the rather small proportion of women imprisoned recently has begun to rise to unprecedented heights, with Black female bodies increasingly subjected to a process of criminalization paralleling that of their male counterparts.

Given the recent emergence of super-maximum prisons and the increasingly punitive character of US prisons in general—which, in the 1990s, were being divested of educational, recreational, and other programs historically associated with rehabilitation projects—it is important to recall that in their early history, prisons were proposed as radical alternatives to the bodily pain that then comprised the dominant mode of punishment. The penitentiary—the historical manifestation of the prison as a site for punishment (rather than as a holding facility for people awaiting trial and punishment)—was conceived architecturally and theoretically as a plan for the moral reformation of the individual. As such it expressed the overarching Enlightenment-age assumption that reason formed the core of every human being. It also expressed modernity's vision of inevitable progress. However, as philosopher David Goldberg points out, the "defining of humanity in relation to rationality clearly prefaces modernity's emphasis on rational capacity as a crucial differentia of racial groups."[8] In fact, modernity's construction of rational humanity was not only racialized, it was gendered as well.

Although it has been argued that the origin of the term "penitentiary" is related to a plan in England to incarcerate "penitent" prostitutes,[9] the penitentiary as an institution for the reformation of criminals was aimed largely at white men. In the United States this is significant in that the birth of the penitentiary occurred during the last half-century or so of slavery, a period that also witnessed intense contestations over the future of women's rights.

Reflecting modernity's relegation of women of all racial backgrounds, and men of color, to reason's antithesis—nature, instinct, and the senses—the putative universality of reason masked strong racial and gendered assumptions about the bodies in which universal reason resided. During much of the nineteenth century, white women had no autonomous juridical status, and they were punished largely within the domestic sphere. As daughters, they were subjected to corporal punishment by their fathers, and as wives, by their husbands. White women deemed "criminal" and brought into the criminal justice system were considered "fallen" and, as such, beyond the pale of moral rehabilitation.

Until the abolition of slavery, most Black men and women were under the authority of their slave masters, who developed punishment regimes designed simultaneously to inflict severe bodily pain and to safeguard the *body* as a laboring and thus profitable commodity. An example of this was the digging of holes in which pregnant women could lay their stomachs in order to protect their unborn children—who were grist for the mills of slave labor—while being flogged.[10] In this context, punishment was entirely detached from the goal of moral reformation. Because slave laborers were valued largely in relation to their size and strength, the value of male slaves was generally higher than that of female slaves, a probable consequence of which was the privileging of the male body for labor and punishment. This is not to dismiss the horrors to which women were subjected under slavery, which included sexualized forms of punishment such as rape as well as gendered forms of punishment related to the control and preservation of women's reproductive labor.

During the post–Civil War era, extralegal lynching along with the legalized Black Codes identified the bodies of Black people as the loci of punishment. In this way, Black men and women continued to be excluded, on the grounds of both race and gender, from the moral realm within which punishment in the penitentiary was equated with rehabilitation. Black men were barred from the individuality and masculinity with which even the criminal citizen was imbued. Black women, on the other hand, were barred from the femininity that tended to protect many white women from imprisonment. The birth of the English and American penitentiaries, whose most ardent advocates were passionately opposed to harsh corporal punishment, had little impact on the punishment regimes to which enslaved people were subjected. Neither did they effectively alter the ways in which white women were punished. As such they were implicitly racialized and gendered as new and less cruel modes of white male punishment.

The most widely publicized penitentiary design was the panopticon engineered for total observation and proposed by utilitarian philosopher Jeremy Bentham. Although few prisons actually were constructed according to its strict standards, its discursive impact was such that it was linked closely to the project of prison rehabilitation. Between 1787 and 1791, Bentham published a series of letters describing in detail a new architectural design for prisons and other institutions requiring the surveillance and control of large numbers of people. Bentham's panopticon was supposed to guarantee the ubiquitous monitoring and the imposition of discipline he thought criminals needed in order to internalize productive labor habits. According to Bentham's plan, which he hoped would win him a contract with the government to build and operate a penitentiary, prison inmates would be housed in solitary cells situated on circular tiers, all of which would face a multilevel guard tower. Bentham suggested the use of venetian blinds, combined with a rather complex interplay of light and darkness, to guarantee that the prisoners—whose cells were arranged so that they could not see each other—also would be unable to see the warden in the guard tower. The warden's vantage point, on the other hand, would allow him a clear view of all the prisoners. However—and this was the most significant aspect of Bentham's mammoth panopticon—because each individual prisoner would never be able to determine where the warden's gaze was focused, each one would be compelled to behave as if he were being watched at all times.

The most consistent attempt to implement Bentham's panopticon design took place in the United States at Stateville Penitentiary, located near Joliet, Illinois, which officially opened on March 9, 1925. It took shape as a direct result of a reform movement, begun in 1905, that exposed the state of Illinois for maintaining "brutal and inhumane conditions" at the old Joliet prison, built in 1860.[11] When a legislative committee returned from a trip to Europe to examine prison planning abroad, they announced that they were most impressed by Bentham's panopticon. Although Stateville was partially constructed as a panopticon, by the time construction was entering its last phase, the state had given up on the circular plan and completed the prison with rectangular cell houses. For the first twenty-five years of its history, Stateville held a majority white prison population. However, by the mid-1950s, the prison population was majority Black.[12]

As theorist Michel Foucault later pointed out, the prisoner of the panopticon "is seen, but he does not see; he is the object of information, never a subject in communication . . . [a]nd this invisibility is a guarantee of order."[13] Moreover, the crowd—a compact mass, a locus of multiple exchanges, individualities merging together, a collective effect—is abolished and replaced by a collection of separated individualities. From the point of view of the guardian, the crowd is replaced by a multiplicity that can be numbered and supervised; from the point of view of the inmates, by a sequestered and observed solitude.[14]

This process of individualization via the panopticon assumed that the prisoner was at least a potentially rational being whose criminality merely evidenced deviation from that potential. This architecture and regime also assumed that the individual to be reformed panoptically was in possession of mental and moral faculties that could be controlled and transformed by the experience of imprisonment. White women were theoretically exempt from this process, since in Britain and in the United States at the turn of the nineteenth century the overdetermining ideology of the "fallen woman" constructed female criminals as having no prospect of moral rehabilitation. Black men and women, on the other hand, were ideologically barred from the realm of morality and, unlike white women, were not even acknowledged as ever having been epistemological subjects and moral agents. Thus, they could not even fall from grace, a state they were deemed incapable of attaining in the first place.

Slaves were not accorded the social status of individuals. If they were granted any individuality at all, it was corporal in nature, defined by their value on the market, their laboring potential, and the punishment they received. As a consequence, they often were not even subject to the gender differentiation operative in the dominant culture. Women's quotas in the plantation fields, for example, where their tasks were essentially the same as men's, were established in connection with their size and weight, rather than with their gender. Women also were targets of the whip and the lash, the major weapons of punishment during slavery.

As Black people began to be integrated into southern penal systems in the aftermath of the Civil War—and as the penal system became a system of penal servitude—the punishment associated with slavery became integrated into the penal system. "Whipping," as author Matthew Mancini has observed, "was the preeminent form of punishment under slavery; and the lash, along with the chain, became the very emblem of servitude for slaves and prisoners."[15] Many Black people were imprisoned under the laws assembled in the various Black Codes of the southern states, which, because they were rearticulations of the Slave Codes, tended to racialize penalty and link it closely with previous regimes of slavery. The expansion of the convict lease system and the county chain gang meant that the antebellum criminal justice system, which focused far more intensely on Black people than on whites, largely defined southern criminal justice as a means of controlling Black labor. According to Mancini:

> Among the multifarious debilitating legacies of slavery was the conviction that Blacks could only labor in a certain way—the way experience had shown them to have labored in the past: in gangs, subjected to constant supervision, and under the discipline of the lash. Since these were the requisites of slavery, and since slaves were Blacks, Southern whites almost universally concluded that Blacks could not work unless subjected to such intense surveillance and discipline.[16]

Scholars who have studied the convict lease system point out that in many important respects, convict leasing was far worse than slavery; the title of Mancini's study is *One Dies, Get Another* and the title of David Oshinsky's work on Parchman Prison is *Worse Than Slavery*. The concern slave owners necessarily expressed for individual slaves because of their particular individual value no longer applied to convicts, who were leased out en masse and could be worked literally to death without affecting the profitability of a convict crew. According to descriptions by contemporaries, the conditions under which leased convicts and county chain gangs lived were far worse than those under which Black people had lived as slaves. The records of Mississippi plantations in the Yazoo Delta during the late 1880s indicate that

> the prisoners ate and slept on bare ground, without blankets or mattresses, and often without clothes. They were punished for "slow hoeing" (ten lashes), "sorry planting" (five lashes) and "being light with cotton" (five lashes). Some who attempted to escape were whipped "till the blood ran down their legs"; others had a metal spur riveted to their feet. Convicts dropped from exhaustion, pneumonia, malaria, frostbite, consumption, sunstroke, dysentery, gunshot wounds, and "shackle poisoning" (the constant rubbing of chains and leg irons against bare flesh).[17]

The US penitentiaries, as they developed according to the Pennsylvania and Auburn systems, envisioned labor as a rehabilitative activity; *convict* labor in the South, overwhelmingly Black, was designed to reap the largest possible profits. Rehabilitation had little or nothing to do with the punishment industry as it developed there. Thus, the theory of punishment associated with the new US penitentiaries and with the Benthamian conception of the panopticon was entirely at odds with the forms of punishment meted out to newly freed Black people.

In the contemporary era, the emergent prison industrial complex, which is fueled increasingly by privatization trends, recalls the early efforts to create a profitable punishment industry based on the new supply of "free" Black male laborers in the aftermath of the Civil War. Steven Donziger, drawing from the work of Norwegian criminologist Nils Christie, argues that

> companies that service the criminal justice system need sufficient quantities of raw materials to guarantee long-term growth. . . . In the criminal justice field, the raw material is prisoners, and industry will do what is necessary to guarantee a steady supply. For the supply of prisoners to grow, criminal justice policies must ensure a sufficient number of incarcerated Americans regardless of whether crime is rising or the incarceration is necessary.[18]

Just as newly freed Black men and a significant number of Black women constituted a virtually endless supply of raw material for the embryonic southern punishment industry and provided much-needed labor for the southern states as they attempted to recover from the devastating impact of the Civil War—so in the contemporary era do unemployed Black men, along with increasing numbers of Black women, constitute an unending supply of raw material for the prison industrial complex.

According to 1997 Bureau of Justice Statistics, African Americans as a whole now represent the majority of state and federal prisoners, with a total of 735,200 Black inmates—10,000 more than the total number of white inmates. As the rate of increase in the incarceration of Black prisoners continues to rise, the racial composition of the incarcerated population is approaching the proportion of Black prisoners to white during the era of the southern convict lease and county chain gang systems. Whether this human raw material is used for its labor or as the forced consumers of commodities provided by corporations directly implicated in the prison industrial complex, it is clear that Black male bodies are considered dispensable within the "free world." They are also a major source of profit in the prison world. This relationship recapitulates in complicated new ways the era of convict leasing.

The privatization characteristic of convict leasing also has its contemporary parallels, as companies like Corrections Corporation of America and Wackenhut* literally run prisons for profit. In the late 1990s, the seventeen private prison companies operating in the United States (and sometimes also abroad) have constructed approximately one hundred jails and prisons in which 50,000 inmates are incarcerated. Private prisons have multiplied at four times the rate of the expansion of public prisons. Observers of the private prison phenomenon have estimated that there will be three times as many private facilities by the turn of the century and that their revenues will be more than $1 billion.[19] In arrangements reminiscent of the convict lease system, federal, state, and county governments pay private companies a fee for each inmate; thus private companies have a stake in retaining prisoners as long as possible and in keeping their facilities filled.

In the state of Texas, there are thirty-four government-owned, privately run jails in which approximately 5,500 out-of-state prisoners are incarcerated. These facilities generate about $80 million annually for Texas.[20] Capital Corrections Resources, Inc., operates the Brazoria Detention Center, a government-owned facility located forty miles outside of Houston, Texas. Brazoria came to public attention in August 1997 when a videotape broadcast on national

* Now known as CoreCivic and G4S, respectively.

television showed prisoners there being bitten by police dogs and viciously kicked in the groin and stepped on by guards. The inmates, forced to crawl on the floor, also were being shocked with stun guns as guards—who referred to one Black prisoner as "boy"—shouted "Crawl faster!"[21] After the tape's release, the state of Missouri withdrew the 415 prisoners it housed in the detention center. Although accompanying news reports made few references to the indisputably racialized character of the guards' behavior, in the section of the Brazoria videotape that was shown on national television, Black male prisoners were seen to be primary targets of the guards' attacks.

The thirty-two-minute Brazoria tape, which jail authorities stated was a training tape showing corrections officers "what *not* to do," was made in September 1996. Important evidence of the abuse that takes place behind the walls and gates of private prisons came to light in connection with a lawsuit filed by one of the prisoners who was bitten by a dog; he was suing Brazoria County for $100,000 in damages. The Brazoria jailers' actions—which, according to prisoners there, were far worse than depicted on the tape—were indicative not only of the ways in which many prisoners throughout the country are treated but of generalized attitudes toward people locked up in jails and prisons; it is believed that, by virtue of their imprisonment, they deserve this kind of severe corporal punishment. According to an Associated Press news story, once the Missouri inmates had been transferred back to their home state from Brazoria, they told the *Kansas City Star* that "guards at the Brazoria County Detention Center used cattle prods and other forms of intimidation to win respect and force prisoners to say, 'I love Texas.'" "What you saw on tape wasn't a fraction of what happened that day," said inmate Louis Watkins, referring to the videotaped cellblock raid of September 18, 1996. "I've never seen anything like that in the movies."[22]

It is interesting that this prisoner compared what he saw during the detention center raid to cinematic representations of prison experience. One of my arguments is that prison experience, in popular representational practices, is a quintessentially Black male experience. Whether brutal punishment within penal settings is inflicted on white, Latino/a, Asian, Native, or African American men or women, the typical prisoner—and the target of this brutality—is generally considered to be a Black man. The gross violations of prisoners' civil and human rights, in this sense, are very much connected with the generalized equation of "criminal" or "prisoner" with a Black male body.

The current construction and expansion of state and federal super-maximum security prisons, whose purpose is to address disciplinary problems within the penal system, draws on the historical conception of the panopticon. Again, Black men are vastly overrepresented in these super-max prisons and control units, the first of which emerged when federal correctional authorities began to send prisoners whom they deemed to be "dangerous" to the prison in Marion, Illinois. In 1983 the entire prison was "locked down," which meant that prisoners were confined to their cells twenty-three hours a day.[23] Today there are at least fifty-seven super-maximum security federal and state prisons located in thirty-six states.[24] A description of super-maxes in a 1997 report by Human Rights Watch sounds chillingly like Bentham's panopticon. What is different, however, is that all references to individual rehabilitation have disappeared:

> Inmates in super-maximum security facilities are usually held in a single cell lock-down, what is commonly referred to as solitary confinement. . . . [C]ongregate activities with other prisoners are usually prohibited; other prisoners cannot even be seen from an inmate's cell; communication with other prisoners is prohibited or difficult (consisting, for example, of shouting from cell to cell); visiting and telephone privileges are limited. The new generation of super-maximum security facilities also rely on state-ofthe-art technology for monitoring and controlling prisoner conduct and movement, utilizing, for example, video monitors and remote-controlled electronic doors. These prisons represent the application of

> sophisticated, modern technology dedicated entirely to the task of social control, and they isolate, regulate and surveil more effectively than anything that has preceded them.[25]

Some of these super-max prisons house inmates in cells with solid steel gates rather than bars—an arrangement that recalls the railroad cars used in the past to house leased convicts—so that prisoners literally see nothing. They are fed through a slot in the gate, unable even to see the guards who bring their food. According to Jerome Miller, "The disproportionate percentage of Black men in the general prison populations is outstripped by the much greater percentage of Black men housed in super-max prisons."[26] Miller refers to a study by researcher William Chambliss, who found that on one day in 1993, 98 percent of the inmates confined in the super-max prison in Baltimore, Maryland, were African Americans.[27]

The danger of super-max prisons resides not only in the systematically brutal treatment of the prisoners confined therein but also in the way they establish standards for the treatment of all prisoners. They solidify the move away from rehabilitative strategies and do so largely on the backs of Black men. Moreover, as prisons become more repressive and as this repression becomes more remote from—and, by default, accepted within—the "free world," they promote retrograde tendencies in educational institutions that serve the populations most likely to move from schools into prisons. These educational institutions begin to resemble prisons more than schools. In poor Black communities, for example, schools tend to direct resources needed to address educational crises toward security and discipline. Rather than preparing students for college, middle and high schools in these communities are fast becoming prep schools for prison, molding Black children into raw material for punishment and coerced labor.

The extent to which Black men today function as the main human raw material for the prison industrial complex only highlights the many ways in which the prison system in the United States in general resembles and recapitulates some of the most abhorrent characteristics of the slavery and convict lease systems of the late nineteenth century. As mentioned earlier, the rampant exploitation of prison labor in an increasingly privatized context is a modern-day form of convict leasing. While Black men are not the only population vulnerable to this exploitation, the overwhelming numbers of Black men imprisoned in the United States make them by far the most threatened members of our society when it comes to the new form of enslavement being implemented through the prison system.

The fact that we can draw these connections between latter-twentieth-century imprisonment practices in the United States and various systems and practices in place a century ago is largely a result of the racism woven into the history of the prison system in this country. The ultimate manifestation of this phenomenon can be found in the super-max prison. Its main function is to subdue and control "problematic" imprisoned populations—again, comprised largely of Black men—who, having been locked away in the most remote and invisible of spaces, are no longer thought of as human. The absolute authority exercised over these disappeared populations[28] by super-max administrators and staff—and the lack of accountability on the part of private corporations in the prison business and/or that benefit from prison labor—is reminiscent of the impunity with which slave owners, overseers, and, later, patrons of the convict lease system routinely disregarded the humanity connected with the Black bodies they systematically abused.

In this sense, the super-max draws on, even as it also serves to feed, the perpetuation of racism at every level of our society. This is true, in fact, of the entire prison system; the continued practice of throwing away entire populations depends on the popular imagination viewing those populations as public enemies. It is precisely this relationship between racism and imprisonment that requires anti-racist activists and prison activists to work together; on the eve of the twenty-first century, these two movements are inseparable.

PART III

Disarticulating Crime and Punishment

Emerging Abolitionist Frameworks

CHAPTER 5

Race and Criminalization

Black Americans and the Punishment Industry*

In this post–civil rights era, as racial barriers in high economic and political realms are apparently shattered with predictable regularity, race itself becomes an increasingly proscribed subject. In the dominant political discourse, it is no longer acknowledged as a pervasive structural phenomenon, requiring the continuation of such strategies as affirmative action, but rather is represented primarily as a complex of prejudicial attitudes, which carry equal weight across all racial boundaries. Black leadership is thus often discredited and the identification of race as a public, political issue itself called into question through the invocation of, and application of, the epithet "Black racist" to such figures as Louis Farrakhan and Khalid Abdul Muhammad. Public debates about the role of the state that once focused very sharply and openly on issues of "race" and racism are now expected to unfold in the absence of any direct acknowledgment of the persistence—and indeed further entrenchment—of racially structured power relationships. Because race is ostracized from some of the most impassioned political debates of this period, their racialized character becomes increasingly difficult to identify, especially by those who are unable—or do not want—to decipher the encoded

* First published in *The House That Race Built: Original Essays by Toni Morrison, Angela Y. Davis, Cornel West, and Others on Black Americans and Politics in America Today*, ed. Wahneema H. Lubiano (New York: Vintage, 1997), 264–79. Speech originally delivered at "Race Matters" conference at Princeton University in April 1994.

language. This means that hidden racist arguments can be mobilized readily across racial boundaries and political alignments. Political positions once easily defined as conservative, liberal, and sometimes even radical therefore have a tendency to lose their distinctiveness in the face of the seductions of this camouflaged racism.

President Clinton chose the date of the Million Man March, convened by Minister Louis Farrakhan of the Nation of Islam, to issue a call for a "national conversation on race," borrowing ironically the exact words of Lani Guinier (whose nomination for assistant attorney general in charge of civil rights he had previously withdrawn because her writings focused too sharply on issues of race).[1] Guinier's ideas had been so easily dismissed because of the prevailing ideological equation of the "end of racism" with the removal of all allusions to race. If conservative positions argue that race consciousness itself impedes the process of solving the problem of race—i.e., achieving race blindness—then Clinton's speech indicated an attempt to reconcile the two, positing race consciousness as a means of moving toward race blindness: "There are too many today, white and Black, on the left and the right, on the street corners and radio waves, who seek to sow division for their own purposes. To them I say: 'No more. We must be one.'"

While Clinton did acknowledge "the awful history and stubborn persistence of racism," his remarks foregrounded those reasons for the "racial divide" that "are rooted in the fact that we still haven't learned to talk frankly, to listen carefully and to work together across racial lines." Race, he insisted, is not about government but about the hearts of people. Of course, it would be absurd to deny the degree to which racism infects in deep and multiple ways the national psyche. However, the relegation of race to matters of the heart tends to render it increasingly difficult to identify the deep structural entrenchment of contemporary racism.

When the structural character of racism is ignored in discussions about crime and the rising population of incarcerated people, the racial imbalance in jails and prisons is treated as a contingency, at best as a product of the "culture of poverty," and at worst as proof of an assumed Black monopoly on criminality. The high proportion of Black people in the criminal justice system is thus normalized and neither the state nor the general public is required to talk about and act on the meaning of that racial imbalance. Thus Republican and Democratic elected officials alike have successfully called for laws mandating life sentences for three-time "criminals," without having to answer for the racial implications of these laws. By relying on the alleged "race blindness" of such laws, Black people are surreptitiously constructed as racial subjects, thus manipulated, exploited, and abused, while the structural persistence of racism—albeit in changed forms—in social and economic institutions, and in the national culture as a whole, is adamantly denied.

Crime is thus one of the masquerades behind which "race," with all its menacing ideological complexity, mobilizes old public fears and creates new ones. The current anti-crime debate takes place within a reified mathematical realm—a strategy reminiscent of Malthus's notion of the geometrical increase in population and the arithmetical increase in food sources, thus the inevitability of poverty and the means of suppressing it: war, disease, famine, and natural disasters. As a matter of fact, the persisting neo-Malthusian approach to population control, which, instead of seeking to solve those pressing social problems that result in real pain and suffering in people's lives, calls for the elimination of those suffering lives, finds strong resonances in the public discussion about expurgating the "nation" of crime. These discussions include arguments deployed by those who are leading the call for more prisons and employ statistics in the same fetishistic and misleading way as Malthus did more than two centuries ago. Take for example James Wooten's comments in the *Heritage Foundation State Backgrounder*:

> If the 55 percent of the estimated 800,000 current state and federal prisoners who are violent offenders were subject to serving 85 percent of their sentence, and assuming that those

> violent offenders would have committed 10 violent crimes a year while on the street, then the number of crimes prevented each year by truth in sentencing would be 4,000,000. That would be over 2/3 of the 6,000,000 violent crimes reported.[2]

In *Reader's Digest,* senior editor Eugene H. Methvin writes: "If we again double the present federal and state prison population—to somewhere between 1 million and 1.5 million and leave our city and county jail population at the present 400,000, we will break the back of America's 30 year crime wave."[3] The real human beings—a vastly disproportionate number of whom are Black and Latino/a men and women—designated by these numbers in a seemingly race-neutral way are deemed fetishistically exchangeable with the crimes they have or will allegedly commit. The real impact of imprisonment on their lives need never be examined. The inevitable part played by the punishment industry in the reproduction of crime need never be discussed. The dangerous and indeed fascistic trend toward progressively greater numbers of hidden, incarcerated human populations is itself rendered invisible. All that matters is the elimination of crime—and you get rid of crime by getting rid of people who, according to the prevailing racial common sense, are the most likely people to whom criminal acts will be attributed. Never mind that if this strategy is seriously and consistently pursued, the majority of young Black men and a fast-growing proportion of young Black women will spend a good portion of their lives behind walls and bars in order to serve as a reminder that the state is aggressively confronting its enemy.[4]

While I do not want to locate a response to these arguments on the same level of mathematical abstraction and fetishism I have been problematizing, it is helpful, I think, to consider how many people are presently incarcerated or whose lives are subject to the direct surveillance of the criminal justice system. There are already approximately 1 million people in state and federal prisons in the United States, not counting the 500,000 in city and county jails, the 600,000 on parole, the 3 million people on probation, or the 60,000 young people in juvenile facilities. Which is to say that there are presently over 5.1 million people either incarcerated, on parole, or on probation. Many of those presently on probation or parole would be behind bars under the conditions of the recently passed crime bill. According to the Sentencing Project, even before the passage of the crime bill, Black people were 7.8 times more likely to be imprisoned than whites.[5] The Sentencing Project's most recent report[6] indicates that 32.2 percent of young Black men and 12.3 percent of young Latino men between the ages of twenty and twenty-nine are either in prison, in jail, or on probation or parole. This is in comparison with 6.7 percent of young white men. A total of 827,440 young African American males are under the supervision of the criminal justice system, at a cost of $6 billion per year. A major strength of the 1995 report, as compared to its predecessor, is its acknowledgment that the racialized impact of the criminal justice system is also gendered and that the relatively smaller number of African American women drawn into the system should not relieve us of the responsibility of understanding the encounter of gender and race in arrest and incarceration practices. Moreover, the increases in women's contact with the criminal justice system have been even more dramatic than those of men:

> The 78 percent increase in criminal justice control rates for Black women was more than double the increase for Black men and for white women, and more than nine times the increase for white men. . . . Although research on women of color in the criminal justice system is limited, existing data and research suggest that it is the combination of race and sex effects that is at the root of the trends which appear in our data. For example, while the number of Blacks and Hispanics in prison is growing at an alarming rate, the rate of increase for women is even greater. Between 1980 and 1992 the female prison population increased 276 percent, compared to 163 percent for men. Unlike men of color, women of color thus belong to two

groups that are experiencing particular dramatic growth in their contact with the criminal justice system.[7]

It has been estimated that by the year 2000 the number of people imprisoned will surpass 4 million, a grossly disproportionate number of whom will be Black people, and that the cost will be over $40 billion a year,[8] a figure that is reminiscent of the way the military budget devoured—and continues to devour—the country's resources. This out-of-control punishment industry is an extremely effective criminalization industry, for the racial imbalance in incarcerated populations is not recognized as evidence of structural racism but rather is invoked as a consequence of the assumed criminality of Black people. In other words, the criminalization process works so well precisely because of the hidden logic of racism. Racist logic is deeply entrenched in the nation's material and psychic structures. It is something with which we all are very familiar. The logic, in fact, can persist, even when direct allusions to "race" are removed.

Even those communities that are most deeply injured by this racist logic have learned how to rely upon it, particularly when open allusions to race are not necessary. Thus, in the absence of broad, radical grassroots movements in poor Black communities so devastated by new forms of youth-perpetrated violence, the ideological options are extremely sparse. Often there are no other ways to express collective rage and despair but to demand that police sweep the community clean of crack and Uzis, and of the people who use and sell drugs and wield weapons. Ironically, Carol Moseley-Braun, the first Black woman senator in our nation's history, was an enthusiastic sponsor of the Senate Anti-Crime Bill, whose passage in November 1993 paved the way for the August 25, 1994, passage of the bill by the House. Or perhaps there is little irony here. It may be precisely because there is a Carol Moseley-Braun in the Senate and a Clarence Thomas in the Supreme Court—and concomitant class differentiations and other factors responsible for far more heterogeneity in Black communities than at any other time in this country's history—that implicit consent to anti-Black racist logic (not to speak of racism toward other groups) becomes far more widespread among Black people. Wahneema Lubiano's explorations of the complexities of state domination as it operates within and through the subjectivities of those who are the targets of this domination facilitates an understanding of this dilemma.[9]

Borrowing the title of Cornel West's recent work, race matters.[10] Moreover, it matters in ways that are far more threatening and simultaneously less discernible than those to which we have grown accustomed. Race matters inform, more than ever, the ideological and material structures of US society. And, as the current discourses on crime, welfare, and immigration reveal, race, gender, and class matter enormously in the continuing elaboration of public policy and its impact on the real lives of human beings.

And how does race matter? Fear has always been an integral component of racism. The ideological reproduction of a fear of Black people, whether economically or sexually grounded, is rapidly gravitating toward and being grounded in a fear of crime. A question to be raised in this context is whether and how the increasing fear of crime—this ideologically produced fear of crime—serves to render racism simultaneously more invisible and more virulent. Perhaps one way to approach an answer to this question is to consider how this fear of crime effectively summons Black people to imagine Black people as the enemy. How many Black people present at this conference have successfully extricated ourselves from the ideological power of the figure of the young Black male as criminal—or at least seriously confronted it? The lack of a significant Black presence in the rather feeble opposition to the "three strikes, you're out" bills, which have been proposed and/or passed in forty states already, evidences the disarming effect of this ideology.

California is one of the states that has passed the "three strikes, you're out" bill. Immediately after the passage of that bill, Governor Pete Wilson began to argue for a "two strikes, you're out" bill. Three, he said, is too many. Soon we will hear calls for "one strike, you're out." Following this mathematical regression, we can imagine that at some point the hardcore anti-crime advocates will be arguing that to stop the crime wave, we can't wait until even one crime is committed. Their slogan will be: "Get them before the first strike!" And because certain populations have already been criminalized, there will be those who say, "We know who the real criminals are—let's get them before they have a chance to act out their criminality."

The fear of crime has attained a status that bears a sinister similarity to the fear of communism as it came to restructure social perceptions during the fifties and sixties. The figure of the "criminal"—the racialized figure of the criminal—has come to represent the most menacing enemy of "American society." Virtually anything is acceptable—torture, brutality, vast expenditures of public funds—as long as it is done in the name of public safety. Racism has always found an easy route from its embeddedness in social structures to the psyches of collectives and individuals precisely because it mobilizes deep fears. While explicit, old-style racism may be increasingly socially unacceptable—precisely as a result of antiracist movements over the last forty years—this does not mean that US society has been purged of racism. In fact, racism is more deeply embedded in socioeconomic structures, and the vast populations of incarcerated people of color are dramatic evidence of the way racism systematically structures economic relations. At the same time, this structural racism is rarely recognized as "racism." What we have come to recognize as open, explicit racism has in many ways begun to be replaced by a secluded, camouflaged kind of racism, whose influence on people's daily lives is as pervasive and systematic as the explicit forms of racism associated with the era of the struggle for civil rights.

The ideological space for the proliferations of this racialized fear of crime has been opened by the transformations in international politics created by the fall of the European socialist countries. Communism is no longer the quintessential enemy against which the nation imagines its identity. This space is now inhabited by ideological constructions of crime, drugs, immigration, and welfare. Of course, the enemy within is far more dangerous than the enemy without, and a Black enemy within is the most dangerous of all.

Because of the tendency to view it as an abstract site into which all manner of undesirables are deposited, the prison is the perfect site for the simultaneous production and concealment of racism. The abstract character of the public perception of prisons militates against an engagement with the real issues afflicting the communities from which prisoners are drawn in such disproportionate numbers. This is the ideological work that the prison performs—it relieves us of the responsibility of seriously engaging with the problems of late capitalism, of transnational capitalism. The naturalization of Black people as criminals thus also erects ideological barriers to an understanding of the connections between late-twentieth-century structural racism and the globalization of capital.

The vast expansion of the power of capitalist corporations over the lives of people of color and poor people in general has been accompanied by a waning anticapitalist consciousness. As capital moves with ease across national borders, legitimized by recent trade agreements such as NAFTA and GATT, corporations are allowed to close shop in the United States and transfer manufacturing operations to nations providing cheap labor pools. In fleeing organized labor in the US to avoid paying higher wages and benefits, they leave entire communities in shambles, consigning huge numbers of people to joblessness, leaving them prey to the drug trade, destroying the economic base of these communities—thus affecting the education system and social welfare—and turning the people who live in those communities into perfect candidates for prison. At the same time, they create an economic demand for prisons, which stimulates the economy, providing jobs in the correctional industry for people who often come from the very populations that are criminalized by this process. It is a horrifying and self-reproducing cycle.

Ironically, prisons themselves are becoming a source of cheap labor that attracts corporate capitalism—as yet on a relatively small scale—in a way that parallels the attraction unorganized labor in Third World countries exerts. A statement by Michael Lamar Powell, a prisoner in Capshaw, Alabama, dramatically reveals this new development:

> I cannot go on strike, nor can I unionize. I am not covered by workers' compensation of the Fair Labor Standards Act. I agree to work late-night and weekend shifts. I do just what I am told, no matter what it is. I am hired and fired at will, and I am not even paid minimum wage: I earn one dollar a month. I cannot even voice grievances or complaints, except at the risk of incurring arbitrary discipline or some covert retaliation.
>
> You need not worry about NAFTA and your jobs going to Mexico and other Third World countries. I will have at least five percent of your jobs by the end of this decade.
>
> I am called prison labor. I am The New American Worker.[11]

This "new American worker" will be drawn from the ranks of a racialized population whose historical superexploitation—from the era of slavery to the present—has been legitimized by racism. At the same time, the expansion of convict labor is accompanied in some states by the old paraphernalia of ankle chains that symbolically links convict labor with slave labor. At least three states—Alabama, Florida, and Arizona—have reinstituted the chain gang. Moreover, as Michael Powell so incisively reveals, there is a new dimension to the racism inherent in this process, which structurally links the superexploitation of prison labor to the globalization of capital.

In California, whose prison system is the largest in the country and one of the largest in the world, the passage of an inmate labor initiative in 1990 has presented businesses seeking cheap labor with opportunities uncannily similar to those in Third World countries.

As of June 1994, a range of companies were employing prison labor in nine California prisons. Under the auspices of the Joint Venture Program, work now being performed on prison grounds includes computerized telephone messaging, dental apparatus assembly, computer data entry, plastic parts fabrication, electronic component manufacturing at the Central California Women's facility at Chowchilla, security glass manufacturing, swine production, oak furniture manufacturing, and the production of stainless steel tanks and equipment. In a California Corrections Department brochure designed to promote the program, it is described as "an innovative public-private partnership that makes good business sense."[12] According to the owner of Tower Communications, whom the brochure quotes,

> The operation is cost effective, dependable and trouble free. . . . Tower Communications has successfully operated a message center utilizing inmates on the grounds of a California state prison. If you're a business leader planning expansion, considering relocation because of a deficient labor pool, starting a new enterprise, look into the benefits of using inmate labor.

The employer benefits listed by the brochure include

> federal and state tax incentives; no benefit package (retirement pay, vacation pay, sick leave, medical benefits); long term lease agreements at far below market value costs; discount rates on Workers Compensation; build a consistent, qualified work force; on call labor pool (no car breakdowns, no babysitting problems); option of hiring job-ready ex-offenders and minimizing costs; becoming a partner in public safety.

There is a major, yet invisible, racial supposition in such claims about the profitability of a convict labor force. The acceptability of the superexploitation of convict labor is largely based on the historical conjuncture of racism and incarceration practices. The already disproportionately Black convict labor force will become increasingly Black if the racially imbalanced incarceration practices continue.

The complicated yet unacknowledged structural presence of racism in the US punishment industry also includes the fact that the punishment industry that sequesters ever-larger sectors of the Black population attracts vast amounts of capital. Ideologically, as I have argued, the racialized fear of crime has begun to succeed the fear of communism. This corresponds to a structural tendency for capital that previously flowed toward the military industry to now move toward the punishment industry. The ease with which suggestions are made for prison construction costing in the multibillions of dollars is reminiscent of the military buildup: economic mobilization to defeat communism has turned into economic mobilization to defeat crime. The ideological construction of crime is thus complemented and bolstered by the material construction of jails and prisons. The more jails and prisons are constructed, the greater the fear of crime, and the greater the fear of crime, the stronger the cry for more jails and prisons, ad infinitum.

The law enforcement industry bears remarkable parallels to the military industry (just as there are anticommunist resonances in the anti-crime campaign). This connection between the military industry and the punishment industry is revealed in a *Wall Street Journal* article entitled "Making Crime Pay: The Cold War of the '90s":

> Parts of the defense establishment are cashing in, too, scenting a logical new line of business to help them offset military cutbacks. Westinghouse Electric Corp., Minnesota Mining and Manufacturing Co., GDE Systems (a division of the old General Dynamics) and Alliant Techsystems Inc., for instance, are pushing crime-fighting equipment and have created special divisions to retool their defense technology for America's streets.

According to the article, a conference sponsored by the National Institute of Justice, the research arm of the Justice Department, was organized around the theme "Law Enforcement Technology in the 21st Century." The secretary of defense was a major presenter at this conference, which explored topics like "the role of the defense industry, particularly for dual use and conversion":

> Hot topics: defense-industry technology that could lower the level of violence involved in crime fighting. Sandia National Laboratories, for instance, is experimenting with a dense foam that can be sprayed at suspects, temporarily blinding and deafening them under breathable bubbles. Stinger Corporation is working on "smart guns," which will fire only for the owner, and retractable spiked barrier strips to unfurl in front of fleeing vehicles. Westinghouse is promoting the "smart car," in which minicomputers could be linked up with big mainframes at the police department, allowing for speedy booking of prisoners, as well as quick exchanges of information.[13]

Again, race provides a silent justification for the technological expansion of law enforcement, which, in turn, intensifies racist arrest and incarceration practices. This skyrocketing punishment industry, whose growth is silently but powerfully sustained by the persistence of racism, creates an economic demand for more jails and prisons and thus for similarly spiraling criminalization practices, which, in turn, fuels the fear of crime.

Most debates addressing the crisis resulting from overcrowding in prisons and jails focus on male institutions. Meanwhile, women's institutions and jail space for women are proportionately proliferating at an even more astounding rate than men's. If race is largely an absent factor in the discussions about crime and punishment, gender seems not even to merit a place carved out by its absence. Historically, the imprisonment of women has served to criminalize women in a way that is more complicated than is the case with men. This female criminalization process has had more to do with the marking of certain groups of women as undomesticated and hypersexual, as women who refuse to embrace the nuclear family as paradigm. The current liberal-conservative discourse around welfare criminalizes Black single mothers, who are represented as deficient, manless, drug-using breeders of children, and as reproducers of an attendant culture of poverty. The woman who does drugs is criminalized both because she is a drug user and because, as a consequence, she cannot be a good mother. In some states, pregnant women are being imprisoned for using crack because of possible damage to the fetus.

According to the US Department of Justice, women are far more likely than men to be imprisoned for a drug conviction.[14] However, if women wish to receive treatment for their drug problems, often their only option if they cannot pay for a drug program is to be arrested and sentenced to a drug program via the criminal justice system. Yet when US Surgeon General Joycelyn Elders alluded to the importance of opening discussion on the decriminalization of drugs, the Clinton administration immediately disassociated itself from her remarks. Decriminalization of drugs would greatly reduce the numbers of incarcerated women, for the 278 percent increase in the numbers of Black women in state and federal prisons (as compared to the 186 percent increase in the numbers of Black men) can be largely attributed to the phenomenal rise in drug-related and specifically crack-related imprisonment. According to the Sentencing Project's 1995 report, the increase in convictions for both men and women amounted to 828 percent.[15]

Official refusals to even consider decriminalization of drugs as a possible strategy that might begin to reverse present incarceration practices further bolsters the ideological staying power of the prison. In his well-known study of the history of the prison and its related technologies of discipline, Michel Foucault pointed out that an evolving contradiction is at the very heart of the historical project of imprisonment: "For a century and a half, the prison has always been offered as its own remedy: . . . the realization of the corrective project as the only method of overcoming the impossibility of implementing it."[16] As I have attempted to argue, within the US historical context, racism plays a pivotal role in sustaining this contradiction. In fact, Foucault's theory regarding the prison's tendency to serve as its own enduring justification becomes even more compelling if the role of race is also acknowledged. Moreover, moving beyond the parameters of what I consider the double impasse implied by his theory—the discursive impasse his theory discovers and that of the theory itself—I want to conclude by suggesting the possibility of radical race-conscious strategies designed to disrupt the stranglehold of criminalization and incarceration practices.

In the course of a recent collaborative research project with UC Santa Barbara sociologist Kum-Kum Bhavnani, in which we interviewed thirty-five women at the San Francisco County Jail, the complex ways in which race and gender help to produce a punishment industry that reproduces the very problems it purports to solve became dramatically apparent. Our interviews focused on the women's ideas about imprisonment and how they themselves imagine alternatives to incarceration. Their various critiques of the prison system and of the existing "alternatives," all of which are tied to reimprisonment as a last resort, led us to reflect more deeply about the importance of retrieving, retheorizing, and reactivating the radical abolitionist strategy first proposed in connection with the prison-reform movements of the sixties and seventies.

We are presently attempting to theorize women's imprisonment in ways that allow us to formulate a radical abolitionist strategy departing from, but not restricted in its conclusions to, women's jails and prisons. Our goal is to formulate alternatives to incarceration that substantively reflect the voices and agency of a variety of imprisoned women. We wish to open up channels for their involvement in the current debates around alternatives to incarceration, while not denying our own role as mediators and interpreters and our own political positioning in these debates. We also want to distinguish our explorations of alternatives from the spate of "alternative punishments" or what are now called "intermediate sanctions" presently being proposed and/or implemented by and through state and local correctional systems.

This is a long-range project that has three dimensions: academic research, public policy, and community organizing. In other words, for this project to be successful, it must build bridges between academic work, legislative and other policy interventions, and grassroots campaigns calling, for example, for the decriminalization of drugs and prostitution—and for the reversal of the present proliferation of jails and prisons.

Raising the possibility of abolishing jails and prisons as the institutionalized and normalized means of addressing social problems in an era of migrating corporations, unemployment and homelessness, and collapsing public services—from health care to education—can hopefully help to interrupt the current law-and-order discourse that has such a grip on the collective imagination, facilitated as it is by deep and hidden influences of racism. This late-twentieth-century "abolitionism," with its nineteenth-century resonances, may also lead to a historical recontextualization of the practice of imprisonment. With the passage of the Thirteenth Amendment, slavery was abolished for all except convicts—and in a sense the exclusion from citizenship accomplished by the slave system has persisted within the US prison system. Only three states allow prisoners to vote, and approximately four million people are denied the right to vote because of their present or past incarceration. A radical strategy to abolish jails and prisons as the normal way of dealing with the social problems of late capitalism is not a strategy for abstract abolition. It is designed to force a rethinking of the increasingly repressive role of the state during this era of late capitalism and to carve out a space for resistance.

CHAPTER 6

Changing Attitudes toward Crime and Punishment*

Attitudes toward crime and punishment historically have been informed by prevailing ideas about class, gender, race, and nation. They rarely have reflected strict legal definitions of crime but rather have been influenced by political discourses, economic conditions, ideological circumstances, and the means by which ideas are publicly disseminated. In the late twentieth century, representations of crime through the mass media have encouraged an uncritical attitude of fear toward racially- and class-defined communities as the main perpetrators of crime, deflecting attention away from corporate, white-collar, government, and police crime, as well as domestic violence against women. The history of the prison reveals that this institution, which has emerged as the dominant mode of punishment, has been unable to solve the problem of crime but rather has become a site for violence, assaults on human rights, and the perpetuation of racism. Nevertheless, it has expanded in the industrialized countries—especially in the United States—to the extent that we now can speak of an emergent prison industrial complex. Oppositional attitudes toward penal systems have emerged in transnational organizations, including abolitionist perspectives toward both prisons and the death penalty.

---

* First published in *Encyclopedia of Violence, Peace, and Conflict*, ed. Lester Kurtz (San Diego: Academic Press, 1999), vol. 1, 473–86.

I. Representations of Crime

During the late twentieth century, increasing evocations of "the crime problem" in the discourse of elected officials, the centrality accorded crime reportage in the print and electronic news media, and the mounting popularity of literary, televisual, and cinematic representations of fictionalized crime all have tended to create a crime-saturated social environment. New genres such as Court TV have helped to transform high-profile trials, such as that of O. J. Simpson, into global media events. The formation of popular attitudes toward crime—and specifically the fascination with and fear of crime—in fact is more an outgrowth of these representational practices than of the actual risk of becoming a victim of crime.

Crime, as it is perceived on the level of common sense, is only indirectly related to its legal definition, which covers a range of actions so vast as to make it difficult to identify commonalities among them beyond the fact that "criminal actions" are those proscribed by law and those for which courts can impose punishments. What is considered a crime during one historical period in another may become neutral behavior in which criminal justice systems have no apparent interest. The penal codes of different countries, as well as state penal codes within the United States, frequently are at variance with each other. Moreover, while numerous surveys indicate that a vast majority of most populations have engaged at one point or another in behavior proscribed by law, only a small percentage of these acts ever is addressed by criminal justice systems. In some countries, spousal battery, a historically sanctioned behavior, has been recognized relatively recently as a punishable crime. Although this and other crimes committed by victims' relatives and acquaintances over time have constituted the great majority of violent crimes, the widespread fear of crime is directed not toward such commonplace events but rather toward the specter of an assault by a stranger. Historically, the construction of this imagined anonymous stranger has been class and/or race inflected.

The deployment of military metaphors in governmental anti-crime policy has helped to legitimize a discourse on crime that constructs the criminal as an enemy to be conquered. In the United States, the "war on crime," as articulated by former president Richard Nixon, developed alongside—and, in many ways, as an appendage to—the war against communism. If communism was represented as an external threat to the security of the nation, crime represented the internal threat. During the era of the 1960s, when the US civil rights movement and social movements that opposed the Vietnam War and raised demands for student rights acquired a dramatic visibility throughout the world, anti-crime campaigns frequently were conflated with strategies to counter political dissent. Through the law-and-order themes that, since the Nixon presidency, have become recurring ingredients in US election campaigns, crime and the call for ever-more-stringent punishments have become increasingly politicized. Similar patterns can be found throughout North America and in many European, African, South American, and Asian countries. China's 1996 "Strike Hard" campaign, which specifically targeted drug-related crime, has been associated with the more than four thousand state-sanctioned executions that year. Japan, on the other hand, has thus far avoided official "tough on crime" postures and, in recent years, has reduced its rate of imprisonment, which is less than one-tenth that of the United States. Although President Nelson Mandela has described crime in the new South Africa as "out of control," he insisted in 1996 that his government's "short-term tactics to deal with crime" should not eclipse the fact that their most effective long-term anti-crime strategy resides in their plans to eradicate poverty. Moreover, under Mandela's leadership, the death penalty was abolished in South Africa.

As criminologists and historians have pointed out, the "crime waves" that, according to public officials, demand the staging of wars against crime almost always have referred to specific kinds of crime, usually anonymous, violent, and—in the late twentieth century—drug-related street crime. White-collar crime, corporate crime, police crime, and government crime rarely have been included in evocations of crime waves or in the statistics produced to evidence the rise and fall of crime. British sociologist and cultural critic Stuart Hall has emphasized that crime statistics function in deeply ideological ways, seeming to ground elusive information for the media and the public at large by transforming complex, disparate, and often contradictory information into numerical data and incontestable facts. In reality, statistics do not always reflect the actual volume of crime committed.

The history of anti-crime campaigns in the United States is closely linked with the production of FBI crime statistics. Despite serious weaknesses in the FBI's Uniform Crime Reports, some of which were detected immediately after the UCR began to be issued in 1930, these figures—which measure reported crime as it is mediated by police interpretations—have continued to be the primary source upon which public perceptions about crime are based. Police information forwarded to the FBI is based on citizens' reports and may include crimes for which no suspect is identified, as well as crimes that go uninvestigated. That factors related to race, class, gender, and sexuality often determine what crimes are reported, and how law enforcement officials respond to reports of crime, is not reflected in crime statistics.

II. Class, Gender, Race, and the Production of Crime

Crime as a legal category is defined as behavior proscribed by law and subject to governmental punishment. Poverty and crime often have been conflated in the popular imagination—as well as in public policy—as a result of punishment historically being meted out disproportionately to poor populations. Vagrancy laws frequently have functioned to reinforce the idea that poverty is synonymous with criminality. In 1798, Thomas Malthus published his *Essay on the Principle of Population*, lending support to political efforts to revise the English Poor Law, which provided for welfare assistance by the parishes of those in need. Malthus contended that state charity was little more than a public encouragement of poverty, and that the state should leave the poor to their natural fate. The English Poor Law of 1834 embodied Malthus's idea and, according to Karl Marx, reflected the view that workers are responsible for their own poverty. Moreover, Marx claimed, the passage of this law encouraged the attitude that poverty is not a misfortune but rather a crime requiring punishment. The new poor law called for confinement in workhouses or poorhouses, where labor was coerced and unpaid.

The earliest model of imprisonment as punishment rather than detention was the workhouse opened in Brideswell, London, in 1555, which later inspired the Act of 1576 calling for the creation of workhouses or "brideswells" in other counties. On the European continent, the Rasphuis of Amsterdam, opened in 1596, was used as a place of confinement and forced labor for beggars and young people labeled as malefactors. In the United States, the poorhouse developed during the early nineteenth century; it was not entirely differentiated from the jail either in its function or in the way it was popularly perceived. Both impoverished people and criminals were viewed as dangerous elements who threatened social stability and needed to be locked away.

A. Patriarchy and Criminality

Patriarchal structures and ideologies also have tended to produce assumptions of criminality, particularly in relation to women who have violated social norms defining women's "place." The most popular examples of this patriarchal production of criminality can be found in the figure of Jeanne d'Arc, in the witch hunts in Europe during the Middle Ages, and in the execution in 1792 of accused witches in Salem, Massachusetts. From the fourteenth to the seventeenth centuries, among the many thousands of people accused of witchcraft, 80 to 90 percent were women. Moreover, feminist historians have uncovered evidence of severe corporal punishments inflicted on women accused of adultery, while the behavior of male adulterers simply was normalized. With the rise of professionalized medicine, women healers in Europe and the United States often were criminalized and punished.

The conflation of criminal and immoral, that is, sexual, activity among girls rendered permeable the borders between "crime" and "unfeminine" behavior. In the late nineteenth century, one girl was committed at the Lancaster Reformatory, the first girls' reformatory in the United States, because her father accused her of engaging in masturbation. As it turned out, she merely was trying to alleviate, by scratching, the chronic genital rash from which she suffered. Adult women tended to be treated similarly. Rather than legally being accused of crimes, many deviant women were locked away in almshouses, workhouses, or asylums for the insane. Prevailing social attitudes during the seventeenth and eighteenth centuries reflected a belief that most women were incapable of intentionally violating the law—and that there was no hope of reform for women who were deemed depraved and criminal—but that they *could* be afflicted with poverty and madness, both of which were sufficient grounds for incarceration. In the twentieth century, women inclined toward or engaging in lesbian sexual practices still could be committed to mental institutions in many countries. In Egypt in 1981, feminist writer and physician Nawal El Saadawi, the first African woman to speak publicly against genital mutilation, was arrested for alleged "crimes against the state."

B. Race and Criminalization in the United States

Particularly in the United States, race has played a central role in constructing presumptions of criminality. After the abolition of slavery, former slave states passed new legislation revising the Slave Codes in order to regulate the behavior of free Blacks in ways similar to those that had existed during slavery. The new Black Codes proscribed a range of actions—such as vagrancy, absence from work, breach of job contracts, the possession of firearms, and insulting gestures or acts—

that were criminalized only when the actor was Black. In light of the provision in the Thirteenth Amendment that abolished slavery and involuntary servitude "except as a punishment for crime, whereof the party shall have been duly convicted," there were crimes defined by state law for which only Blacks could be "duly convicted," and thus sentenced to involuntary servitude. Black people thereby became the prime targets of the developing convict lease system, in many ways a reincarnation of slavery. The Mississippi Black Codes, for example, declared vagrant "anyone/who was guilty of theft, had run away [from a job, apparently], was drunk, was wanton in conduct or speech, had neglected job or family, handled money carelessly, and . . . all other idle and disorderly persons." Thus vagrancy was coded as a Black crime, one punishable by incarceration and forced labor, sometimes on the very plantations that previously had thrived on slave labor.

Identifying the racialization of crime, Frederick Douglass wrote in 1883 of the South's tendency to "impute crime to color." When a particularly egregious crime was committed, he noted, not only was guilt frequently assigned to a Black person regardless of the perpetrator's race, but white men sometimes sought to escape punishment by disguising themselves as Black. Douglass would later recount one such incident that took place in Granger County, Tennessee, in which a man who appeared to be Black was shot while committing a robbery. The wounded man, however, was discovered to be a respectable white citizen who had colored his face Black.

Legal scholar Cheryl Harris has argued that a property interest in whiteness emerged from the conditions of slavery. According to Harris, since white identity was owned as property, rights, liberties, and self-identity were affirmed for whites while being denied for Blacks, whose only access to whiteness was through "passing." Douglass's comments indicate how this property interest in whiteness was easily reversed in schemes to deny Black people their rights to due process. Interestingly, cases similar to the one Douglass discusses above emerged in the United States during the 1990s: in Boston, Charles

Stuart murdered his pregnant wife and attempted to blame an anonymous Black man, and in Union, South Carolina, Susan Smith killed her children and claimed they had been abducted by a Black carjacker. The racialization of crime—the tendency to "impute crime to color," to use Frederick Douglass's words—is operative not only in the United States but in other countries such as Brazil and South Africa, which have their own distinct histories of racial subjugation.

C. The Drug Wars

A racialized disjuncture further characterizes the relationship, in contemporary campaigns against drugs, between illicit drug use and interventions of the criminal justice system. The general context of this disjuncture has resulted from the ways in which the multinational pharmaceutical industry advertises a range of licit drugs—particularly those that have psychotropic effects, such as Prozac—as panaceas for emotional disorders, while the use of drugs that circulate outside of corporate and governmental sanctions is defined as criminal. Because of the prevailing association of drug use and illegal drug dealing with people of color, Black, Latino, and immigrant communities in the United States, Canada, and Europe have become disproportionately vulnerable to prosecution. "Wars on drugs"—which, like the various "wars on crime," evoke the violence of military maneuvers—have thus played a pivotal role in criminalizing these populations. The Dutch Ministry of Justice, for example, which until the 1980s had managed to prevent increases in—and, during many years, to reduce—its incarcerated population, has begun to construct more prison space largely in response to drug trafficking. Among those sentenced to prison on drug trafficking charges, a disproportionate number are first- or second-generation immigrants from the Netherlands' former colonies in the Caribbean and Asia, as well as Latin Americans involved in the drug economy. In the United States, the war on drugs is responsible for soaring numbers of imprisoned individuals. In 1996, drug defendants made up 61 percent of the US federal prison population, up from 23 percent in 1980. In the state prison systems, by 1991, nearly one in three women were incarcerated for drug offenses.

In the United States, sentencing disparities in cases involving crack and powdered cocaine result in much more prison time for crack users than for cocaine users. This distinction is highly racialized: the majority of crack cases involve Black defendants—according to a 1992 report by the US Sentencing Commission, 91.3 percent of defendants sentenced for federal crack offenses were Black—and the majority of powdered cocaine cases involve white defendants. The result is the criminalization and incarceration of many more people of color for offenses comparable to those committed by their more leniently treated white counterparts.

D. Violence against Women

Another disjuncture between crime commission and the response of the criminal justice system can be discovered in the historical treatment of women who have been targets of domestic violence. Before the advent of feminist movements, spousal assault—and in earlier eras, gynecide—was not addressed within the realm of criminal law. Thus violent assaults in the public sphere were criminalized, while male violence enacted within the domestic sphere was privatized and thus shielded from state intervention. This historically dichotomous relationship between the public and private realms has positioned gender at the center of many contradictions in the ideological production of crime and the practical implementation of punishment. One particularly dramatic example is the pattern of murder convictions and excessively long sentences—currently contested by feminist movements in many countries—meted out to battered women who have killed their male batterers. For much of the history of criminal justice, men have killed and assaulted their wives and partners with impunity, whereas women who fight back have been defined as assailants and murderers. Currently, feminist movements are calling upon state and national governments to recognize "battered women's syndrome" as a viable legal defense.

III. Punishment and the Prison: A Historical Overview

Although noncapital corporal punishment still prevails in some countries, imprisonment is by far the most widely employed mode of punishment. Fines, and in some cases (the US, for example) the death penalty—the most violent state assault on the body—complete the spectrum of punishment. However, the prominence of incarceration is a relatively recent historical development and incarceration itself has been theorized during different eras as accomplishing very different goals. Prison reform movements have criticized the brutality associated with imprisonment for as long as prisons have existed.

The United Nations' Standard Minimum Rules for the Treatment of Prisoners, approved in 1957, reflect many decades of organizing and advocacy of international prison reform toward the reduction of, among other things, torture and injurious living conditions. In this context it is ironic that the institution of the prison itself originally emerged in part as a response to Enlightenment-era opposition to the cruelty of corporal punishment. Michel Foucault opens his germinal study, *Discipline and Punish: The Birth of the Prison*, with a graphic description of a 1757 execution in Paris. The court had sentenced the unfortunate murderer to undergo a series of formidable tortures before he was finally put to death. Red-hot pincers were used to burn away the flesh from his limbs, and molten lead, boiling oil, burning resin, and other substances were melted together and poured onto the wounds. Finally, he was drawn and quartered, his body burned, and the ashes tossed into the wind.

This gruesome execution reflects the extent to which the body was a target of torture, which in this instance—although not always—was terminated by death. Other modes of corporal punishment have included the stocks and pillories, whippings, brandings, and amputations. Prior to the historical birth of the prison, such punishment was designed to have its most profound effect not so much on the person punished as on the crowd of spectators. Punishment was, in essence, public spectacle.

When women were punished within the domestic domain, instrumentalities of torture were sometimes imported by authorities into the household. In seventeenth-century Britain, women whose husbands identified them as quarrelsome and unaccepting of male dominance were punished by means of a gossip's bridle or branks, a headpiece with a chain attached and an iron bit that was introduced into the woman's mouth. Although the branking of women was often linked to a public parade, this contraption was sometimes hooked to a wall of the house, where the punished woman remained until her husband decided to release her.

Although the conceptualization of punishment as the infliction of physical pain on the body is associated with precapitalist eras, there are conspicuous exceptions to this pattern. The extralegal lynching of Black Americans well into the twentieth century, although not directly sanctioned by law, was nonetheless condoned by the political structures of the southern states. These lynchings, like the community spectacles of the US colonial period and Europe of the Middle Ages, were frequently public events with a carnivalesque character.

Other modes of punishment that predated the rise of the prison included banishment, forced labor in galleys, transportation, and appropriation of the accused's property. The punitive transportation of large numbers of people from England facilitated the initial colonization of Australia. The North American colony of Georgia also was settled by transported English convicts. During the early 1700s, one in eight transported convicts were women, and the work they were forced to perform often consisted of prostitution.

Imprisonment was not employed as a principal mode of punishment until the eighteenth century in Europe and the nineteenth century in the United States. European prison systems were instituted in Asia and Africa as an important component of colonial rule. In India, for example, the English prison system was introduced during the second half of the eighteenth century, when jails were established in the regions of Calcutta and Madras.* In Europe, the penitentiary movement reflected new intellectual tendencies associated with the Enlightenment, activist interventions by Protestant reformers, and structural transformations associated with the rise of industrial capitalism. In Milan in 1764, Cesare Beccaria published his essay *On Crimes and Punishments*, which was strongly influenced by notions of equality advanced by the philosophes—especially Voltaire, Rousseau, and Montesquieu. Beccaria argued that punishment should never be a private matter, nor should it be arbitrarily violent; rather, it should be public, swift, and as lenient as possible. Beccaria identified what was then a distinctive feature of imprisonment, its imposition prior to the defendant's guilt or innocence being decided. Eventually, when incarceration became more a function of the sentence rather than of pretrial detention, it emerged as the predominant form of punishment, revealing a shift in the valuation of the individual. Prior to the Enlightenment, before the individual was perceived as a bearer of formal rights and liberties, the deprivation of rights and liberties through imprisonment could not be understood as punishment. The prison sentence as punishment invokes the abstraction of time in a way that resonates with the role of labor-time as the basis for computing commodity value. Marxist theorists of punishment have noted that the historical period during which the commodity form arose is the same one in which the penitentiary emerges as the paradigmatic mode of punishment.

Georg Rusche and Otto Kirchheimer's *Punishment and Social Structure*, first published in 1939 by the Institute for Social Research, attempted to establish a relationship between penal policy and labor market conditions, particularly those prevailing during different phases of capitalist development. While their model has been crit-

* Now Kolkata and Chennai.

icized for its economism and reductionism, it has greatly influenced Marxist criminologists and historians of punishment, some of whom argue that Rusche and Kirchheimer underestimated the role of ideology. Feminist critics such as Adrian Howe, author of *Punish and Critique: Toward a Feminist Analysis of Penality*, have observed that most political economies of punishment are profoundly masculinist, failing to account for the women who are in prison and ignoring feminist contestations of traditional Marxist categories.

The fact that convicts punished by imprisonment in emergent penitentiary systems were primarily male reflected the deeply gender-biased structure of legal, political, and economic rights. Since women were largely denied public status as rights-bearing individuals, they could not be punished by the deprivation of those rights through imprisonment. This was especially true of married women, who had no standing before the law. According to English common law, marriage resulted in a state of "civil death," as symbolized by the wife's assumption of the husband's name. Consequently, she tended to be punished for revolting against her domestic duties rather than for failure in her meager public responsibilities. The relegation of women to domestic economies, where use value prevailed, prevented them from playing a significant role in the emergent commodity realm, which was defined by exchange value. This was especially true because the wage reflected the exchange value of labor power, typically gendered as male and racialized as white. Thus corporal punishment for women survived long after these modes of punishment had become obsolete for (white) men. The persistence of domestic violence painfully attests to historical modes of gendered punishment.

A. The Penitentiary

Ironically, as some scholars have argued, the word *penitentiary* may have been used first in connection with plans outlined in England in 1758 to house "penitent prostitutes." In 1877, John Howard, the leading Protestant proponent of penal reform in England, published *The*

State of the Prisons in which he conceptualized imprisonment as an occasion for religious self-reflection and self-reform. Between 1787 and 1791, the utilitarian philosopher Jeremy Bentham published his letters on a prison model he called the panopticon, which would facilitate the total surveillance and discipline he claimed criminals needed in order to internalize productive labor habits. Prisoners were to be housed in single cells on circular tiers, all facing a multilevel guard tower. By means of blinds and a complicated play of light and darkness, the prisoners—who would not see each other at all—would be unable to see the warden; from his vantage point, on the other hand, the warden would be able to see all of the prisoners. However—and this was the most significant aspect of Bentham's mammoth panopticon—because each individual prisoner would never be able to determine where the warden's gaze was focused, each prisoner would be compelled to act, that is, work, as if he were being watched at all times. Howard's ideas were incorporated in the Penitentiary Act of 1799, which opened the way for the modern prison. While Bentham's ideas influenced the development of the first national English penitentiary, located in Millbank and opened in 1816, the first full-fledged effort to create a panopticon prison was in the United States. The Western State Penitentiary in Pittsburgh, based on a revised architectural model of the panopticon, opened in 1826.

Pennsylvania's Walnut Street Jail housed the first state penitentiary in the United States when a portion of the jail was converted in 1790 from a detention facility to an institution housing convicts whose prison sentences simultaneously became punishment and occasions for penitence and reform. Walnut Street's austere regime—total isolation in single cells, where prisoners lived, ate, worked, read the Bible (if, indeed, they were literate), and supposedly reflected and repented came to be known as the Pennsylvania system. This regime would constitute one of that era's two major models of imprisonment. Although the other model, developed in Auburn, New York, was viewed as a rival to the Pennsylvania system, the philosophical basis of the two models did not differ substantively. The Pennsylvania model, which eventually crystallized in the Eastern State Penitentiary in Cherry Hill—the plans for which were approved in 1821—emphasized total isolation, silence, and solitude, whereas the Auburn model called for solitary cells and silent congregate labor. Because of its more efficient labor practices, the Auburn model eventually achieved hegemony.

B. Women's Prisons

The relatively small proportion of women among incarcerated populations is often invoked as a justification for the scant attention accorded women prisoners by policymakers, scholars, and activists. In most countries, the female percentage of prison populations usually hovers around 5 percent. Ideologically, the small numbers of women prisoners tend to bolster the view that imprisoned women must be a great deal more aberrant and far more threatening to society than their numerous male counterparts.

That women, historically, have constituted a far greater number of inmates in mental institutions than in prisons suggests that while jails and prisons have been dominant institutions for the control of men, mental institutions have served a similar purpose for women. That is, deviant men have been constructed as criminal, while deviant women have been constructed as insane. Prior to the emergence of the penitentiary and thus of the notion of punishment as "doing time," the employment of places of confinement to control beggars, thieves, and the insane tended to conflate these categories of deviancy. As the discourse on criminality and the corresponding institutions to control it distinguished the "criminal" from the "insane," the distinction focused largely on men, leaving deviant women in the category of the insane.

Quaker reformers in the United States—especially the Philadelphia Society for Alleviating the Miseries of Public Prisons, founded in 1787—played a pivotal role in campaigns to substitute imprisonment for corporal punishment. Following in the tradition established by Elizabeth Fry in England, Quakers were also responsible for extended crusades to institute separate prisons for women. Fry formulated principles governing prison reform for women in her 1827 work, *Observations on the Visiting, Superintendence and Government of Female Prisoners*, which were taken up in the United States by women such as Josephine Shaw Lowell and Abby Hopper Gibbons. Prevailing attitudes toward women convicts differed from those toward men convicts, who were assumed to have forfeited rights and liberties that women generally could not claim. Although some women were housed in penitentiaries, the institution itself was gendered as male. As a consequence, male punishment was linked to penitence and reform. The very forfeiture of rights and liberties implied that with self-reflection, religious study, and work, male convicts could achieve redemption and could recover these rights and liberties. Since women were not acknowledged as ever in possession of them, however, they were not eligible to participate in this process of redemption.

According to the prevailing views, women convicts were irrevocably fallen women, with no possibility of salvation. If male criminals were considered to be public individuals who had simply violated the social contract, female criminals were seen as having transgressed fundamental moral principles of womanhood. The reformers who, following Elizabeth Fry, argued that women were capable of redemption, did not really contest these ideological assumptions about women's place. In opposing the idea that fallen women could not be saved, they advocated separate facilities and a specifically female approach to punishment. Their approach called for an architectural design replacing cells with cottages and "rooms" designed to infuse domesticity into prison life. This model facilitated a regime devised to reintegrate criminalized women into the domestic roles of wife and mother. A female custodial staff, the reformers argued, would minimize the sexual temptations that they believed were often at the root of female criminality.

The US women's prison reform movement unfolded within the context of a larger developing social movement demanding women's rights. Like the women's suffrage movement, it tended to accept the prevailing class- and race-inflected discourse on womanhood, which privileged the social conditions of white, middle-class women. Since imprisoned white women came largely from working-class communities, the domestic strategy associated with the women's prison reform movement—while putatively training female convicts to be better wives and mothers—in fact tended to mark them as domestic servants. This outcome of domestic prison regimes was even more pronounced for women of color.

Although it is widely assumed that women prisoners are most often incarcerated in separate women's facilities, in many countries—and indeed in local jails in the United States—they are housed together with men. In a widely publicized case in the mid-1970s, Joan Little was charged with the murder of a male guard, who had raped her in her cell in a men's jail where she was being held. India is one example of a country where there are very few separate institutions for women, although there are women's sections of central prisons that primarily house men.

C. The Punishment Debate: Deterrence, Retribution, Rehabilitation

The history of the prison and attendant attitudes toward punishment have been shaped by debates regarding the ultimate objective of imprisonment. Does it deter those in the "free world" from committing the crimes that will lead them to prison? Is its primary purpose that of rehabilitating the individual who has broken the social (or domestic) contract by committing a crime? Or is it simply meant to ensure that the person convicted of criminal behavior receives his/her just deserts? In the fields of criminology, penology, and philosophy of punishment, myriad discussions have been devoted to justificatory arguments rationalizing imprisonment on the basis of one or more of these objectives. These scholarly concerns have directly influenced policymaking, especially with respect to sentencing practices and prison conditions. Rehabilitative strategies, for example, may demand educational and vocational programs, as well as more humane living conditions than retributive imprisonment. However, as some critics have pointed out, rehabilitation has led to coercive psychiatric treatment and indeterminate sentences, since the prisoner may not be released until he/she has been "rehabilitated." As the limits of modern discourses on punishment have been established by this conceptual triumvirate of deterrence, rehabilitation, and retribution, popular attitudes toward punishment also have tended to move along these triangular axes.

At the beginning of the intellectual tradition of advocating imprisonment as the primary mode of punishment, the prison was represented as a site for the reformation of the individual. Reformers who opposed the violence and cruelty of corporal punishment proposed confinement under conditions designed to morally reshape the offender. According to Foucault, with the birth of the prisons, the locus of punishment shifted from the body to the soul or psyche, and the prison became the disciplinary apparatus par excellence, one that was most appropriate to a historical era in which a disciplined working class was required by the developing industrial capitalist economy. In this sense, the institution of the prison had the same aim as educational and military institutions. Bentham claimed that his panopticon could be applied to any institution in which people were subject to surveillance—penitentiaries, workhouses, poorhouses, insane asylums, places of quarantine, factories, hospitals, and schools. As Foucault would observe, it is not surprising that prisons recall schools, factories, military barracks, and hospitals, all of which, in turn, recall prisons.

For a number of reasons—among them recidivism and the continued lack of proof that prisons curtail crime—the great historical penitentiary projects in England, France, and the United States have been acknowledged as failures by advocates and critics alike. Foucault points out that this failure did not follow a period during which the penitentiary was recognized for its successes, but rather it was denounced as a monumental failure from the very beginning of its history. He further argues that reform campaigns were so inextricably tied to ideological assumptions that the prison was the only effective strategy for countering crime that the prison repeatedly is proposed as the remedy for its own failure. Thus even in its failure to inhibit crime—indeed, to rehabilitate criminals—the prison is self-perpetuating.

The project of rehabilitation itself underwent transformation—from the religious model of the early penitentiaries to the medical model of the twentieth century without any significant increase in the effectiveness of the prison. The philosophical debate about the purpose of the prison has been deeply ensconced in this dilemma—the failure of the prison combined with the inability to conceptualize penal strategies that move beyond the discursive and material space of the prison. Popular attitudes also reflect the assumption that as brutal as prisons may appear, public order will always depend on the existence of prisons, whether they are represented as places of rehabilitation, deterrence, or retribution.

The dominance until the 1970s of arguments for rehabilitation can be explained by the seductiveness of the medical model, which defines criminals as "ill" and thus in need of a cure. However, with the increase and globalization of drug trafficking—which some scholars and journalists have linked to government involvement or sanction—and the attendant "wars" on drugs and crime, imprisoned populations soared to unprecedented heights. As the primary but ineffective weapon in these "wars," the prison again tends to perpetuate its own failures, thereby becoming self-perpetuating.

D. Proliferation of Imprisoned Populations

The United States and other industrialized countries have experienced what John Irwin and James Austin call an imprisonment binge. Between 1980 and 1995, the US federal and state prison populations increased 235 percent (from 329,821 to 1,104,074). They point out that in 1995 the imprisoned population in the United States equaled or exceeded the populations of 13 states and many major US cities. While the United States, South Africa, China, and Russia have had the highest rates of incarceration, the incarceration rate in a country like the Netherlands—which has an international reputation for a humane penal system and for implementing strategies of decarceration—has increased from 20 per 100,000 in 1975 to 40 in 1988, and is in excess of 50 in the 1990s. Dutch criminologist Willem de Haan has observed that the corresponding tendency to build more prisons in the Netherlands may well interrupt a 125-year-old pattern of decarceration, or consistent reduction of prison populations.

In the United States, there has been great resistance to the idea of decriminalizing drug use, while in the Netherlands, drug decriminalization has been an important part of criminal justice policy for many years. Moreover, while many states in the United States have implemented "three strikes and you're out" sentencing policies providing for long mandatory sentences after the commission of three felonies, Dutch sentencing policies call for much shorter sentences and emphasize prisoners' rights to move to "half-open" and "open" prisons after completion of a certain percentage of their sentences. (Other countries, including Cuba, use similar rehabilitative strategies of progressive reintroduction of prisoners into the "free world.") In general, US criminal justice policies have all but discarded the traditional goal of prison rehabilitation, emphasizing unembellished punishment as the objective of imprisonment. In the Netherlands, on the other hand, rehabilitation, and the ultimate reincorporation of the individual into society, remains the goal of the Dutch penal system.

Even with these vast differences between the United States and the Netherlands—and although the rate of incarceration in the Netherlands is 50 per 100,000, while in the United States it is more than 10 times that amount—both countries have embarked upon a path of prison construction, to which there is no apparent end in sight.

Furthermore, in spite of progressive approaches in the Netherlands, a disproportionate number of incarcerated individuals in both countries have been convicted on drug charges, and both the Dutch and US prison populations consist of a preponderance of people of color.

IV. The Prison Industrial Complex

Social historian Mike Davis first used the term "prison industrial complex" in relation to California's penal system, which, he observed, already had begun in the 1990s to rival agribusiness and land development as a major economic and political force. The United States has the largest prison complex in the world. According to the 1995 Census of State and Federal Correctional Facilities conducted under the auspices of the Bureau of Justice Statistics, between 1990 and 1995 more than 280,000 beds were added in 213 prisons, representing a 41 percent increase in prison capacity. In 1995 there were 1,500 state facilities (up from 1,287) and 125 federal facilities (up from 80). The Census indicated that 327,320 persons were employed by these facilities, up from 264,201 in 1990. Almost two-thirds of correctional employees were in custodial or security positions. The US penal system differs from that of most other countries in that county jails, which are excluded from the BJS Census, are used to detain accused persons awaiting trial as well as to house misdemeanants whose sentences are less than 1 year. In 1994, there were more than 9.8 million admissions to the more than 3,300 county jails. Irwin and Austin have calculated that nearly 1 in every 25 adults in the United States goes to jail each year.

Punishment has developed into a vast industry, and its presence in the US economy is expanding continually. This presence not only includes the federal and state prison facilities and county jails but also a significant population under the direct supervision of correctional authorities such as parole and probation officers. If these latter figures are added to those representing prison and jail populations (over 1.5 million), then in 1994 over five million adults were under the direct surveillance and supervision of the US criminal justice system. In other words, 1 in 37 adults was marked in this way as "criminal." The corresponding ratio in 1980 was 1 in 91 adults. (It should be pointed out that these statistics do not reflect the increasing imprisonment of teenagers and children.) In the United Kingdom a similar trend can be detected. The 1994/1995 prison population of England and Wales was 49,300—6,000 higher than in the previous two years. In 1997, that population had risen to 56,900 and was rising at a rate of 1,000 per month.

Such statistics as have been reported in this section do not create a full picture of the emergence of a US prison industrial complex. As astounding as they may appear by themselves, they do not reveal the disproportionate surge in the population of incarcerated women and the phenomenal rise in the numbers of Black men who are under the direct control of correctional systems. Although women in the United States—as in every other country—constitute a relatively small minority of convicted persons, during the last two decades of the twentieth century, the number of women sentenced to state and federal prisons increased by 386 percent, as compared with a 214 percent increase among their male counterparts. The twentieth-century history of women's prison facilities reveals that between 1930 and 1950 only 2 or 3 prisons were built or established per decade. In the 1960s, 7 more were created, 17 in the 1970s, and 34 in the 1980s.

In 1990, the Washington-based Sentencing Project published a study of US populations in prison and jail and on parole and probation that concluded that 1 in 4 Black men between the ages of 20 and 29 were among these numbers. Five years later, a second study revealed that this percentage had soared to almost 1 in 3 (32.2 percent). Moreover, more than 1 in 10 Latino men in this same age range was in jail or prison, or on probation or parole. The second study also revealed that the group experiencing the greatest increase was Black women, whose imprisonment increased by 78 percent. According to BJS, African Americans as a whole now represent the majority of state and federal prisoners, with a total of 735,200 Black inmates—10,000 more than the total number of white inmates.

The concept of the prison industrial complex, first employed by Mike Davis—or the correctional industrial complex, the term used by Irwin and Austin—attempts to capture not only the phenomenal expansion of prisons and jails and the enormous increase in the numbers of people of color subject to the surveillance and supervision of the criminal justice system, but also the increasingly symbiotic relationship between the corporate structure and the prison industry, the relationship between corrections and economic vitality in many communities, and the mounting political influence of the correctional community.

A. Prisons and Private Industry

Recapitulating the nineteenth-century post-slavery leasing of mostly Black convicts to individuals and companies in the southern states, the contemporary pattern of privatization has established prisons as a source of corporate profit. By the late 1990s, there were approximately 50,000 private prison beds in the United States, the largest private prison company being Corrections Corporation of America (CCA). CCA managed twenty-one prisons in the US, Australia, and Britain. Wackenhut, the second largest private prison corporation, was also under contract in Britain, where, as of 1997, there were plans for at least twelve private prisons.

Private corporations not only seek out prison labor but also constitute markets for their goods and services. In 1993 among the many advertisements in a prominent trade journal, a cellular phone company proposed that convicts under house arrest and monitored by electronic bracelets—but possessing no home telephones—could be provided with cellular phones to facilitate constant contact with authorities. The growth of privately run operations within prisons throughout the United States further consolidates connections between the corporate economy and prisoners who are perceived in this context as constituting attractively cheap labor pools. Structurally, prison labor is vulnerable to exploitation in much the same way as Third World labor, which has become a seductive alternative for US-based transnational corporations seeking relief from the demands of domestic organized labor. While the US labor movement has forcefully protested prison labor in China and has spoken out against the use of prison labor by private corporations in the United States, by and large, it has not been persuaded to demand the unionization of prison labor.

In Britain, advocates of privatization have pointed to the fact that privately managed prisons have introduced progressive changes that have been taken up by the public sector, such as more lenient visiting policies. Moreover, they claim that the privatization of entire institutions has not introduced profit into the penal realm, but rather is merely an extension of the solidly anchored presence of private enterprise, long a provider of goods and services to prisons. Among those who have expressed opposition to privatization is criminologist Sir Leon Radzinowicz, who counters this argument by pointing out that provision of goods and services by private companies whose primary interest is commercial is quite a different question from possession by these same companies of the power of coercion over human beings.

V. Prison Activism and Abolitionist Strategies

The concept of the prison industrial complex has been taken up by intellectuals and activists in the United States whose work focuses on issues of criminalization and punishment. The term's growing popularity among these groups in the 1990s is linked in part to its historical resonance with the concept of a military industrial complex, a term first employed by Dwight Eisenhower and appropriated by radical activists and scholars in the 1960s who invoked it in their opposition to the military buildup during the Vietnam War and to the resulting ties between the corporate, academic, and military sectors. While radical prison activism has its most immediate roots in this same period, it should be acknowledged that the tradition of prison activism is as old as the institution of the prison itself. What differentiates the contemporary activist tradition from its predecessors is its attempt not only to protest inhumane conditions of imprisonment but to challenge the very necessity of prisons as the major mode of addressing such social problems as poverty, drug use, and racial dominance.

In the 1960s and 1970s, activist movements took shape around political prisoners associated with antiracist, antiwar, and anticolonialist movements, including the campaigns for civil rights in Northern Ireland and against apartheid in South Africa. In the United States, governmental repression of civil rights leaders, student organizers, Native American activists, and Black Power advocates led to the formation of campaigns to free political prisoners such as Huey Newton, Leonard Peltier, myself, and Ericka Huggins. The more generalized opposition to the prison structure began to form as a result of growing awareness of the political character of imprisonment.

In September 1971, a rebellion of prisoners at Attica Correctional Facility was put down militarily by the New York National Guard, under the command of then Governor Nelson Rockefeller. Forty-three people, including eleven guards, were killed during the retaking of the prison yard. An inquiry into the events revealed that none of the prisoners were directly responsible for any of the deaths. The prisoners had seized control of the institution by taking civilian hostages, and had presented a list of demands that included, alongside demands for improved prison conditions, the rights to reading materials and religious freedom. The demands were prefaced with an appeal to "conscientious citizens" to help abolish prisons as institutions that "would enslave and exploit the people of America."

The Attica Rebellion was the most publicized—and most brutally suppressed—of a great number of similar episodes during that period in prisons throughout the United States and in Europe. In connection with a series of uprisings in French prisons during the early 1970s, Michel Foucault helped to establish a center for information on prisons and in the process was inspired to write *Discipline and Punish: The Birth of the Prison*. A member of the Norwegian pressure group KROM during the late 1960s, Thomas Mathiesen later emerged as a prominent theorist of prison abolitionism. In the United States, some prisoners developed their own theories of imprisonment. George Jackson, for example, linked his analysis of criminality to a transformative strategy whereby the political education of prisoners would seek to abolish criminal mentalities and encourage radical consciousness and resistance. Assata Shakur's autobiography includes important insights on the gendered nature of imprisonment. Puerto Rican political prisoners such as Alexandrina Torres, Ida Luz Rodriguez, and Dylcia Pagan have addressed race, nation, gender, and imprisonment. Mumia Abu-Jamal, a Black journalist who in 1997 had spent fifteen years on Pennsylvania's death row, has emerged as a prominent opponent of the death penalty. The extensive international campaign organized around his case has helped to publicize widely his critiques of capital punishment.

A. International Prison Activism

Worldwide campaigns to support political prisoners often have been linked to transnational movements for penal reform. The most prominent transnational prisoner-oriented organization, Amnesty International, seeks the release of prisoners of conscience, defined as individuals who have not used or advocated violence and are detained on the basis of their beliefs, race, ethnic origin, language, and/or religion. Historically criticized for failing to take up cases such as Nelson Mandela's, it now calls for fair and prompt trials for all political prisoners. Moreover, Amnesty International opposes the death penalty, torture, and other forms of cruel and degrading treatment of all prisoners. The organizing principles driving AI's work are taken from the United Nations Universal Declaration of Human Rights.

Other transnational organizations have organized around more specific UN policies. The nongovernmental organization Penal Reform International, for example, has developed a campaign based on the UN's Standard Minimum Rules for the Treatment of Prisoners (SMRs). Approved in 1957 by the Economic and Social Council, the SMRs encompass a broad range of principles governing conditions of imprisonment and treatment of prisoners, based on the notion that while prisoners are deprived of their liberty, they should not be divested of their human rights. The most fundamental principle of the SMRs is that individuals convicted of crimes are sent to prison *as* punishment, not *for* punishment. It is the loss of liberty—not the treatment meted out by the institution—that is meant to constitute the penalty. According to the SMRs, when a court sentences an offender to imprisonment, the punishment it imposes is inherently afflictive; prison conditions should not intentionally aggravate this inherent affliction. Thus, prisons should not constitute a danger to life, health, or personal integrity.

Specifically, the SMRs require that prison activities focus as much as possible on assisting prisoners to rejoin society after the prison sentence has been served. For this reason, the SMRs state that prison rules and regimes should not limit prisoners' freedoms, external social contacts, and possibilities for personal development more than is absolutely necessary. They recommend that prison regimes attempt to reduce as much as possible those differences between the prison world and the free world that render prisoners dependent or violate their dignity as human beings. In general, good prison practice should not accentuate prisoners' isolation from the community but rather facilitate their continuing connections with it. Although some countries, such as the Netherlands, use these principles as the basis for developing their own penal practices, many others—the United States among them—are in perpetual violation of the Standard Minimum Rules.

B. Prison Abolitionism

An international conference of activists and academics who associate themselves with campaigns to abolish prisons met eight times between 1982 and 1997. Originally designated as the International Conference on Prison Abolition, its advocacy has extended to penal abolition since 1987—when it became the International Conference on Penal Abolition. ICOPA thus not only opposes prisons but proposes that all punitive and retributive practices be replaced with criminal justice systems that promote peacemaking, reconciliation, and healing for victims, offenders, and communities. In related contexts, Indigenous models of addressing crime associated with peaceful societies have been examined for the lessons they may reveal for such efforts. ICOPA Conferences have been held in Canada, the Netherlands, Poland, Costa Rica, the United States, and New Zealand. Leading theorists include criminologists Herman Bianchi, Harold Pepinsky, Nils Christie, Louk Hulsman, Thomas Mathiesen, and Willem de Haan. While ICOPA emphasizes theories and practices of complete penal abolition, it also encourages theoretical and activist interventions around specific issues relating to penal systems. In the resolutions of its eighth conference, held in Auckland, New Zealand, in 1997, it opposed the privatization of incarceration and detention and demanded an end to killings in and by prisons.

C. Death Penalty Abolitionism

While prison abolitionism is still a minor discourse and movement, death penalty abolitionism has been widely embraced since the organized campaign against capital punishment took shape during the nineteenth century. Historical opponents of the death penalty have included Cesare Beccaria, considered the founder of the abolitionist movement, Jeremy Bentham, and Victor Hugo. In 1965, only 12 countries had abolished the death penalty, but by 1997, 57 countries had abolished the death penalty entirely and 15 had eliminated it for all but exceptional crimes, for example, crimes committed during wartime. In 20 countries that retained capital punishment there had been no executions for 10 or more years. However, during 1996, according to documentation by Amnesty International, there were at least 5,300 prisoners executed in 39 countries. China's 4,173 executions accounted for the vast majority, followed by 167 in Ukraine and 140 in Russia. The United States carried out 45 executions during this same time period. Although South Africa—which, prior to the fall of apartheid, claimed one of the highest rates of execution in the world—abolished capital punishment in 1995, the United States regularly sentences a significant proportion of capital defendants to death. In 1997, there were more than 3,000 prisoners on death row, approximately 40 percent of whom were Black.

Racist patterns in the application of capital punishment have long been central to opposition to the death penalty in the United States. Opponents have pointed out that since 1930 54 percent of all executions involved people of color, and that 89 percent of individuals executed for rape when it was a capital offense were Black. In 1972, the US Supreme Court decided in the case of *Furman v. Georgia*—which involved a Black man who committed a murder in the course of a burglary—that the practice of granting juries the discretion of determining which offenders were to be sentenced to death was "pregnant with discrimination." The impact of *Furman* was to require all prisoners to be removed from death rows. However, because most of the justices joining the majority decision hinged their argument on the due process principle of the Fourteenth Amendment—only a minority among the majority argued that the death penalty was inherently cruel and unusual punishment—the states soon began to develop nondiscretionary and putatively nondiscriminatory principles for the application of the death penalty. Since 1972, new death penalty statutes have been enacted in thirty-one states.

Although, during the late twentieth century, death penalty advocacy consistently has been losing ground internationally—and the overwhelming majority of Western industrialized nations have abolished it—public opinion polls indicate that the majority of people in the United States still favor capital punishment, the reason most often evoked for its continued existence. Yet when the framing of questions in such polls is considered, their reliability becomes suspect. More nuanced questions in some surveys have indicated, for example, that a majority of responding death penalty supporters would favor life sentences for murderers if the money earned by prisoners during their incarceration went to victims' families.

Both internationally and within the United States, death penalty abolitionists are far more organized than its advocates. Organized support for capital punishment in the United States tends to develop around specific cases, with family members of murder victims at the center of pro–death penalty campaigns and aided by operations such as the Washington Legal Foundation. On the other hand, numerous organizations, such as the American Civil Liberties Union, the NAACP Legal Defense and Educational Fund, and the National Coalition to Abolish the Death Penalty, have established long records of abolitionist practice.

VI. Conclusion

Ironically, forms of punishment designed to minimize crime—and especially its violent manifestations—themselves promote and perpetuate violence. Capital punishment is only the most extreme example of state-sanctioned violence; many lesser punitive measures—solitary confinement, for instance—represent a form of political violence that rarely receives critical attention because it is obscured by the physical and ideological boundaries that separate the world of the prison from the free world. In the United States, the construction and expansion of state and federal super-maximum security prisons, whose purpose is to address disciplinary problems within the penal system, are structured around the imposition of continuous solitary confinement and sensory deprivation—including extremely limited visiting and telephone privileges—on prisoners deemed a danger to correctional order. The US model of the "super-max" currently is being imported to other countries as well. Moreover, as the phenomenon of prison privatization escalates, more and more punishment—beyond that which is called for in sentencing—is being meted out to prisoners by private companies that have even less public accountability than their public counterparts. This is in direct violation of the guiding principle of the UN Standard Minimum Rules of the Treatment of Prisoners, that individuals are sentenced to prison *as* punishment, not *for* punishment.

Scholars and activists who work toward the eradication of governmental and corporate violence within penal settings have mounted productive campaigns around both prison reform and penal abolition. The limited successes of penal reform and abolitionist campaigns in many countries can be attributed to the degree to which the ideology of crime has eclipsed the social realities that direct vast numbers of people throughout the world into prisons and jails. Critiques of expanding imprisonment should not ignore the existence of individuals sentenced to prison and to death who have committed appalling crimes of violence, nor should they dismiss the importance of security. These problems cannot be solved, however, through the ideological equation of perpetrators of heinous violence with all who are criminalized by virtue of having committed relatively minor criminal acts, having been imprisoned, or belonging to communities that predominate in the prisons. Moreover, the construction of a class- and/or race-inflected "criminal" as the enemy and as a deserving target of often violent punishment—a phenomenon that can result in the false imprisonment of innocent people—diverts attention from social problems such as poverty, homelessness, deteriorating education and health care, and drug use, thereby siphoning off the collective energy needed to solve them.

CHAPTER 7

Public Imprisonment and Private Violence

Reflections on the Hidden Punishment of Women*

Over the last twenty-five years, feminist research and activism on sexual assault and domestic violence have generated campaigns and services on local, national, and international levels and an increasingly popular culture of resistance, which has helped to unveil the global pandemic of violence against women. At the same time, research and activism have developed on a much smaller scale around women in prison. The work in these two areas has intersected in a number of important ways, including the amnesty campaigns for women convicted of killing abusive spouses or partners. Moreover, one of the salient themes in the current literature on women in prison is the centrality of physical abuse in the lives of women subject to state punishment. Even so, the domestic violence and women's prison movements remain largely separate.

Considering the enormous increase in the numbers of imprisoned women during this contemporary era of the US prison industrial complex, we need to examine the potential for establishing deeper and more extensive alliances between the anti-violence movement and the larger women's prison movement. Therefore, this article explores preliminarily some of the historical and philosophical connections

* First published in *New England Journal on Criminal and Civil Confinement* 24, no. 2 (Summer 1998), 339–51.

between domestic violence and imprisonment as two modes of gendered punishment—one located in the private realm, the other in the public realm. This analysis suggests that the women's anti-violence movement is far more integrally related to the women's prison movement than is generally recognized.

The history of prison reform reveals multiple ironies. While imprisonment is now the dominant mode of public punishment and is associated with egregious human rights abuses, it was once regarded as a promise of enlightened moral restoration and thus, as a significant improvement over forms of punishment that relied on the infliction of corporal pain. In the era of flogging, pillories, and stocks, reformers called for the penitentiary as a more humane alternative to the cruelty of corporal punishment. During the nineteenth century, however, even as (mostly white) men in Europe and the United States convicted of violating the law were increasingly sentenced to prison, as opposed to being subjected to torture and mutilation, (white) women's punishment remained emphatically linked to corporal violence inflicted upon them within domestic spaces. These patriarchal structures of violence affected Black women in different ways, primarily through the system of slavery. Today, it is easy to see how the gender and race limitations of the nineteenth-century discourse on punishment reform ruled out the possibility of linking domestic torture with public torture, and thus of a related campaign against the gendered violence visited on women's bodies.

Sometimes, however, the boundaries between private and public punishment were blurred. Long before the emergence of the reform movement that succeeded in establishing imprisonment as generalized punishment, there was a prison for women—the first documented prison for women, in fact—in the Netherlands.[1] Amsterdam's Spinhuis, which opened in 1645, contained cells for women who could not "be kept to their duties by parents or husbands."[2] In seventeenth-century Britain, use of the branks—sometimes known as the scold's or gossip's bridle—to punish women who did not respect patriarchal authority[3] also indicates the permeability of borders between public and private. According to Russell Dobash et al.,

> The branks was an iron cage placed over the head, and most examples incorporated a spike or pointed wheel that was inserted into the offender's mouth in order to "pin the tongue and silence the noisiest brawler." This spiked cage was intended to punish women adjudged quarrelsome or not under the proper control of their husbands. The common form of administering this punishment was to fasten the branks to a woman and parade her through the village, sometime [*sic*] chaining her to a pillar for a period of time after the procession. Although these were public chastisements, they were integrally linked to household domination. In some towns arrangements were made for employing the branks within the home . . . [M]en often used the threat of the branks to attempt to silence their wives, "If you don't rest with your tongue, I'll send for the [town jailor] . . . to hook you up." In this example, we see how patriarchal domination and state domination were intricately intertwined.[4]

When early reformers like John Howard and Jeremy Bentham called for systems of punishment that would putatively minimize violence against the human body, prevailing ideas about the exclusion of women from public space did not allow for the emergence of a reform movement that also contested the ubiquitous violence against women. Such movements did not develop until the late twentieth century. Ironically, as "private" sexual and physical assaults against women are increasingly constructed as "crimes" and, therefore, subject to "public" sanctions, the "public" imprisonment of women remains as hidden as ever. At the same time, greater numbers of women, especially women of color, are subjected to the public punishment of prison as they simultaneously experience violence in their intimate and family relationships. The two modes of punishment remain as disarticulated in both popular and scholarly discourse as they were over a century ago.

Today, as structural racism becomes more entrenched and simultaneously more hidden, these two forms of punishment together camouflage the impact of racism on poor women of color. Domestic violence as a form of punishment is rarely perceived as integrally connected to the modes of punishment implemented by the state. Many recent studies recognize that large numbers of imprisoned women are survivors of family violence. Joanne Belknap's study, *The Invisible Woman: Gender, Crime and Justice*, which looks at the impact of the criminal justice system on women, insightfully examines both imprisonment and battering.[5] As a criminologist, however, Belknap necessarily frames her study with the categories—rarely problematized in criminological and legal discourses—of "female offender" and "female victim."[6] Her examination of women's imprisonment constructs women prisoners as "female offenders," while her analysis of male violence against women constructs women as "victims" of crime.[7] In the first instance, women are perpetrators and in the second, they are victims. Belknap develops a range of important feminist critiques of traditional criminological theories and sheds light on the ways women tend to suffer more from imprisonment practices than do their male counterparts. She also makes valuable observations on the continued invisibility of male violence, even in an era of expanding campaigns, services, and feminist theorizing around these issues. This article suggests, however, that her work can also encourage us to think more deeply about the patriarchal power circuits from the state to the home, which are disconnected by the ideological division of the "public" and the "private," thus, rendering the underlying complexities of women's punishment invisible.

Pat Carlen's 1983 study, *Women's Imprisonment: A Study in Social Control*, highlights the coconstitutive character of women's public and private punishment.[8] This case study on the Scottish women's prison, Cornton Vale, argues that both violent and nonviolent informal disciplining in the home are as important to the construction of domestic life as the parallel, often similar, and indeed symbiotically related discipline that is the foundation of prison practices:[9] "In general, the motto of those charged with the penal regulation of deviant women has been 'discipline, medicalise and feminise'! Women's imprisonment both in Great Britain and in the United States has traditionally been characterized by its invisibility, its domesticity and its infantalisation."[10] In Scotland, the inhabitants of Cornton Vale are largely working-class white women and, as Carlen points out, the intersection of public and private axes of domination is very much class-determined. While Carlen's study does not put into the foreground the influence of race—which is no less important to an understanding of white women's imprisonment than of the imprisonment of women of color—it should be pointed out that throughout the urban areas of Europe and the United States, a vastly disproportionate number of women prisoners come from racially marginalized communities. What Carlen refers to as a "fusion of the private and public realms of family discipline with the penological regulation of deviant women [which] has, in fact, received nominal recognition[,]"[11] then, becomes even more complex when race is taken into consideration.

Sociologist Beth Richie, who has also attempted to link the private and public punishment of women, has studied what she calls the "gender entrapment" of Black women, who are, in many instances, "compelled to crime" and subsequently, imprisoned by the same conditions that inform their subjection to violence within their personal relationships.[12] She writes about

> African American women from low-income communities who are physically battered, sexually assaulted, emotionally abused, and involved in illegal activity. Their stories vividly contradict the popular impression—perpetuated by mainstream social scientists, human service providers, public policy analysts and legislators—that the escalating rates of violence against women, poverty, addiction and women's participation in crime is because of women's psychological, moral, or social inadequacies.[13]

Richie chose to translate the legal category "entrapment" into the theoretical paradigm "gender entrapment" because it allows her to examine the intersections of gender, race, and violence. This paradigm also facilitates an understanding of the ways in which women who experience poverty and violence in their personal lives end up being punished for a web of social conditions over which they have no control.[14] While Richie presents a provocative analysis of the means by which women can be led to engage in illegal activities, as a direct result of either the violence in their intimate relationships or the threat of it, it is not within the purview of her sociological study to examine the historical continuum between domestic and state-inflicted punishment of women.

In much of the historical literature on women's imprisonment, the emergence of a "domestic model" of imprisonment for women toward the end of the nineteenth century is represented as the advent of a specifically female approach to public punishment. This relocation of domestic punishment regimes to the public sphere did not result in any less punishment in the home. The continued social sanctioning of private violence against women historically has minimized the numbers of women subject to public punishment. Because of the ironclad ideological connection between "crime" and "punishment," women's punishment is seldom disarticulated from the unlawful activities that lead them to prison, which makes it all the more difficult to articulate "private" and "public" punishment. The assumption that women constitute a relatively small portion of the imprisoned population simply because they commit fewer crimes continues to reign over common sense and over criminological discourse. Therefore, the fact that women are punished in venues other than prison and in accordance with authority not directly assumed by the state might begin to explain the relatively small numbers of imprisoned women.

State-sanctioned punishment is informed by patriarchal structures and ideologies that have tended to produce historical assumptions of female criminality linked to ideas about the violation of social norms defining a "woman's place." Feminist historians have uncovered evidence of severe corporal punishment inflicted on women accused of adultery, for example, while the behavior of male adulterers has been normalized. At the same time, violence against women inflicted within domestic spaces has only recently begun to be "criminalized." Considering the fact that as many as half of all women are assaulted by their husbands or partners,[15] combined with dramatically rising numbers of women sentenced to prison, it may be argued that women in general are subjected to a far greater magnitude of punishment than men. Even though women are still represented as negligible targets of the prison system, the continued pandemic of private punishment, connected with the soaring numbers of women being sent to prison, combine to create a picture of the lives of poor, working-class, and racially marginalized women as overdetermined by punishment. This is not to dismiss the extent to which middle-class women are also victims of violence in their families and intimate relationships. They are not, however, "entrapped"—to use Richie's term—in the same web of social conditions that places many poor women of color on the track that leads to prison and thus, causes them to experience surplus punishment.

Paradoxically, prison reform movements in general have tended to bolster, rather than diminish, the stronghold of prisons on the lives of the individuals whom they hold captive. Michel Foucault has pointed out that from the beginning, reform has always been linked to the evolution of the prison, which, in turn, has become more entrenched due in part precisely to the effectiveness of reforms.[16]

> [T]he movement for reforming the prisons, for controlling their functioning is not a recent phenomenon. It does not even seem to have originated in a recognition of failure. Prison "reform" is virtually contemporary with the prison itself: it constitutes, as it were, its programme. From the outset, the prison was caught up in a series of accompanying mechanisms, whose purpose was apparently to correct it, but which seem to form part of its very functioning, so closely have they been bound up with its existence throughout its long history.[17]

In other words, prison reform campaigns, focusing on men's as well as women's institutions, generally have called for the improvement of prisons, but rarely have problematized the role of prisons as the dominant mode of punishment. Thus, as reforms have been instituted, prison systems have become more entrenched both structurally and ideologically. Today, when punishment in the United States has become a veritable industry consolidating the linkages between government and transnational corporations in ways that mirror and strengthen the military industrial complex, it is as difficult to question the need for prisons on such a large scale as it is to question the need for such a vast military machine.

When the reform movement calling for separate prisons for women emerged in England and the United States during the nineteenth century, Elizabeth Fry, Josephine Shaw, and other advocates argued against the prevailing conception that criminal women were beyond the reach of moral rehabilitation. Like male convicts, who presumably could be "corrected" by rigorous prison regimes, female convicts, they suggested, could also be molded into moral beings by differently gendered imprisonment regimes. Architectural changes, domestic regimes, and an all-female custodial staff were implemented in the reformatory program proposed by reformers,[18] and eventually, women's prisons became as strongly anchored to the social landscape as men's prisons. Their relative invisibility was as much a reflection of the domestic space reinscribed on women's public punishment, as it was of the relatively small numbers of women incarcerated in these new institutions.

This feminization of public punishment in England and the United States was explicitly designed to reform white women. Twenty-one years after the first reformatory in England was established in London in 1853, the first US reformatory for women was opened in Indiana.[19] As Richie writes,

> [The] aim was to train the prisoners in the "important" female role of domesticity. Thus, an important part of the

> reform movement in women's prisons was to encourage and ingrain "appropriate" gender roles, such as vocational training in cooking, sewing, and cleaning. To accommodate these goals, the reformatory cottages were usually designed with kitchens, living rooms, and even some nurseries for prisoners with infants.[20]

This feminized public punishment, however, did not affect all women in the same way. When Black women were imprisoned in reformatories, they often were segregated from white women. Moreover, they tended to be disproportionately sentenced to serve time in men's prisons. In the southern states in the aftermath of the Civil War, Black women endured the cruelties of the convict lease system unmitigated by the feminization of punishment; neither their sentences, nor the labor they were compelled to do, were lessened by virtue of their gender. As the US prison system evolved during the twentieth century, feminized modes of punishment—the cottage system, domestic training, etc.—were designed, ideologically, to reform white women, relegating women of color, in large part, to realms of public punishment that made no pretense of offering them femininity.

Moreover, as Lucia Zedner has pointed out, sentencing practices for women within the reformatory system often required women to do more time than men for similar offenses. "This differential was justified on the basis that women were sent to reformatories not to be punished in proportion to the seriousness of their offense but to be reformed and retrained, a process that, it was argued, required time."[21] At the same time, Zedner points out, this tendency to send women to prison for longer terms than men was accelerated by the eugenics movement, "which sought to have 'genetically inferior' women removed from social circulation for as many of their childbearing years as possible."[22] Although Nicole Rafter points out that racism may not be the primary explanatory factor underlying late-nineteenth-century eugenic criminology,[23] the eugenic discourses that presumed to define white normalcy against white deviancy—intellectual impairment, criminality, physical disability, etc.—relied on the same logic of exclusion as racism itself, and therefore, could be easily retooled for racist uses.

In the latter twentieth century, women's prisons have begun to look more like their male counterparts, particularly those that have been constructed in the era of the prison industrial complex. As corporate involvement in punishment begins to mirror corporate involvement in military production, rehabilitation is becoming displaced by penal aims of incapacitation. Now that the population of prisons and jails is approaching two million, the rate of increase in the numbers of women prisoners has surpassed that of men. As criminologist Elliott Currie has pointed out,

> For most of the period after World War II, the female incarceration rate hovered at around 8 per 100,000; it did not reach double digits until 1977. Today it is 51 per 100,000.... At current rates of increase, there will be more women in American prisons in the year 2010 than there were inmates of both sexes in 1970. When we combine the effects of race and gender, the nature of these shifts in the prison population is even clearer. The prison incarceration rate for Black women today exceeds that for white men as recently as 1980.[24]

A quarter-century ago, in the era of the Attica uprising and the murder of George Jackson at San Quentin, radical movements developed against the prison system as a principal site of state violence and repression. In part as a reaction to the invisibility of women prisoners in this movement, and in part as a consequence of the rising women's liberation movement, specific campaigns developed in defense of the rights of women prisoners. While many of these campaigns put forth, and continue to advance, radical critiques of state repression and violence, those taken up within the correctional community have been influenced largely by liberal constructions of gender equality.

In contrast to the nineteenth-century reform movement, which was grounded in an ideology of gender difference, late-twentieth-century "reforms" have relied on a "separate but equal" model. This "separate but equal" approach often has been applied uncritically, ironically resulting in demands for more repressive conditions in order to render women's facilities "equal" to men's. For example, Tekla Dennison Miller, former warden of Huron Valley Women's Prison in Michigan, identifies her crusade for equality during the 1980s as strongly feminist. The problematic character of such an approach is revealed in her discussion of security.

> Staffing was far leaner at Huron Valley Women's than at men's prisons. When it opened . . . [t]here were no yard officers at Women's, let alone a yard sergeant to watch prisoner movement and yard activities. The yards are the favorite areas for prisoner-on-prisoner assaults. There was also only one Assistant Deputy Warden. Men's prisons were allowed two ADWs, one for security and one for housing, but male central office administration claimed, "Women prisoners pose no security threat. They're just basic pains in the ass and are mostly interested in painting their nails and harassing us for more personal property. They need a housing deputy, not a security deputy."[25]

In her campaign for gender equality, Miller also criticized security practices for the unequal allocation of weapons:

> Arsenals in men's prisons are large rooms with shelves of shotguns, rifles, hand guns, ammunition, gas canisters, and riot equipment . . . Huron Valley Women's arsenal was a small, five feet by two feet closet that held two rifles, eight shotguns, two bull horns, five hand guns, four gas canisters and twenty sets of restraints.[26]

After a prisoner, intent on escaping, successfully climbed over the razor ribbon and was captured after jumping to the ground on the other side, a local news reporter, whom Miller described as "an unexpected ally in the ongoing fight for parity," questioned the policy of not firing warning shots for women escapees.[27] As a result, Miller observed, "escaping women prisoners in medium or higher [security] prisons are treated the same way as men. A warning shot is fired. If the prisoner fails to halt and is over the fence, an officer is allowed to shoot to injure. If the officer's life is in danger, the officer can shoot to kill."[28]

Paradoxically, demands for parity with men's prisons, instead of creating greater educational, vocational, and health opportunities for women prisoners, often have led to more repressive conditions for women. This is a consequence of not only deploying liberal, that is, formalistic, notions of equality, but more dangerously, allowing male prisons to function as the punishment norm. Miller points out that she attempted to prevent a prisoner, whom she characterizes as a "murderer" serving a long term, from participating in graduation ceremonies at the University of Michigan.[29] (Of course, she does not indicate the nature of the woman's murder charges—whether, for instance, she was convicted of killing an abusive partner, as is the case for a substantial number of women convicted of such charges.) Although Miller did not succeed in preventing the inmate from participating in the commencement ceremony, the prisoner was made to wear leg chains and handcuffs with her cap and gown.[30]

A more widely publicized example of the use of repressive paraphernalia, historically associated with the treatment of male prisoners, to create "equality" for female prisoners, was the 1996 decision by Alabama's prison commissioner to establish women's chain gangs.[31] After Alabama became the first state to reinstitute chain gangs in 1995, then State Corrections Commissioner Ron Jones announced the following year that women would be shackled while they cut grass, picked up trash, and worked a vegetable garden at Julia Tutwiler State Prison for Women. This attempt to institute chain gangs for women was in part a response to lawsuits by male prisoners, who charged that male chain gains discriminated against men by virtue of their gender. Immediately after Jones's announcement, however, he was fired by Governor Fob James, who obviously was pressured to prevent Alabama from acquiring the dubious distinction of being the only US state to have equal opportunity chain gangs.

Four months after Alabama's embarrassing flirtation with the possibility of chain gangs for women, Sheriff Joe Arpaio of Maricopa County, Arizona—represented in the media as "the toughest sheriff in America"—held a press conference to announce that because he was "an equal opportunity incarcerator," he was establishing the country's first female chain gangs.[32] When the plan was implemented, newspapers throughout the country carried a photograph of chained women cleaning Phoenix's streets. While Sheriff Arpaio's policy regarding women prisoners has been criticized as little more than a publicity stunt, the fact that this women's chain gang emerges against the backdrop of a generalized increase in the repression inflicted on women prisoners—including the proliferation of security housing units, which parallel the development of super-maximum security prisons—is cause for alarm. Since the population of women in prison is now comprised of a majority of women of color, the historical resonances of slavery, colonization, and genocide should not be missed in these images of women in chains and shackles.

As the level of repression in women's prisons increases, and, paradoxically as the influence of domestic prison regimes recedes, sexual abuse—which, like domestic violence, is yet another dimension of the privatized punishment of women—has become an institutionalized component of punishment behind prison walls. Although guard-on-prisoner sexual abuse is not sanctioned as such, the widespread leniency with which offending officers are treated suggests that for women, prison is a space in which the threat of sexualized violence that looms in the larger society is effectively sanctioned as a routine aspect of the landscape of punishment behind prison walls.

According to a recent Human Rights Watch report on the sexual abuse of women in US prisons:

> Our findings indicate that being a woman prisoner in U.S. state prisons can be a terrifying experience. If you are sexually abused, you cannot escape from your abuser. Grievance or investigatory procedures, where they exist, are often ineffectual, and correctional employees continue to engage in abuse because they believe they will rarely be held accountable, administratively or criminally. Few people outside the prison walls know what is going on or care if they do know. Fewer still do anything to address the problem.[33]

The following excerpt from the summary of this report, entitled *All Too Familiar: Sexual Abuse of Women in U.S. State Prisons,* reveals the extent to which women's prison environments are violently sexualized, thus recapitulating the familiar violence that characterizes many women's private lives:

> We found that male correctional employees have vaginally, anally, and orally raped female prisoners and sexually assaulted and abused them. We found that in the course of committing such gross misconduct, male officers have not only used actual or threatened physical force, but have also used their near total authority to provide or deny goods and privileges to female prisoners to compel them to have sex or, in other cases, to reward them for having done so. In other cases, male officers have violated their most basic professional duty and engaged in sexual contact with female prisoners absent the use or threat of force or any material exchange. In addition to engaging in sexual relations with prisoners, male officers have used mandatory pat-frisks or room searches to grope women's breasts, buttocks, and vaginal areas and to view them inappropriately while in a state of undress in the housing or bathroom areas. Male correctional officers and staff have also engaged in regular verbal degradation and harassment of female prisoners, thus contributing to a cus-

> todial environment in the state prisons for women which is often highly sexualized and excessively hostile.[34]

This report argues that the prevalence of sexual abuse in women's prisons is in violation of the US Constitution as well as of international human rights law.[35] The upcoming visit in summer 1998 to a number of US women's prisons by the United Nations Special Rapporteur on Violence Against Women further highlights the importance of framing the conditions of imprisoned women within the context of the anti-violence movement and within a larger human rights context. As Linda Burnham has pointed out,

> [t]he intent of the human rights paradigm is to position women's issues central to human rights discourse; negate the tendency to view women's issues as private matters; provide teeth and a structure of accountability for women's oppression that includes but is not limited to the state; and provide an overarching political framework capable of connecting the full range of women's issues and the full diversity of their social identities and circumstances.[36]

The sexual abuse of women in prison is one of the most heinous state-sanctioned human rights violations within the United States today. Women prisoners represent one of the most disfranchised and invisible adult populations in our society. The absolute power and control the state exercises over their lives both stems from and perpetuates the patriarchal and racist structures that for centuries have resulted in the social domination of women. As the prison industrial complex threatens to transform entire communities into targets of state punishment, the relatively small, but rapidly increasing, percentage of imprisoned women should not be used as a pretext for ignoring the complicated web of women's punishment. The moment may very well be ripe for forging alliances and for establishing links with international movements for human rights.

PART IV

Rethinking Incarceration

Identifying the Prison Industrial Complex

CHAPTER 8

Masked Racism

Reflections on the Prison Industrial Complex*

Imprisonment has become the response of first resort to far too many of the social problems that burden people who are ensconced in poverty. These problems often are veiled by being conveniently grouped together under the category "crime" and by the automatic attribution of criminal behavior to people of color. Homelessness, unemployment, drug addiction, mental illness, and illiteracy are only a few of the problems that disappear from public view when the human beings contending with them are relegated to cages.

Prisons thus perform a feat of magic. Or rather the people who continually vote in new prison bonds and tacitly assent to a proliferating network of prisons and jails have been tricked into believing in the magic of imprisonment. But prisons do not disappear problems, they disappear human beings. And the practice of disappearing vast numbers of people from poor, immigrant, and racially marginalized communities has literally become big business.

The seeming effortlessness of magic always conceals an enormous amount of behind-the-scenes work. When prisons disappear human beings in order to convey the illusion of solving social problems, penal infrastructures must be created to accommodate a rapidly swelling population of caged people. Goods and services must be provided to keep imprisoned populations alive. Sometimes these

* First published in *Colorlines* 1, no. 2 (Fall 1998).

populations must be kept busy and at other times—particularly in repressive super-maximum prisons and in Immigration and Naturalization Service detention centers—they must be deprived of virtually all meaningful activity. Vast numbers of handcuffed and shackled people are moved across state borders as they are transferred from one state or federal prison to another.

All this work, which used to be the primary province of government, is now also performed by private corporations, whose links to government in the field of what is euphemistically called "corrections" resonate dangerously with the military industrial complex. The dividends that accrue from investment in the punishment industry, like those that accrue from investment in weapons production, only amount to social destruction. Taking into account the structural similarities and profitability of business-government linkages in the realms of military production and public punishment, the expanding penal system can now be characterized as a "prison industrial complex."

Almost two million people are currently locked up in the immense network of US prisons and jails. More than 70 percent of the imprisoned population are people of color. It is rarely acknowledged that the fastest growing group of prisoners are Black women and that Native American prisoners are the largest group per capita. Approximately five million people—including those on probation and parole—are directly under the surveillance of the criminal justice system.

Three decades ago, the imprisoned population was approximately one-eighth its current size. While women still constitute a relatively small percentage of people behind bars, today the number of incarcerated women in California alone is almost twice what the nationwide women's prison population was in 1970. According to Elliott Currie, "The prison has become a looming presence in our society to an extent unparalleled in our history—or that of any other industrial democracy. Short of major wars, mass incarceration has been the most thoroughly implemented government social program of our time."

To deliver up bodies destined for profitable punishment, the political economy of prisons relies on racialized assumptions of criminality—such as images of Black welfare mothers reproducing criminal children—and on racist practices in arrest, conviction, and sentencing patterns. Colored bodies constitute the main human raw material in this vast experiment to disappear the major social problems of our time. Once the aura of magic is stripped away from the imprisonment solution, what is revealed is racism, class bias, and the parasitic seduction of capitalist profit. The prison industrial system materially and morally impoverishes its inhabitants and devours the social wealth needed to address the very problems that have led to spiraling numbers of prisoners.

As prisons take up more and more space on the social landscape, other government programs that have previously sought to respond to social needs—such as Temporary Assistance for Needy Families—are being squeezed out of existence. The deterioration of public education, including prioritizing discipline and security over learning in public schools located in poor communities, is directly related to the prison "solution."

As prisons proliferate in US society, private capital has become enmeshed in the punishment industry. And precisely because of their profit potential, prisons are becoming increasingly important to the US economy. If the notion of punishment as a source of potentially stupendous profits is disturbing by itself, then the strategic dependence on racist structures and ideologies to render mass punishment palatable and profitable is even more troubling.

Prison privatization is the most obvious instance of capital's current movement toward the prison industry. While government-run prisons are often in gross violation of international human rights standards, private prisons are even less accountable. In March of this year [1998], the Corrections Corporation of America, the largest US private prison company, claimed 54,944 beds in 68 facilities under contract or development in the US, Puerto Rico, the United Kingdom, and Australia. Following the global trend of subjecting more women to public punishment, CCA recently opened a women's prison outside Melbourne. The company recently identified California as its "new frontier."

Wackenhut Corrections Corporation (WCC), the second largest US prison company, claimed contracts and awards to manage 46 facilities in North America, the UK, and Australia. It boasts a total of 30,424 beds as well as contracts for prisoner health care services, transportation, and security. The stocks of both CCA and WCC are doing extremely well. Between 1996 and 1997, CCA's revenues increased by 58 percent, from $293 million to $462 million. Its net profit grew from $30.9 million to $53.9 million. WCC raised its revenues from $138 million in 1996 to $210 million in 1997. Unlike public correctional facilities, the vast profits of these private facilities rely on the employment of nonunion labor.

But private prison companies are only the most visible component of the increasing corporatization of punishment. Government contracts to build prisons have bolstered the construction industry. The architectural community has identified prison design as a major new niche. Technology developed for the military by companies like Westinghouse is being marketed for use in law enforcement and punishment.

Moreover, corporations that appear to be far removed from the business of punishment are intimately involved in the expansion of the prison industrial complex. Prison construction bonds are one of the many sources of profitable investment for leading financiers such as Merrill Lynch. MCI charges prisoners and their families outrageous prices for the precious telephone calls that are often the only contact prisoners have with the free world.

Many corporations whose products we consume on a daily basis have learned that prison labor power can be as profitable as Third World labor power exploited by US-based global corporations. Both relegate formerly unionized workers to joblessness and many even wind up in prison. Some of the companies that use prison labor are IBM, Motorola, Compaq, Texas Instruments, Honeywell, Microsoft, and Boeing. But it is not only the high-tech industries that reap the profits of prison labor. Nordstrom department stores sell jeans that are marketed as "Prison Blues," as well as T-shirts and jackets made in Oregon prisons. The advertising slogan for these clothes is "made on the inside to be worn on the outside." Maryland prisoners inspect glass bottles and jars used by Revlon and Pierre Cardin, and schools throughout the world buy graduation caps and gowns made by South Carolina prisoners.

"For private business," write Eve Goldberg and Linda Evans (a political prisoner inside the Federal Correctional Institution at Dublin, California),

> prison labor is like a pot of gold. No strikes. No union organizing. No health benefits, unemployment insurance, or workers' compensation to pay. No language barriers, as in foreign countries. New leviathan prisons are being built on thousands of eerie acres of factories inside the walls. Prisoners do data entry for Chevron, make telephone reservations for TWA, raise hogs, shovel manure, make circuit boards, limousines, waterbeds, and lingerie for Victoria's Secret—all at a fraction of the cost of "free labor."

Although prison labor—which ultimately is compensated at a rate far below the minimum wage—is hugely profitable for the private companies that use it, the penal system as a whole does not produce wealth. It devours the social wealth that could be used to subsidize housing for the homeless, to ameliorate public education for poor and racially marginalized communities, to open free drug-rehabilitation programs for people who wish to kick their habits, to create a national health care system, to expand programs to combat HIV, to eradicate domestic abuse, and, in the process, to create well-paying jobs for the unemployed.

Since 1984 more than twenty new prisons have opened in California, while only one new campus was added to the California State

University system and none to the University of California system. In 1996–97, higher education received only 8.7 percent of the state's general fund while corrections received 9.6 percent. Now that affirmative action has been declared illegal in California, it is obvious that education is increasingly reserved for certain people, while prisons are reserved for others. Five times as many Black men are presently in prison as in four-year colleges and universities. This new segregation has dangerous implications for the entire country.

By segregating people labeled as criminals, prison simultaneously fortifies and conceals the structural racism of the US economy. Claims of low unemployment rates—even in Black communities—make sense only if one assumes that the vast numbers of people in prison have really disappeared and thus have no legitimate claims to jobs. The numbers of Black and Latino men currently incarcerated amount to two percent of the male labor force. According to criminologist David Downes, "Treating incarceration as a type of hidden unemployment may raise the jobless rate for men by about one-third, to 8 percent. The effect on the Black labor force is greater still, raising the [Black] male unemployment rate from 11 percent to 19 percent."

Mass incarceration is not a solution to unemployment, nor is it a solution to the vast array of social problems that are hidden away in a rapidly growing network of prisons and jails. However, the great majority of people have been tricked into believing in the efficacy of imprisonment, even though the historical record clearly demonstrates that prisons do not work. Racism has undermined our ability to create a popular critical discourse to contest the ideological trickery that posits imprisonment as key to public safety. The focus of state policy is rapidly shifting from social welfare to social control.

Black, Latino, Native American, and many Asian youth are portrayed as the purveyors of violence, traffickers of drugs, and as envious of commodities that they have no right to possess. Young Black and Latina women are represented as sexually promiscuous and as indiscriminately propagating babies and poverty. Criminality and deviance are racialized. Surveillance is thus focused on communities of color, immigrants, the unemployed, the undereducated, the homeless, and in general on those who have a diminishing claim to social resources. Their claim to social resources continues to diminish in large part because law enforcement and penal measures increasingly devour these resources. The prison industrial complex has thus created a vicious cycle of punishment that only further impoverishes those whose impoverishment is supposedly "solved" by imprisonment.

Therefore, as the emphasis of government policy shifts from social welfare to crime control, racism sinks more deeply into the economic and ideological structures of US society. Meanwhile, conservative crusaders against affirmative action and bilingual education proclaim the end of racism, while their opponents suggest that racism's remnants can be dispelled through dialogue and conversation. But conversations about "race relations" will hardly dismantle a prison industrial complex that thrives on and nourishes the racism hidden within the deep structures of our society.

The emergence of a US prison industrial complex within a context of cascading conservatism marks a new historical moment, whose dangers are unprecedented. But so are its opportunities. Considering the impressive number of grassroots projects that continue to resist the expansion of the punishment industry, it ought to be possible to bring these efforts together to create radical and nationally visible movements that can legitimize anticapitalist critiques of the prison industrial complex. It ought to be possible to build movements in defense of prisoners' human rights and movements that persuasively argue that what we need is not new prisons but new health care, housing, drug programs, jobs, and education. To safeguard a democratic future, it is possible and necessary to weave together the many and increasing strands of resistance to the prison industrial complex into a powerful movement for social transformation.

CHAPTER 9

Race, Gender, and the Prison Industrial Complex

California and Beyond*

with Cassandra Shaylor

Women's Rights as Human Rights

A central achievement of the 1995 United Nations Fourth World Conference on Women in Beijing was the emphatic articulation of women's rights as human rights. In specifically identifying violence against women in both public and private life as an assault against women's human rights, the Beijing Conference helped to deepen awareness of violence against women on a global scale. Yet, even with this increasing attention, the violence linked to women's prisons remains obscured by the social invisibility of the prison. There, violence takes the form of medical neglect, sexual abuse, lack of reproductive control, loss of parental rights, denial of legal rights and remedies, the devastating effects of isolation, and, of course, arbitrary discipline.

Recent reports by international human rights organizations have begun to address the invisibility of women prisoners and to highlight the severity of the violence they experience. For example,

* From the Report to the UN World Conference Against Racism, Racial Discrimination, Xenophobia, and Related Intolerance (Durban, South Africa), first published in *Meridians* 2, no. 1 (2001), 1–25.

Human Rights Watch and Amnesty International have specifically focused on the widespread problem of sexual abuse in US prisons. In 1998 the UN Special Rapporteur on Violence Against Women issued a report on her findings—which were even more disturbing than prison activists had predicted—from visits to eight women's prisons in the United States. In general, although international human rights standards rarely are applied in the US context, particularly in the legal arena, UN documents (such as the International Covenant on Civil and Political Rights and the Standard Minimum Rules for the Treatment of Prisoners) have been used productively by activists to underscore the gravity of human rights violations in women's prisons.

The Prison Industrial Complex

As prison populations have soared in the United States, the conventional assumption that increased levels of crime are the cause of expanding prison populations has been widely contested. Activists and scholars who have tried to develop more nuanced understandings of the punishment process—and especially racism's role—have deployed the concept of the "prison industrial complex" to point out that the proliferation of prisons and prisoners is more clearly linked to larger economic and political structures and ideologies than to individual criminal conduct and efforts to curb "crime." Indeed, vast numbers of corporations with global markets rely on prisons as an important source of profit and thus have acquired clandestine stakes in the continued expansion of the prison system. Because the overwhelming majority of US prisoners are from racially marginalized communities, corporate stakes in an expanding apparatus of punishment necessarily rely on and promote old as well as new structures of racism.

Women especially have been hurt by these developments. Although women comprise a relatively small percentage of the entire prison population, they constitute, nevertheless, the fastest-growing segment of prisoners. There are now more women in prison in the state of California alone than there were in the United States as a whole in 1970.[1] Because race is a major factor determining who goes to prison and who does not, the groups most rapidly increasing in number are Black, Latina, Asian American, and Indigenous women.

Globalization of capitalism has precipitated the decline of the welfare state in industrialized countries such as the United States and Britain and structural adjustment in the countries of the southern region. As social programs in the United States such as Aid to Families with Dependent Children (AFDC) have been drastically curtailed, imprisonment has simultaneously become the most self-evident response to many of the social problems previously addressed by institutions such as AFDC. In other words, in the era of the disestablishment of social programs that have historically served poor communities, and at a time when affirmative action programs are being dismantled and resources for education and health are declining, imprisonment functions as the default solution. Especially for women of color, who are hardest hit by the withdrawal of social resources and their replacement with imprisonment, these draconian strategies—ever longer prison sentences for offenses that are often petty—tend to reproduce and, indeed, exacerbate the very problems they purport to solve.

There is an ironic but telling similarity between the economic impact of the prison industrial complex and that of the military industrial complex, with which it shares important structural features. Both systems simultaneously produce vast profits and social destruction. What is beneficial to the corporations, politicians, and state entities involved in these systems brings blight and death to poor and racially marginalized communities throughout the world. In the case of the prison industrial complex, the transformation of imprisoned bodies of color into consumers and/or producers of an immense range of commodities effectively transforms public funds into profit, leaving little in the way of social assistance to bolster the efforts of women and men who want to overcome barriers erected by poverty and racism. For example, when women who spend many years in prison are released, instead of jobs, housing, health care and education, they are offered a small amount of release money, which covers little more than a bus ride and two nights in an inexpensive hotel. In the "free world," they are haunted by the stigma of imprisonment, which renders it extremely difficult for a "felon" to find a job. Thus they are inevitably tracked back into a prison system that in this era of the prison industrial complex has entirely dispensed with even a semblance of rehabilitation.

The emergence of a prison industrial complex means that whatever rehabilitative potential the prison may have previously possessed (as implied by the bizarre persistence of the term "corrections"), the contemporary economics of imprisonment privilege the profitability of punishment at the expense of human education and transformation. State budgets increasingly are consumed by the costs of building and maintaining prisons while monies dedicated to sustaining and improving communities are slashed. A glaring example of the misplaced financial investment in punishment is the decreasing state support for public education: for example, in California in 1995 the budget for prisons exceeded that for higher education.

Corporations are intimately linked to prison systems in both the public and the private sector. The trend toward privatization is only one manifestation of a growing involvement of corporations in the punishment process. While a myopic focus on private prisons in activist campaigns may tend to legitimate public prisons by default, placing this development within the context of a far-reaching prison industrial complex can enhance our understanding of the contemporary punishment industry. In the United States, there are currently 26 for-profit prison corporations that operate approximately 150 facilities in 28 states.[2] The largest of these companies, Corrections Corporation of America and Wackenhut, control 76.4 percent of the private prison market globally. While CCA is headquartered in Nashville, Tennessee, its largest shareholder is the multinational headquartered in Paris, Sodexho Marriott, which provides catering services at many US colleges and universities. Currently, CCA, Wackenhut, and the other smaller private prison companies together bring in $1.5 to 2 billion a year.[3]

Though private prisons represent a fairly small proportion of prisons in the United States, the privatization model is quickly becoming the primary mode of organizing punishment in many other countries.[4*] These companies have tried to take advantage of the expanding population of women prisoners, both in the United States and globally. In 1996, the first private women's prison was established by CCA in Melbourne, Australia. The government of Victoria "adopted the US model of privatization in which financing, design, construction, and ownership of the prison are awarded to one contractor and the government pays them back for construction over twenty years. This means that it is virtually impossible to remove the contractor because that contractor owns the prison."[5]

But to understand the reach of the prison industrial complex, it is not enough to evoke the looming power of the private prison business. Of course, by definition, those companies court the state within and outside the United States for the purpose of obtaining prison contracts. They thus bring punishment and profit into a menacing embrace. Still, this is only the most visible dimension of the prison industrial complex, and it should not lead us to ignore the more comprehensive corporatization that is a feature of contemporary punishment. As compared to earlier historical eras, the prison economy is no longer a small, identifiable, and containable set of markets. Many corporations, whose names are highly recognizable by "free world" consumers, have discovered new possibilities for expansion by selling their products to correctional facilities.

---

* Julia Sudbury offers an analysis of the growing trend toward privatization of prisons in England in particular.

> In the 1990s, the variety of corporations making money from prisons is truly dizzying, ranging from Dial Soap to Famous Amos cookies, from AT&T to health-care providers. . . . In 1995 Dial Soap sold $100,000 worth of its product to the New York City jail system alone. . . . When VitaPro Foods of Montreal, Canada, contracted to supply inmates in the state of Texas with its soy-based meat substitute, the contract was worth $34 million a year.[6]

The point here is that even if private prison companies were prohibited—an unlikely prospect, indeed—the prison industrial complex and its many strategies for profit would remain intact.

Moreover, it is not only the private prison—CCA and Wackenhut in particular—that gets reproduced along the circuits of global capital and insinuates itself into the lives of poor people in various parts of the world. Connections between corporations and public prisons, similar to those in the United States, are currently emerging throughout the world and are being reinforced by the contemporary idea, widely promoted by the United States, that imprisonment is a social panacea. The most obvious effects of these ideas and practices on women can be seen in the extraordinary numbers of women arrested and imprisoned on drug charges throughout the world. The US-instigated war on drugs has disproportionately claimed women as its victims inside the United States, but also elsewhere in Europe, South America, the Caribbean, Asia, and Africa.[7] In what can be seen as the penal equivalent of ambulance chasing, architectural firms, construction companies, and other corporations are helping to create new women's prisons throughout the world.

Race, Gender, and the Prison Industrial Complex

Activist opposition to the prison industrial complex has insisted on an understanding of the ways racist structures and assumptions facilitate the expansion of an extremely profitable prison system, in turn helping to reinforce racist social stratification. This racism is always gendered, and imprisonment practices that are conventionally considered to be "neutral"—such as sentencing, punishment regimes, and health care—differ in relation to the ways race, gender, and sexuality intersect.*

The women most likely to be found in US prisons are Black, Latina, Asian American, and Native American women. In 1998, one out of every 109 women in the United States was under the control of the criminal justice system.[8] But where these women are located within the system differs according to their race: while about two-thirds of women on probation are white, two-thirds of women in prison are women of color. An African American woman is eight times more likely to go to prison than a white woman; a Latina woman is four times more likely. African American women make up the largest percentage of women in state prisons (48 percent) and federal detention centers (35 percent), even though they are only approximately 13 percent of the general population.[9] As the population of Latinas in the United States grows, so does their number in prisons. In California for example, though Latinas comprise 13 percent of the general population, they make up around 25 percent of women in prison.[10] Though there is no official data maintained on the numbers of Native American women in prison, numerous studies document that Native Americans are arrested at a higher rate than whites and face discrimination at all levels of the criminal justice system.[11]

Given the way in which US government statistics fail to specify racial categories other than "white," "Black," and "Hispanic"—figures regarding women who self-identify as Native American, Vietnamese, Filipina, Pacific Islander, or as from any other racially marginalized community, are consolidated into a category of "other"—it is difficult to provide precise numbers of women from these groups in prison.[12] However, advocates for women prisoners

---

* For a discussion of intersectional analysis, see Kimberlé Crenshaw, "Mapping the Margins: Intersectionality, Identity Politics, and Violence Against Women of Color."

report that the numbers of Asian women, including Vietnamese, Filipinas, and Pacific Islanders, are growing in women's prisons.[13]

The vast increase in the numbers of women of color in US prisons has everything to do with the war on drugs. Two African American women serving long federal sentences on questionable drug charges—Kemba Smith and Dorothy Gaines—were pardoned by President Bill Clinton during his last days in office. In the cases of both Smith, who received a twenty-four-and-a-half-year sentence, and Gaines, whose sentence was nineteen years and seven months, their sole link to drug trafficking was their involvement with men who were accused traffickers.[14]

Considering only the federal system, between 1990 and 1996, 84 percent of the increase in imprisoned women (2,057) was drug related. In the entire complex of US prisons and jails, drug-related convictions are largely to blame for the fact that Black women are imprisoned at rates that are twice as high as their male counterparts and three times the rate of white women.[15] Harsh sentencing laws, such as mandatory minimums attached to drug convictions and "three-strikes" laws, which can result in a life sentence for a relatively minor drug offense, have created a trap door through which too many women of color have fallen into the ranks of disposable populations.

Violence Against Women in Prison

Dorothy Gaines and Kemba Smith were fortunate, but they are only two of the women incarcerated during the Clinton years, during which more women than ever were sentenced to prison. What happens to the vast numbers of women behind walls? In the first place, contrary to international human rights standards, imprisonment means much more than just a loss of freedom. Women's prisons are located on a continuum of violence that extends from the official practices of the state to the spaces of intimate relationships. Both public and private incarnations of this violence are largely hidden from public view. But while domestic violence increasingly is an issue of concern in public life, the violence of imprisonment rarely is discussed. Prisons are places within which violence occurs on a routine and constant basis; the functioning of the prison depends upon it. The threat of violence emanating from prison hierarchies is so ubiquitous and unpredictable that some women have pointed out the striking structural similarities between the experiences of imprisonment and battering relationships.[16]

Though many women prisoners have indeed experienced intimate violence, the profile of "the women prisoner" tends to imply that this victimization in the "free world" is the cause of imprisonment. Such a simplistic causal link fails to recognize the complex set of factors related to the social and political legitimation of violence against women, emphasizing *domestic* violence at the expense of an understanding of *state* violence—both in the "free world" and in the world of prison.

Violence in prison is directed at the psyche as well as the body. Increasingly prisons in the United States are becoming a primary response to mental illness among poor people. The institutionalization of mentally ill people historically has been used more often against women than against men. However, for women who do not enter prison with mental health issues, extended imprisonment is sure to create them. According to Penal Reform International, "Long term prisoners may develop mental and psychic disturbances by imprisonment itself and by being cut off from their families. Mental problems also arise and may become chronic in big prisons, where there is much overcrowding; where there are few activities; where prisoners have to stay long time in their cells in daytime."[17] Thus, this organization interprets the Standard Minimum Rules for the Treatment of Prisoners as not only proscribing the incarceration of mentally ill persons in prisons, but as also calling for compassionate care by medical, psychological, and custodial staff of those who suffer mental and emotional problems as a consequence of imprisonment.

Most women in prison experience some degree of depression or post-traumatic stress disorder. Very often they are neither diagnosed nor treated, with injurious consequences for their mental health in and outside prison. Many women report that if they ask for counseling, they are offered psychotropic medications instead. Despite legal challenges, prison regimes construct prisoners who suffer the effects of institutionalization as "sick" and in need of treatment with psychotropic drugs.[18] Historically, this "medicalization model" has been most widely used against women.[19]

As technologies of imprisonment become increasingly repressive and practices of isolation become increasingly routine, mentally ill women often are placed in solitary confinement, which can only exacerbate their condition. Moreover, women prisoners with significant mental illnesses frequently do not seek treatment because they fear harsh procedures (such as being placed in a "strip cell" if they say they are suicidal) and/or overmedication with psychotropic drugs. While women who have mental health concerns are mistreated, women with serious physical conditions often are labeled mentally ill in order to preempt their complaints—sometimes with grave consequences.*

Medical Neglect

At the historic legislative hearings recently conducted inside California women's prisons,† prisoner Gloria Broxton declared: "They don't have the right to take my life because they thought I was worthless. I

* For example, Jody Fitzgerald died in November 2000 at the Central California Women's Facility. In legal interviews with staff of Legal Services for Prisoners with Children, several women prisoners testified that prison staff ignored Ms. Fitzgerald's serious physical symptoms—claiming they were "all in her head"—and sent her to a psychiatric unit where she subsequently died.

† Legislative hearings were conducted at Valley State Prison for Women on October 11, 2000 and at California Institution for Women on October 12, 2000. Twenty women provided testimony about medical neglect, sexual abuse and harassment, separation from their children and communities, and criminalization of battered women.

didn't come here to do my death sentence. I did a stupid thing, but I should not have to pay for it with my life."[20*] As Broxton's words indicate, she would probably not be dying of endometrial cancer today had she been granted earlier treatment. Violence is promoted by prison regimes, which also divest prisoners of the agency to contest them. The most salient example of this habitual violence is the lack of access to decent health care—in prison, medical neglect can result in death. Widely accepted interpretations of UN documents such as the Convention Against Torture and Other Cruel, Inhuman or Degrading Treatment or Punishment and the International Covenant on Civil and Political Rights (Articles 6.1 and 7), and the Standard Minimum Rules for the Treatment of Prisoners emphasize the importance of health care in prisons. "The level of health care in prison and medication should be at least equivalent to that in the outside community. It is a consequence of the government's responsibility for people deprived of their liberty and thus fully dependent on state authority."[21]

Women in California prisons overwhelmingly have identified lack of access to medical information and treatment as their primary concern. At the hearings on conditions in women's prisons in California, witnesses reported that they often wait months to see a doctor and weeks for prescriptions to be refilled. For women with heart disease, diabetes, asthma, cancer, seizures, and HIV/AIDS, such delays in medication can cause serious medical complications or premature death. For example, Sherrie Chapman, an African American woman imprisoned at the California Institution for Women, testified about extreme delays in treatment that have led to the development of a terminal condition. Chapman sought diagnosis of breast lumps for ten years and was denied

* The contributions of women prisoners to this report were drawn from a number of sources: public testimony at legislative hearings; legal interviews with attorneys at Justice Now and Legal Services for Prisoners with Children; and oral histories recorded by community activists Cynthia Chandler and Carol Kingery. Names of women prisoners are used only when they offered public testimony or when they gave explicit permission for their names to be used. Otherwise the authors have assigned pseudonyms to protect their privacy.

access to medical care. By the time she received treatment, she was subjected to a double mastectomy, and ten months later a total hysterectomy. Despite the fact that her cancer had metastasized to her head and neck, she was consistently denied adequate pain management. As she testified: "I can't just go to the doctor and ask for help without being looked at and thought of as a manipulator, a drug seeker."[22] Her requests for a compassionate release—in order to live with her mother until she dies—have been denied, and she will likely die in prison.

Tragically, all too often medical neglect in prison results in premature death. As Beverly Henry, a prisoner peer educator, testified:

> I have seen women die on my yard, women that I was very close to and women that I knew. If I could see that the whites of their eyes were as yellow as a caution sign, why couldn't somebody else? I watched a woman's waist grow from approximately 27 inches to 67 inches because her liver was cirrhoted [a sign of advanced liver failure]. She could not wear shoes, she looked nine months pregnant, and every day she asked me: "Am I gonna die here? Am I gonna die here? Do you think this is what is gonna happen to me?" And she died. And there was nothing we could do about it. And I know that something could have been done.[23]

During an eight-week period at the end of 2000, nine women did in fact die in the Central California Women's facility (CCWF) in Chowchilla, California. Though these women died of a variety of illnesses, all of their deaths were in some way attributable to severe medical neglect on the part of the prison.* One of these women was Pamela Coffey, a 46-year-old African American woman who complained of a mass on her side and swelling in her abdomen for several months but was denied

* Based on extensive interviews with women prisoners, reviews of medical records, and reports of outside doctors, legal advocates at Justice Now and Legal Services for Prisoners with Children concluded that all of the deaths of women at CCWF were attributable to medical neglect in one form or another.

medical treatment. On the night she died, she complained of extreme abdominal pain, swelling in her face and mouth, and numbness in her legs. Her roommates called for medical help, and for three hours no one came. She collapsed on the bathroom floor in her cell, and when a Medical Technical Assistant (MTA)—a guard with minimal medical training—finally arrived, he failed to examine her or to call for medical help. He left the cell and Coffey's condition deteriorated. Her cellmates again called for help, but by the time the MTA arrived thirty minutes later, Coffey was dead. Prison staff then left her body in the cell for over an hour, further traumatizing her cellmates. Pamela Coffey's death exemplifies the severe medical neglect many women prisoners face, as well as the punishment all women are subjected to in an environment in which medical neglect is rampant. Many women are forced to watch other women deteriorate and sometimes die, and as a result must live in fear that they or someone they care about will be next.

Following the deaths, prison officials attempted to further criminalize the women who died by claiming that their deaths were attributable to illicit drug use in prison, despite the fact that there was no evidence to support such a claim. Prison administrators thus easily relied on widely circulating stereotypes of women prisoners as drug addicts—stereotypes fueled by the war on drugs—to demonize women who died as a result of medical neglect. Prison staff also instituted a new practice of treating the cell of a woman who called for medical help after hours as a "crime scene," which meant searching all of the women, upending the cell, and seizing property. Such a practice serves to make women fearful of calling for help because they or their cellmates will be punished. All of the women who died at CCWF were determined to have died of "natural" causes. Given that these premature deaths were preventable, these deaths cannot be considered to be "natural." On the other hand, given that women prisoners are systematically denied appropriate health care leading to the development of serious illnesses and premature death, medical neglect and death in prison have become, sadly, all too "natural."

Women prisoners are consistently accused of malingering, and medical staff often uses intimidation to dissuade them from seeking treatment. In order to complain about inadequate medical care, a woman must first file a written grievance with the staff person with whom she has a problem. In other words, the recipient of the complaint is the only person who ostensibly can provide them with the care they need. Because there is only one doctor on each prison yard, women prisoners explain to outside advocates that they rarely complain in order to avoid retaliation and the denial of treatment altogether. This process clearly violates the spirit of rule 36 of the SMR, which encourages prison authorities to make confidential channels available to prisoners who decide to make complaints.[24]

Beyond the ongoing epidemic of medical neglect of individual women prisoners, prisons also operate to create and exacerbate public health crises such as Hepatitis C Virus (HCV) and HIV. Lack of treatment and callous disregard for individual women's lives is even more frightening within the context of such massive infectious disease epidemics. HIV rates are at least ten times higher among prisoners than among people outside of prison, and the rate is higher among women prisoners than men.[25] Hepatitis C has reached epidemic levels in California prisons—the California Department of Corrections estimates that 40 percent of the prison population is infected.[26] Because the Department of Corrections regularly fails to test women for HCV or to provide information about prevention, advocates for women prisoners believe the numbers to be considerably higher. Not only is there is a dearth of access to treatment but also to information about prevention. Women report that even when they request to be tested for communicable diseases, they often do not get the results, even if they test positive. By virtue of this medical neglect, the prison promotes the spread of these diseases both inside the prisons and in the communities outside of prison to which women go when they are released.

Medical neglect in prison reflects and extends the lower value society places on the provision of preventative care and treatment to poor women of color outside of the prison. The abuse of women prisoners through medical neglect recapitulates a long history of inadequate health care for women, particularly women of color, which is often based in obsolete sexist and racist ideologies.

Reproductive Rights

Reproductive health care in prisons is equally informed by these ideologies and often equally abysmal. Pregnant women are provided limited prenatal care and in several US jurisdictions, women are shackled during labor.[27] Women prisoners wait months, and sometimes years, to receive routine gynecological examinations that protect against the development of serious health conditions.* For some women these delays, combined with a consistent failure of prison medical staff to address treatable conditions early, result in the development of serious reproductive health problems. Theresa Lopez, a young Latina in her twenties, developed and died of cervical cancer, a condition that is treatable in its early stages, because prison medical staff failed to provide her with basic medical treatment.†

In an interview with community activists recording women prisoners' oral histories, Davara Campbell described the politics of reproductive health in prisons:

> In the 1970s I was suffering severe menstrual cramps and a tilted uterus. As a young woman in the criminal justice system serving a life sentence complicated by medical female "disorders" and subject to misdiagnoses by questionable, unprofessional, unethical medical personnel, it was recommended I

* Legal interviews conducted by lawyers at Justice Now and Legal Services for Prisoners with Children with hundreds of women at Valley State Prison for Women, Central California Women's Facility, and California Institution for Women reveal a pattern and practice of extreme neglect of women's reproductive health in prisons.

† Theresa Lopez was a client of Justice Now who was granted compassionate release a few days before she died.

> have a hysterectomy. I was maybe 20-years-old. Having some enlightenment about genocide, I felt that the prospect of my being able to have a family was being threatened, so I escaped from prison to have a child. I had a son. He is now 28 years old, and I have four grandchildren who I would not have if I had given up my rights. Any imposition upon reproductive rights is an injustice against the well-being of family units—the rights of women, children, and grandchildren, or the promise of the future.[28]

As this account highlights, gynecological and reproductive health services in prisons are inadequate at best, dangerous and life-threatening at worst. Inside prisons, women are subject to substandard gynecological care that often results in loss of reproductive capacity or leads to premature death. Often, this inadequate care amounts to practices of sterilization, as Campbell's analysis highlights. The use of sterilization as a "solution" to women's gynecological problems resonates with racist practices women of color in the United States have experienced historically.

In the contemporary efforts to justify the abolition of welfare, continuing accusations of over-reproduction directed at African American and Latina single mothers legitimize differential claims to reproductive rights. Racist ideologies circulating outside prisons then enable the kinds of assaults on women's reproductive capacities inside prisons that are reminiscent of earlier historical eras, such as the forced sterilization of Puerto Rican and Native American women and forced reproduction of enslaved Black women. Thus prisons operate as a site where those reproductive rights putatively guaranteed to women in the "free world" are often systematically ignored, especially where women of color are concerned.

Gynecology is one of the most problematic areas in prison health care. Historical connections with racist gynecological practices continue to live on within the prison environment. More generally, to say that imprisonment deleteriously affects the health of women is clearly a criticism of health care in women's prisons, conditions that have been abundantly documented by legal and human rights organizations. But it is also to raise questions about the inertia that appears to prevent significant change in health care conditions, even when there is acknowledgment that such change is necessary. Why, for example, do accusations of sexual abuse continue to hover around medical regimes in women's prisons? Why have women prisoners complained for many decades about the difficulty of gaining access to skilled medical personnel? One of the ways to answer these questions is to look at the prison as a receptacle for obsolete practices—a site where certain practices, even when discredited in the larger society, acquire a second life.

There are children and families left behind in the "free world" on whom the imprisonment of women undoubtedly has a devastating impact. Almost 80 percent of women in prison have children for whom they were the primary caretakers before their imprisonment.[29] The removal of a significant number of women of color, coupled with the alarming rates of incarceration for their male counterparts, has a disabling effect on the ability of poor communities to support families, whatever their constellation.* When mothers are arrested, children are often placed in foster care and, in line with new laws, such as the Adoption and Safe Families Act of 1997, many are streamlined into adoption. All ties with birth mothers and extended families are thus systematically severed. In many instances, this process tracks children into juvenile detention centers and from there into adult prisons. For women who are reunited with their children upon

---

* Approximately two million people are currently being held in state and federal prisons and in county jails. According to the Bureau of Justice Statistics, about half of those in prison are Black. In 1990, the Washington-based Sentencing Project published a study of US populations in prison, jail, and on parole and probation, which concluded that one in four Black men between the ages of twenty and twenty-nine were among these numbers. Five years later, a second study revealed that this percentage had soared to almost one in three (32.2 percent). Moreover, more than one in ten Latino men in this same age range was in jail, in prison, or on probation or parole.

release, the challenges for them are amplified by new welfare reform guidelines that prevent a former prisoner from receiving public benefits, including housing assistance. When previously imprisoned women are divested of their rights to social services—a move related to the political disenfranchisement of former prisoners in many states—they are effectively tracked back into the prison system. This is one of the modes of reproduction of the prison industrial complex.

Sexual Harassment and Abuse

The development of putatively "feminist" campaigns by prison administrators has had deleterious consequences for women in prison. The assumption that formal gender equality inevitably leads to better conditions for women is contradicted by the recent pattern of modeling the architecture, regimes, and staff of women's prisons after their male counterparts. The current tendency, for example, is to place gun towers in women's maximum-security units in order to render them equal to similar men's units. The hiring of male custodial staff, who have visual access at all times to women's cells—even when they are changing clothes—and to the showers, creates a climate that invites sexual abuse. In US women's prisons the ratio of male to female corrections staff is often two to one and sometimes three to one. Though this disproportion alone does not inevitably lead to abuse, the administration and culture of the prison create an environment in which sexual abuse thrives.

Partly as a result of these increasingly repressive models, and partly because of the rampant sexist and racist ideologies that support and sustain women's prisons, routine sexual abuse and harassment amounts to a veritable climate of terror. Among the many abuses women prisoners have identified are inappropriate pat searches (male guards pat searching and groping women); illegal strip searches (male guards observing strip searches of women); constant lewd comments and gestures; violations of their right to privacy (male guards watching women in showers and toilets); and, in some instances, sexual assault and rape.[30]

According to international human rights standards, the rape of a woman in custody is an act of torture. Furthermore, violations of rights to privacy and preservation of human dignity are protected by the International Covenant on Civil and Political Rights. Recent studies by human rights organizations have confirmed that these international standards are routinely violated in US prisons. Human Rights Watch, for example, found that sexual abuse is often related to perceived sexual orientations of prisoners.[31] Sexual abuse is also frequently linked to medical practices. Many women in California prisons have indicated that they avoid much-needed medical treatment because male doctors can force them to submit to inappropriate pelvic examinations regardless of their symptoms.[32] However, only a small proportion of sexually harassed women report these incidents to prison authorities, not only because staff perpetrators are rarely disciplined, but also because they themselves may suffer retaliation.

Sexual harassment and abuse are also linked to the new technologies of imprisonment. For example, the rapidly proliferating "super-max units," which isolate prisoners in individual cells for twenty-three out of twenty-four hours a day, render women even more vulnerable to sexual assault and harassment. In a legal interview, Regina Johnson, a thirty-six-year-old African American woman in the Security Housing Unit at Valley State Prison for Women in Chowchilla, CA, reported being required to expose her breasts to a male guard in order to obtain necessary hygiene supplies.[33]

"Cell extractions," a practice linked to the "super-max" structure, involves subduing a prisoner, usually by means of restraints, and performing a strip search before removing her from her cell. The involvement of male guards in these cell extractions—although female guards also participate—especially imbues this practice with a very real potential for sexual abuse.

In the state of Arizona, the sheriff in Maricopa County has installed video cameras in the women's holding and search cells in the county jail; he broadcasts live footage of women in these cells on the internet.[34] Though such prurient monitoring is unacceptable in any detention setting, it is particularly disturbing in the jail setting because many of these women are pretrial detainees who have not been found guilty of any crime and therefore presumably are not yet to be subjected to any form of punishment.

Policing Sexuality

Such sexual harassment of women, in the guise of being "tough on crime," illustrates the myriad ways in which prisons attempt to control women and their sexuality through sexual violence. In the sexualized environment of the prison, prison guards and staff learn not to fear sanctions for being sexually abusive to women. At the same time, women's sexuality, both inside and outside of prison, is policed and punished. A significant number of women enter the prison system as a direct result of the criminalization of sexual practices. Laws against sex work in most US jurisdictions result in the arrest and conviction of thousands of poor women. The workers most often arrested work the streets, as opposed to organized environments such as brothels, parlors, or escort services. Street workers, who are disproportionately women of color, are most likely to land in jail. In several states, there is now a charge of "felony prostitution" for sex workers with a known HIV-positive status, carrying a mandatory minimum sentence of four years. The criminalization of sex work creates a cycle of imprisonment: women are arrested, sentenced to jail time, and often charged heavy fines and court fees, which then force them back onto the streets only to be arrested again.

Such criminalization of women's sexuality begins at a young age; girls are now the fastest-growing population in the juvenile justice system. Most often these girls are arrested for "status offenses," which include truancy, underage drinking, breaking curfew, running away, and prostitution. Boys are less likely to be arrested for similar behavior, reflecting an obvious gender bias, but race determines which girls will actually end up in juvenile hall. As in the prison system, communities of color are represented disproportionately in juvenile justice systems. Almost half of girls in juvenile detention in the United States are African American, and 13 percent are Latina. While seven out of ten cases involving white girls are dropped, only three out of every ten cases involving African American girls are dismissed.[35] This increasing imprisonment of girls occurs despite the fact that the juvenile crime rate, particularly violent crime, has continued to decline since 1994.[36] The targeting of girls of color for imprisonment in juvenile detention is a precursor to their later entrapment in women's prisons, since a majority of women in prison first entered the prison system as girls. The anxieties about women's sexualities that circulate outside of the prison, and often lead to women's criminalization, are exacerbated and foregrounded within the prison. Guards and staff sexualize the space of the prison through their abuse of women, and in so doing cast women prisoners not only as criminal but also as sexually available.

At least since the publication of Rose Giallombardo's *Society of Women: A Study of a Women's Prison* (1966), the most salient characteristic of women's prisons is assumed to be women's intimate and sexual involvement with each other. Yet the ideological presumption of heterosexuality is policed more systematically than in the free world. Women's prisons have rules against "homosecting"—a term used within prisons to refer to same-sex sexual practices among prisoners. The racism and sexism associated with prison regimes intersect in the construction of women of color as hyper-deviant, and the addition of heterosexism means that lesbians of color face a triple jeopardy. A Latina lesbian couple at Valley State Prison for Women reported in a legal interview that masculine-identified prisoners are targeted for verbal harassment and sometime physical assault by male guards, while their feminine-identified partners are sexually harassed by those same guards.[37] This gendered form of harassment exemplifies the ways in which gender identity is rigidly policed inside prisons.

Women's Prisons and Anti-Immigrant Campaigns

Women immigrants to the United States are policed and punished in myriad ways. Racist and xenophobic campaigns against immigrant communities, which particularly target people from Mexico and Central America (and increasingly people from Asian countries), have contributed to the criminalization of immigrants, the militarization of the US-Mexico border, and the buildup of the Immigration and Naturalization Service (INS) as an arm of the prison system.

The INS has shifted its focus from providing services to immigrants seeking refuge in the United States to enforcement and detention of individuals labeled "illegal aliens," thus establishing itself as a significant component of the prison industrial complex. In many cases, immigrants choose to travel to the United States in order to escape economic dislocation produced by global (often US-headquartered corporations) in their own countries. The profit potential of INS detention centers mirrors that of state and federal prisons both for corporations and for state institutions. For example, the INS rents space in public and private prisons, as well as county jails, often paying twice what the state government would pay for the same beds.[38]

Immigrant rights and human rights organizations have documented conditions in INS detention facilities that violate basic human rights: detention of immigrants for inordinately long periods, sometimes years; denial of basic medical treatment; and immigrants forced to sleep on cell floors.[39] Furthermore, the INS practice of purchasing space for detainees in state systems often means that detainees are placed in state prisons and jails that face lawsuits over their conditions. In New Orleans Parish Prison in Louisiana, for example, women detainees are housed in a jail that is being sued for sexual abuse of women prisoners.[40]

Beyond warehousing immigrants for the INS, state and federal prisons in the United States independently play a significant role in criminalizing and punishing women from other countries. In federal prisons, for example, approximately 30 percent of prisoners are foreign nationals,[41] many of whom are in prison for extremely long sentences as a result of the war on drugs. Many of these women face deportation upon conclusion of their prison sentence. In states with larger immigrant populations, prisoners in the state system often confront dilemmas produced by the intersection of xenophobia and criminalization. In California, for example, Sylvia Rodriguez was dying in prison of metastasized cancer, but if legal advocates secured a compassionate release for her, she faced deportation.* She was sixty-seven years old and had moved to the United States from the Philippines when she was nine years old. She knew no one in her country of origin and was suffering from a terminal illness, but the INS would not guarantee that they would allow her to go home to be with her family before she died. In the process of fighting for her release, she died in state custody.

Legal Challenges to Women's Imprisonment

Over the past thirty years, prisoners have faced the steady erosion of laws that ostensibly protect them against the abuses of the punishment system. The Supreme Court of the United States has systematically dismantled civil rights protections for prisoners, making it virtually impossible for prisoners to demonstrate that their mistreatment violates the Eighth Amendment to the US Constitution, a provision that is supposed to protect against "cruel and unusual punishment." In addition to court decisions that detrimentally impact prisoners' access to justice, the US Congress has also undermined legal protections for prisoners. In 1996, with little opposition, the

* Ms. Rodriguez was a client of Justice Now.

legislature passed the Prison Litigation Reform Act (PLRA), which creates almost insurmountable legal barriers to prisoners and their advocates seeking remedies in court.

One of the most difficult provisions of the PLRA requires a prisoner to "exhaust available administrative remedies" before seeking assistance from a court. This requirement fails to acknowledge how systematically the prison denies prisoners agency and basic human rights. Indeed, it establishes a double bind for the women who must fulfill it. The PLRA states that if there is any procedure in place, however flawed, a prisoner must prove that she has fulfilled the requirements of that procedure. In California, for example, a woman must first file a grievance form with the person with whom she has a complaint (the guard who sexually assaulted her or the doctor on whom she relies for treatment, for example) and then pursue the complaint up several levels of review. Many women report that they never see the complaint again after they submit it at the first level. Others have described guards tearing up the complaints in their faces. But regardless of how fruitless the process may be, and considering that it ultimately most often fails, the fact remains that a woman cannot take a complaint to court without completing the procedure.

This process encapsulates as it perpetuates the abuse of women inside. As the space of the prison becomes increasingly repressive, prison litigation "reform" serves to deny gross human and legal rights violations in prison, to exacerbate the suffering of women inside, and to facilitate the expansion of the prison industrial complex. As a result, women in prison in the United States, the so-called "free" world, are neither free nor able to pursue legal remedies deemed basic and necessary human rights by international standards.

Organizing for Change

Despite the significant obstacles encountered by those who want to challenge conditions of their confinement, especially through traditional legal methods, women prisoners find many ways to meaningfully organize and contest the injustices of imprisonment. In many states, women prisoners organize formal or informal peer networks that provide information and support on a wide range of issues including health care prevention and treatment, child custody, labor conditions, and legal rights. In New York, women at Bedford Hills Correctional Facility organized a program called AIDS Counseling and Education (ACE), which provides HIV and AIDS prevention and treatment education and support to women in prison. In California, peer educators have organized against the spread of HIV and HCV in prison and have provided health care information about a variety of medical conditions. Women prisoners have also filed individual and class action lawsuits demanding protection of their legal and human rights. In Washington, DC, Massachusetts, and Michigan, for example, women successfully organized lawsuits challenging systemic sexual abuses in state prisons. The legislative hearings in October 2000 marked the first time in the history of California that proceedings were conducted inside prisons with prisoners serving as the primary witnesses. Approximately twenty women testified at two institutions on medical neglect, sexual assault, battered women's issues, and separation from their children and families. As a result of this testimony, two bills were introduced in the California legislature that potentially will have a far-reaching impact on health care in California prisons.

Advocates for women in prison are increasingly locating their efforts to ameliorate conditions of confinement within the frame of a broader resistance to the prison industrial complex. Human rights instruments are deployed to emphasize the systematic denial of human rights further exacerbated by the contemporary corporatization of punishment. However, the strategic goal of this work is not to create better prisons but rather to abolish prisons insofar as they function as a default solution for a vast range of social problems that need to be addressed by other institutions. It is within this context that the most far-reaching challenges to the racism bolstered by the expansion of prisons are emerging. In California, for example, a number of groups work collaboratively to develop more radical approaches of working with and for women in prison. Justice Now is an organization that actively contests violence against women in prison and its connections to the prison industrial complex by training students, family members, and community members to provide direct services to women prisoners in California in conjunction with community-based education, media, and policy campaigns. The California Coalition for Women Prisoners organizes activist campaigns with and for women prisoners to raise awareness about inhumane conditions and advocate for positive changes. Legal Services for Prisoners with Children provides civil legal services to women prisoners, provides support to prisoner family members, and organizes in the communities from which prisoners come. California Prison Focus investigates and exposes human rights violations in California prisons, in particular those in Security Housing Units and super-max prisons. Critical Resistance (CR) builds national campaigns framed by an analysis of the prison industrial complex that foreground the intersections of race, gender, and class. In the course of these campaigns, CR encourages people to envision social landscapes where ubiquitous state punishment will have been replaced by free education, health care, and drug rehabilitation, as well as affordable housing and jobs.

While national campaigns are rapidly advancing in the United States, the UN World Conference Against Racism, Racial Discrimination, Xenophobia, and Related Intolerance provides a major opportunity to learn from and share experiences with organizations in other parts of the world. Greater emphasis must be placed on the global reach of the prison industrial complex and the further proliferation of the gendered racism it encourages. It is especially important that the punishment industry be seen as a significant component of the developing global political economy. An overarching recommendation for action thus calls for international networking among organizations that acknowledge the link between prisons and racism and that locate the important work of providing services to imprisoned women within a strong anticorporate and antiracist framework.

Further recommendations for action include the decriminalization of drug use and the establishment of free drug-rehabilitation programs that are not tied to criminal justice agencies and procedures. This would drastically decrease the number of women in prison. In conjunction with these decarceration strategies, local and transnational campaigns to prevent the construction of new public and private prisons are also necessary. Legislation is needed that makes state and federal governments, as well as individual perpetrators, responsible for sexual abuse and harassment of women prisoners. In line with human rights standards, women's reproductive and family rights must be guaranteed. This means that civilian boards with enforcement powers should be established to review and act upon women prisoners' grievances, especially those involving medical neglect, arbitrary discipline, and sexual abuse. In general, more widespread educational and media campaigns are needed to expand and deepen awareness of the central role women's prisons play throughout the world in perpetuating misogyny, poverty, and racism.

PART V

Incarcerated Women

The Netherlands, the United States, and Cuba

CHAPTER 10

Women in Prison

Researching Race in Three National Contexts*

with Kum-Kum Bhavnani

Women in prison comprise an enormous, invisible, and silenced population. This chapter draws on research based on interviews with over one hundred imprisoned women in the United States, the Netherlands, and Cuba. Our collaborative research contests their multiple marginalizations, not the least of which is racism, that render them invisible and silent. We also question the ubiquitous status of prisoners (particularly women prisoners of color) as objects of research. In our study, women prisoners' insights about the conditions of their imprisonment have been used to raise new questions, which in turn have informed the ultimate direction of our work.[1]

We are interested in the ways in which presently and formerly incarcerated women can help explain the increasing reliance on public forms of punishment for women who historically have been punished largely within private spheres. We are also interested in the extent to which counter discourses forged by antiracist social movements inform imprisoned women's ability to explicitly theorize the role of racism in imprisonment practices. As women

* First published in *Racing Research, Researching Race: Methodological Dilemmas in Critical Race Studies*, eds. France Winddance Twine and Jonathan W. Warren (New York: New York University Press, 2000), 227–45.

researchers of color—one South Asian and the other African American—who have been involved in antiracist movements in Britain and the United States for many years, our own perspectives are informed both by our experiences as activists in different national contexts and by our commitment to link our academic research to strategies for radical social change. Our study thus begins with the assumption that the overutilization of imprisonment to address a range of social problems—which would more appropriately be dealt with by nonpunitive institutions—constitutes a major contemporary crisis. This means that our work is linked to efforts to transform public policy and to activist strategies that emphasize the importance of including imprisoned women in a new public discourse of resistance to imprisonment rather than to more conventional research agendas to generate knowledge *about* a subjugated group.

In conceptualizing this study of women's imprisonment and our role as researchers, we considered our own racialized backgrounds within the political contexts defining our activist histories. We were—and continue to be—concerned with the possibility of forging feminist alliances across racial boundaries. Whereas Kum-Kum Bhavnani was involved during the seventies and eighties in labor, feminist, and prison activism in Britain at a time when the category "Black" was politically defined as embracing people of African, Asian, and Middle Eastern descent, Angela Y. Davis was active during the same era in a number of campaigns informed by the category "women of color," which addressed political issues affecting Native American, Latina, African American, and Asian American women. The issues addressed were thus not racially exclusive. In imagining the groups of imprisoned women we would interview, we did not establish goals for specific racial *groups* but rather considered the general racialization of imprisonment *practices,* which have a disproportionate impact on women of color and poor white women. We were much more interested in the women's critical perspectives about racialized and gendered prison systems and the way they might help demystify the role of the state than in learning about *individuals* and their relationship to the racial groups with which they identified. The democratic framework in which we attempted to formulate this project is a reflection of our own attempt to render the boundaries between research and activism more permeable.

We chose the three countries where we conducted our interviews for specific reasons. We are most familiar with the penal system in the United States and are concerned with the gendered character of the emergent prison industrial complex, which has resulted in the proliferation of women's prisons and an attendant intensification of penal repression. Within the United States, the number of prisoners per capita far exceeds that of any other capitalist country.[2] The Netherlands, which is experiencing a significant increase in the number of prisoners for the first time in its history, has one of the lowest per capita rates of incarceration, as well as a history of progressive penal reform.[3] As far as Western capitalist countries go, it is at the other end of the spectrum. Finally, we chose Cuba so that we might ascertain the differences, if any, between penal regimes for women in capitalist countries and penal regimes under socialism. While our study of imprisoned women in the United States began with the premise that race played a pivotal role in determining who goes to prison and how long a convicted woman remains behind bars, we set out to discover the significance of race in the other two national settings as well.

It is worth noting that Angela Y. Davis's history as a political prisoner during the early seventies and as an internationally known political activist both obstructed and facilitated our research. We attribute the fact that we were unable to gain access to the California Institution for Women (CIW) to her reputation as a former prisoner and prison activist. As we indicate below, we changed the venue of our US interviews to the San Francisco

County Jail because the warden at CIW never granted us permission to enter the prison. On the other hand, the director of the women's prison in the Netherlands was herself a prison activist and was aware of Angela's history as a former political prisoner and of her work on prisoners' rights. This clearly facilitated our ability to conduct research in the prison she supervised. Our access to women's prisons in Cuba was directly related to Angela's historical connections with the Association of Cuban Women, an organization that had played a major role in organizing the Cuban campaign for her freedom.

While Angela's experiences and history as a former political prisoner facilitated our access to prisons in the Netherlands and in Cuba, it also sometimes led to a tendency on the part of the prison staffs to treat Angela as the primary researcher, which contradicted the egalitarian way we had structured our research relationship. We made it clear that in our collaborative project, we both claimed equal status as coinvestigators. But in spite of tactful reminders, Kum-Kum's name was frequently misspelled and in official documents was listed after Angela's, even though our own practice was to list our names in alphabetical order. On the other hand, the prisoners we interviewed seemed far more sophisticated than their keepers. Even though many of them knew of Angela—one even had a child named after her—they always treated us as equals and never indicated a preference for being interviewed by one of us over the other. Collaborative research relationships rarely unfold without complications. In our case, the assumption of a hierarchal relationship by the prison administrations could have negatively affected our research relationship. However, we talked openly about the impact this behavior might have on our work, thus struggling to preserve our own collaborative spirit.

Explanations for the sparsity of literature on imprisoned women usually point to the relatively small percentage of women in prison compared to their male counterparts. It is true that in most countries women constitute between 5 and 10 percent of imprisoned populations.

> On average only one out of every twenty prisoners is a woman. Women constitute roughly 50 percent of the population of any country, yet provide only 5 percent of its prisoners. . . . This is not specific to any one country or region, but is reflected all over the world. There are variations. In Spain, the proportion of women in prison is 10 percent, in the United States over 6 percent, in France 4 percent, in Russia 3 percent and in Morocco it is 2 percent. But nowhere in the world do women make up more than one in ten of the whole [prison] population.[4]

What is rarely taken into consideration, however, is the fact that modes of punishment are both racialized and gendered in ways that indicate a historical continuum linking women's imprisonment with incarceration in mental institutions and with modes of private punishment such as domestic violence.[5] In the context of a developing global prison industrial complex, the relatively small percentages of imprisoned women are now rising. In the United States, the rate of increase in women's incarceration has surpassed the rate of increase in men's.[6] As international women's movements contest patriarchal structures and ideologies, a new consciousness of women's rights in "private" settings has begun to subvert old attitudes of acquiescence toward misogynist violence. However, even as the private punishment of women becomes less hidden from view and less taken for granted, the state-inflicted punishment of women still remains relatively invisible. In the United States and Europe, as well as in countries in which people of European descent are most dominant, women of color are disproportionately targeted by contemporary modes of public punishment. Thus the hyperinvisibility of women's prisons reflects a larger contemporary tendency to incarcerate structures of racism within those institutions that function in public discourse as sites where expendable populations and problems are deposited and hidden away.

According to Mary Helen Washington, "The class, gender, and racial politics of prisons in this country conspire to make most of us feel, not only separate from the world of prison but indifferent to it, untouched and unconcerned."[7] Racialized socioeconomic patterns are camouflaged by representational practices that criminalize poor people of color, thereby justifying their imprisonment and allowing the racist structures that affect access to employment, health care, education, and housing to go unrecognized. It may not be entirely fortuitous that California, the first state to abolish affirmative action, also has the largest prison population in the country. It is therefore important to view prisons as productive sites for research on racism and an important opportunity to challenge conservative claims regarding the "end of racism."

In the United States, the current shift from a social welfare state to one prioritizing social control[8] has helped to generate the conditions for an emergent prison industrial complex and has caused the numbers of imprisoned women to rise even more strikingly than those of their male counterparts.[9] As government policies in Canada, in many parts of Europe, and in some African and Latin American countries reveal a similar shift toward larger penal systems, the practice of imprisonment disproportionately affects people of color—not only in the United States but on an international level.[10] In the Netherlands, for example, the imprisoned population has begun to increase significantly for the first time in that country's history, due largely to the influx of Black and immigrant populations who can be found disproportionately in the prisons. While our research on and with imprisoned women in the United States, the Netherlands, and Cuba is largely concerned with the ways women prisoners think about alternatives to incarceration, our study also tries to highlight the gendering of racism in imprisonment practices and in general attempts to address the intersections of class, race, gender, and sexuality as they are perceived and theorized by the women with whom we spoke and as we ourselves attempt to theorize these intersections. In this sense, our project attempts to address issues that exceed both conventional research agendas and activist strategies that treat prisoners—and especially women prisoners—as objects of knowledge or as simply the beneficiaries of liberatory movements.

Collaboration and Access

Having previously met each other through political and intellectual work, in the early 1990s we began to explore the possibility of long-term collaborative research that would allow us to productively draw from our respective training in the humanities and social sciences. In 1993, we were awarded resident research fellowships at the University of California Humanities Research Institute (UCHRI) in connection with its Minority Discourse Initiative which that year called upon fellows to think critically about the normalization of certain social science discourses in relation to public policy. It was in this context that we decided to conduct a series of interviews with women prisoners in California. Since the UCHRI is housed on the Irvine campus in Southern California, we planned to interview prisoners at the California Institute for Women, located in Frontera, a relatively short distance from Irvine.

As activists, we were not unaware of the general difficulties of access to prisons. Nevertheless, we assumed that a legitimate and compelling scholarly project would be accepted by the California Department of Corrections (CDC). However, our instincts as scholars did not adequately reflect our sophistication as political activists, for, despite prompt submission of our application, the CDC never granted us permission to enter the prison. After submitting all the necessary documents to the CDC authorities in charge of approving research proposals, we were led to believe that the approval of our project by the warden at CIW was simply a formality. As we made final preparations for our move to Irvine and for our visits to CIW, we waited to hear from the warden. In further communications with the research department of CDC, we were advised to be patient with the department's slow-moving bureaucracy. However, once we arrived in Irvine and still had not received word from CIW, it became obvious to us that more might be at issue than bureaucratic sluggishness. After numerous messages left at the warden's office went unanswered, the director of the Humanities Research Institute intervened for us, under the assumption that his messages would not be so easily disregarded. While he was never allowed to speak with the warden, he was told by an unidentified official in an off-the-record communication that "Angela Davis would never be allowed inside the California Institute for Women." The warden, the official indicated, felt that she had things under control in the prison and would not allow Angela Y. Davis to come in and "rock the boat." We received the official denial of our request after the proposed research period would already have begun.

Because we were determined to pursue our project with imprisoned women, we decided to investigate the possibility of another interview site. Since Angela had previously taught at the San Francisco County Jail, we decided to submit our project proposal to Michael Morcum, the director of the County Jail system's program facility, who had previously served a sentence in San Quentin and was active during the 1970s in the formation of the California Prisoners' Union. The fact that an access permit came through in a matter of days caused us to think in more complex terms about the ways in which individual administrators are interpolated within the correctional system. Ironically, we had applied for the UCHRI fellowship in Irvine because CIW was in the vicinity and had both moved to Irvine to conduct the interviews. Now we would be required to make numerous research trips to the San Francisco Bay Area during the course of our residence in Southern California. Despite these initial difficulties, we soon recognized that given the San Francisco Program Facility's pioneering efforts to minimize racism within the jail, which we discuss later in this essay, the interviews would be extremely productive.

We interviewed thirty-five of the approximately one hundred women at the San Francisco County Jail's Program Facility. In this section of the county jail, located in San Bruno, California, male and female inmates were required to participate in "programs"—that is, in educational classes, cultural programs, Alcoholics or Narcotics Anonymous sessions, and organic gardening classes. Men were housed in four dormitories and women in the remaining two. Our interview pool was comprised of women who volunteered to participate after attending a session during which we described our project. In our introductory statements, we described our activist and academic histories, our desire to use a "grounded theory" approach and generally democratic research methods, as well as our hopes that this work would ultimately help to transform public discourses and policies around women in prison. We explained that we were not interested in the women's legal cases and therefore would not ask them to explain to us why they were in jail. Rather, we wanted them to offer their own perspectives about women's imprisonment and about alternatives to incarceration.

As with the other two sites of our study, we first asked for volunteers to participate in focus groups, to help us think about the kinds of questions that would be most productive. That far more women volunteered than we expected may have been a *result* of our decision not to construct them as research subjects whose criminal histories we wanted to probe. As at the other two sites, women who had not initially volunteered later attempted to join the project as news about the interviews traveled. While we were able to accommodate some of them, we never succeeded in talking to all the women who volunteered. In San Francisco, our interview pool, like the overall jail population, was comprised of an African American majority, but also Latinas, white women, and one Asian American. However, in the individual interviews, we did not ask different questions based on the assumed racial identities of these women.

While the US component of the research presented huge access problems, we gained entrance to the prison in the Netherlands—

Amerswiel Prison for Women—with relative ease. The director, Bernadette van Dam, was herself a well-known advocate of the rights of imprisoned women and, unlike the warden at CIW, welcomed scholarly work designed to make a difference in the lives of women in prison. Angela had visited this prison the previous year and had interviewed the director, as well as several prisoners. When we formally submitted a request to the Dutch Ministry of Justice to conduct interviews at Amerswiel, both the prison director and the Ministry of Justice immediately approved our proposal. While we spent most of our 1996 visit to the Netherlands in Amerswiel, we did have the opportunity to visit two other women's prisons—in Breda and Sevenum—as well as the men's prison in Breda.

Amerswiel Prison is located in the town of Heerhugowaard, thirty miles outside Amsterdam. At the time of our interviews, the prison consisted of four residential units—the Short Term, Long Term, Individual Guidance, and Drug Rehabilitation Units—housing seventy-nine women altogether. With one exception, our interviewees were women in the Short and Long Term Units, which housed twenty-seven and twenty-six women respectively. Approximately half of the women imprisoned in Amerswiel were women of color—of Surinamese, South American, and Asian descent. Our interview pool, consisting of volunteers, comprised approximately the same percentage of women of color.

While our own racial and national backgrounds were sometimes noted by the women we interviewed, it was our status as researchers and prison activists that most interested the women who raised questions about our research project. Virtually all the women we interviewed were aware of the prison director's international advocacy on behalf of women in prison, especially with respect to the rights of imprisoned mothers. In fact, some of the women criticized Bernadette van Dam for devoting more time to public campaigns around imprisoned women than to the women under her direct supervision. They pointed out that they saw more of her on television than in person. In general, however, most of the women expressed their appreciation for her public advocacy. Because of their awareness of the director's work as a prison activist, the prisoners tended to locate our work within a similar political framework. However, when we presented our work to the two groups from which the volunteer pool was selected, we did not attempt to conceal our own leanings toward prison abolitionism. While we were explicit about our interest in the racialization of the prison regime in general and in the awareness of racism exhibited by the prisoners, we raised no specific questions about particular racial groups. In our own discussions about interview strategies, "racial matching" was never really an issue.

Therefore both of us conducted interviews with Black, Asian, South American, and white Dutch prisoners. Since almost all the prisoners were fluent in English, all our interviews, except those with women from Colombia, were conducted in English. We talked with the Colombian women with the aid of a Spanish-English translator.

The organization of the Cuban component of our research was much more complicated, not only because of the general communication difficulties related to the US embargo on Cuba, but also because we were required to obtain a research license from the US State Department in order to legitimately travel to Cuba. Our Cuban sponsor, the Association of Cuban Women, acted as the intermediary to allow us to gain clearance to visit women's prisons there.

Initially, both of us had planned to make the trip to Cuba. However, just as we had scheduled the trip, Kum-Kum, who had been attempting for some time to adopt, was informed that a baby was available for adoption. Consequently, she faced the dilemma, encountered by many women (and some men), of negotiating a balance between her domestic desires and her research passions. Ultimately she decided that she did not want to be separated from her small baby at such a critical stage in the baby's development and decided to forgo the trip. We decided that Angela should go on with the project, accompanied by one of her students, Isabel Velez, whose bilingual skills would allow her to serve as translator. Since we had previously used a translator in the Dutch prison for interviews with women from South America, we felt a translator would be able to help us again.

Angela and Isabel conducted forty-five interviews at women's prisons in three Cuban provinces—Pinar del Rio, Havana, and Camagüey. At the time of the interviews, there were seventy women in the prison in Pinar del Rio, six hundred in Havana, and one hundred and sixty-three in Camagüey. In accordance with the overall conceptualization of our project, our concerns focused less on the racial identities of our interviewees than on the way in which they perceived and characterized the racial dynamics of the prison regimes. However, it was inevitable that questions about racial identification should arise, especially since racial categories in Cuba are far more fluid than in the United States. Some people with whom we talked indicated that their official identity cards listed them as "white," although they would describe themselves as *mulatta* or *jabao*. In fact, many of the women who counted as "white" by Cuban standards would be characterized as "women of color" by US standards. Therefore, our questions regarding the proportion of women of color in the prison and differential treatment based on race could never be simply answered. As a result, the Cuban component of our project raised far more complicated questions regarding race.

Ethical Dilemmas

In the three sets of interviews we conducted, many of the women expressed their appreciation for what they considered to be better conditions of imprisonment than they imagined to exist elsewhere. At the same time, they were emphatic that although they had abundant educational and vocational opportunities, they were still in prison and they had been deprived of their most precious possession, their liberty. That a significant number of the women we interviewed made positive comments about the conditions of their confinement, along with the critiques they proposed, was in part related to the way we chose the sites of our research. In each instance, we had developed relationships either with the authorities directly in charge of the prison or, as in Cuba, had previous relationships with organizations that intervened for us. These relationships were based on our own respect for the comparatively progressive penal methods employed in each of the sites. However, our own prison politics are best described as abolitionist, and at no time did we attempt to conceal our political leanings from the authorities. As a result, the space we negotiated for our research was fraught with contradictions. Like the women prisoners who constantly pointed out—in the Netherlands, for example—that despite the creature comforts they enjoyed, they were still in prison, or—in California—that regardless of the prison's antiracist and antihomophobic policies, they were still in prison, or—in Cuba—that regardless of their prospects of reintegrating themselves into society, they were still in prison, we too continually reminded ourselves that the purpose of our research was to point to the possibility of handling much behavior legally constructed as "crime" without resorting to imprisonment.

As we have reflected on our research, our one overarching dilemma with its methodological and ethical dimensions has been precisely this: how do we balance our abolitionist perspective with our role as scholars and as human beings who clearly recognize that the prisons in which we worked did indeed provide relatively livable conditions for the women who inhabited them? As we conducted our field research, we talked at length about how we might best draw on the progressive aspects of the penal settings and regimes we were studying and simultaneously negotiate a relationship between our ultimate political aims and the need to affirm the importance of humane conditions of confinement for women and men in prison. A constant theme of our discussions was how we might be able to forge a productive research and activist agenda out of the tension between our ultimate goal of prison abolition and our recognition that penal reform is also essential, if only to improve the daily lives of the millions who have been removed from the free world. Given the historical tendency of reform movements to strengthen prison institutions and discourses,[11] we were especially concerned about how to locate our work within a larger long-term political project of opposing the prison industrial complex and of arresting the proliferation of prisons.

Even as we recognized the power circuits that flowed through the research process and through the prison systems we were studying, we tried to forge collaborative relationships in our conversations with the prisoners. By not withholding information about our political motives and goals and by not treating the women as individuals whom we expected to generate knowledge about themselves to be later collectivized by the researchers, we hoped to demonstrate the possibility of more democratic approaches to research. Just as we did not want to address them as representatives of their respective racial groups, nor did we want to treat them as somehow representing a class of prisoners who could benefit from but not act as agents in an emancipatory political project. When it proved difficult for our interviewees to imagine social landscapes in which prisons were not prominent features, we did not assume that it was any easier for us, despite our adherence to abolitionism. As researchers and as prisoners, we struggled with the same overwhelming ideological constraints.

A related dilemma was whether to interview the administrative and custodial staff in the prisons we studied. Because we did not want to convey the impression to our primary interviewees that we were approaching them with preconceptions and biases acquired from the administrators and guards, we initially decided against interviewing prison personnel. Although we did not naively assume that it was possible to obtain ideas from the prisoners that were "pure" and unmediated, we did feel that this was the best way to achieve our goal of involving imprisoned women in a larger conversation about the radical transformation of punishment systems. However, early on in the actual interview process, we realized that we needed certain information that could only be provided by the administrators and guards. As a result, we decided that while we would talk with prison officials, these interviews would take place only after we had completed our interviews with the prisoners.

We did not treat this methodological decision as a satisfactory solution to our quandary, but rather recognized that practical decisions sometimes highlight the artificiality and abstractness of theoretical research frameworks. Seemingly contradictory on-the-ground decisions can open up new paths of inquiry. Moreover, this decision led us to acknowledge that just as we had tried to avoid essentializing the women we interviewed in relation to their racial backgrounds and their status as prisoners, civilian and uniformed prison personnel were also more than representatives of the state. Ironically, this particular decision to interview prison personnel yielded some interesting results, especially with respect to the official contract that prisoners at the San Francisco County Jail Program Facility were required to sign, agreeing to adhere to the announced antiracist, antisexist, and antihomophobic policies of the jail.

Researching Racism

Throughout the world, prisons are predictably the most consistently multiracial and multicultural locations,[12] making them not only important sites for negative inquiry but also productive sites for positive multicultural, multiracial alliance building. Of course, race is understood differently in different national contexts. Based on the long history of antiracist social movements in the United States, racism in this country is often understood to refer to institutional and individual discrimination against Black, Latinx, Native American, and Asian American people. In Europe, *racism* is viewed as synonymous with *xenophobia*. Thus in the Netherlands, which often prides itself—though not always justifiably—as being the least racist country in Europe, responses to our questions about racism tended to focus on attitudes toward foreigners, rather than on racism by white Dutch people against nonwhite Dutch citizens.

In the program facility at the San Francisco County Jail, specific efforts were undertaken to minimize racism, sexism, and homophobia in the operation of the jail. In fact, according to the director, each prisoner was required to sign the following contract upon being booked into the program facility in which they agreed not to engage in racist, sexist, or homophobic behavior: "I understand that I am required to treat others and myself with respect and dignity. I understand that racism, sexism, anti-gay/lesbian remarks, glorification of substance abuse or criminal behavior and any other form of antisocial behavior will result in loss of privileges, extra work duty or removal from the program facility."[13]

This clause in the contract provided jail personnel with the leverage to avoid a more complicated discussion of racism, as jail rules barred prisoners from exhibiting perceptibly racist behavior. Because antiracism was constructed as a jail rule implemented by guards and administrators, it was linked to the regimes of power and surveillance and attributed to the prisoners as subjects of prison authority. Discussions with the jail personnel who thought of themselves as progressive revealed that they were proud of their pioneering roles as overseers charged with identifying potential violations of the antiracist, antisexist, and antihomophobic rule. In a sense, this pattern was a microcosmic reflection of the larger contemporary proclivity to relegate the process of minimizing racism to the US legal sphere—which constitutes the subject as a rational, free *individual*—and to use legal prohibitions as evidence of the decline of racism in civil society.[14]

However, many of the prisoners we interviewed—both women of color and white women—noticed a disparity between the official policy and the treatment they received, thus proposing astute political analyses regarding the persistence of racism within a putatively antiracist framework. One woman said that some guards treated prisoners differently based on their racial backgrounds. Her observations regarding the racism of deputies contested the relegation of racist behavior to the prisoners.[15] She described incidents in which she and other Black women were severely limited in the amount of time they were allowed to use the telephone, whereas the deputies allowed a white prisoner to stay on the pay phone for several hours. She said that she and a group of her Black friends had consciously monitored certain deputies' practices of allowing white prisoners to spend much more time on the telephone than prisoners of color. This was an obvious example of everyday strategies of resistance to racism within the jail.

Given the shifting definitions of racism referred to above, we were not entirely surprised that the questions we asked women prisoners about the impact of racism within the prison setting did not always travel well from one research site to another. Since our questions were informed by popular and scholarly discourses on race in the United States, they were most easily understood by and most directly answered by prisoners, guards, and administrators alike at the jail in San Francisco. One interviewee in the Netherlands indicated that there was little overt discussion of racism in the prison, but that she was planning to raise this issue with the prison authorities in the near future.[16] Responses by a substantial number of our interviewees in the Netherlands helped us understand the implicit xenophobia that informed attitudes and behavior toward prisoners from South America. A Colombian woman said: "There's a lot of racism here. If you're Colombian, Black or from another country they don't give you anything. . . .There's nothing for [Dutch] people . . . in jail, and less if they are Colombian."[17] Another South American woman also criticized the xenophobic attitudes of the custodial personnel when she told us about her skin rash that had gone untreated: "It's not normal that my skin is like this and I've got a rash. It's already twenty days [that I have been] asking for the doctor. If I'd been Dutch, the doctor would have shown up immediately."[18]

A white Dutch woman was critical of the general tendency on the part of the Dutch to represent themselves as egalitarian:

> I always feel attracted to other cultures. But I didn't catch it by birth, because my mother and father are totally white, and they were very . . . yeah, I think my father was a racist, in a way that he doesn't speak it aloud, but in his thinking, like I've seen with many Dutch, they say, "I am not a racist," but if you see their behavior, you can see that their behavior has racist elements.[19]

She also pointed to the pattern among prison guards and administrators of infantilizing prisoners from South America: "So if they deal with the Spanish women, they deal with them like they're not grown-up people. Like they're dealing with children, you know? And I am very much irritated by that type of approach. I hate it. I really hate it."[20] She also indicated that there was a pattern of belittling non-Dutch-speaking prisoners, and particularly women whose cultural and language practices involved gesticulating with their hands. Our interviews in the Dutch prison thus revealed that women of color were not the only prisoners who had thought about the workings of racism. In fact, one white Dutch woman, expressing her solidarity with the women from South America, indicated that she was attempting to learn Spanish in order to communicate with her coprisoners.[21]

In Cuba, the prisoners' reluctance to engage in discussions about race seemed to be linked to the way in which popular discourses on race and racism are overdetermined by the particular history of racism in the United States and by Cuban solidarity with antiracist activists in Black, Puerto Rican, and Native American movements. They talked with ease about such figures as Martin Luther King Jr. and Malcolm X, and although most of the prisoners were too young to have experienced the Cuban solidarity campaign that developed around Angela's case during the early seventies, many of them had learned about her history as well. Because our questions about race and racism were generally understood within a US context, all the interviewees insisted that racism was neither an issue in the prison nor in society at large. When we asked one woman whether she felt there was a way to talk about race that was enlightening and not indicative of discrimination, she answered, "Yes, you can talk about it in order to unify instead of separate or discriminate. The more unity there is between people, white and Black, there would be a better world, more unified."[22] She also felt that people in the United States might learn important lessons from Cuba in the quest for racial equality.

The administrators' observations about the role of race in the prison context both reflected and diverged from prisoners' comments. In Cuba, for example, the prison directors and guards, like the prisoners themselves, tended to interpret questions referring to race as questions about racial discrimination. In San Francisco, questions about race and racism led administrators to refer us to the contract each prisoner was required to sign upon entering the program facility. However, the sheriff of San Francisco, who is in charge of the county jail system, initiated discussion about the disproportionately high numbers of Black and brown prisoners in his jails. He indicated that his responsibility as sheriff required a special sensitivity toward prisoners of color as he instituted social programs for inmates.

Just as administrators of the program facility in San Francisco tended to interpret questions about racism as synonymous with race relations among the prisoners, so in the Netherlands, the director of Amerswiel Prison responded to our questions about racism by focusing on relations between prisoners, especially between white Dutch women and women from South America. Further, her comments suggested to us that the enforced equality of prison—where each one is equally deprived of certain rights and liberties, regardless of race—makes it an interesting test of the limits of liberal thinking around racism.

Conclusion

Many of the contradictions we confronted—our knowledge that prisoners were ubiquitous subjects of research, the discrepancies between official policy and everyday practice, the fact that denials of entry arrived too late to matter, that assurances of equality could proliferate, and that equality was imagined as the morally correct action of each free individual toward the other backed up by the force of a state that would never be analyzed as a subject—were about the nature of a liberal system and the limits of a research methodology that would fail to address its own hegemonic context first and last. The prisoner from the Netherlands who told us she was learning Spanish in order to communicate with her fellow prisoners is a far better example of how to create a just society than a state like California that abolishes affirmative action and bilingual education, while building more prisons to hold those populations who cannot fail to be endlessly misapprehended by the system. Thus, the "results" of our research exceed the scope of most research agendas that can be imagined around prisoners, including even those that might be significant, like gathering information about health care in prison, family relations and social welfare, and even racism.

The prison was our best research site not because conditions are so bad there but because the segmentation of the prison system away from our consciousness allows the liberal state to manage its population. To attempt to solve the problem of racism without considering the most degraded of its subjects would be contrary to any analytic agenda. Still, the information garnered in this process would also outstrip its intended uses, since learning the language of those with whom you seek to build community is a means not only toward bettering conditions in prison but toward their betterment in the free world outside.

CHAPTER 11

Incarcerated Women

Transformative Strategies*

with Kum-Kum Bhavnani

The prison plays a central role in the policing of individuals in capitalist society, and so an attention to the different forms of oppression, which are reproduced through the layering of gender and race upon class exploitation in this institution, should be an important part of the agenda for Marxist psychologists. The development of women's prisons in the United States and Britain over the last 150 years is informed by and in turn informs a history of social attitudes toward women and an attendant history of gendered and racialized punishment practices. Both men's and women's prisons rely upon physical discipline and surveillance, as well as psychological strategies of control and self-surveillance.[1] Psychological strategies emphasizing self-esteem and domestication are especially central in the conceptualization of rehabilitation programs for incarcerated women.

---

* Previously published in *Psychology and Society: Radical Theory and Practice*, ed. Ian Parker and Russell Spears (London: Pluto Books, 1996), 173–83. The authors were assisted at various stages in the production of this chapter by Dana Collins and Stefanie Kelly. We conducted the research on which this chapter is based with the assistance of a resident fellowship from the University of California Humanities Research Institute at UC Irvine. We would like to thank the Institute's director, Mark Rose, as well as the support staff (Sauni Hayes, Deborah Massey, Chris Aschan, and Mia Larson), all of whom went beyond the call of duty to make our stay at the Institute as productive and as pleasant as possible.

Discourses of self-help and counseling permeate much of the literature on women's incarceration. Yet, despite this deployment of psychological techniques of control and rehabilitation—that often are mutually contradictory—feminist and Marxist psychologists have not produced a significant body of work on women's imprisonment. Therefore, we hope that this chapter—tentative though it may be—will stimulate further discussion among feminist psychologists. We collaboratively conducted the research that informs this chapter in order to provoke public debate on the future prospects of abolishing jails and prisons as normal punishment for women.

Even as imprisonment is ideologically represented as the surest way to "keep criminals off the streets" and therefore to assuage the socially constructed fear of crime, the incarceration of greater numbers of people has never had the result of diminishing the number of potential prisoners. On the contrary, the very efforts to invoke the prison as the solution to crime have always resulted in the expansion of carceral institutions and the populations they contain. The number of imprisoned individuals has spiraled steadily in the United States: between 1980 and 1992, the male prison population increased 160 percent; the female population during the same period increased 275 percent. While women constitute a relatively small minority of all prisoners—in 1991, there were 87,000 women in state and federal prisons[2]—the rate of increase among women is proportionately higher than among men. Rather than recognizing this alarming tendency toward ever-larger incarcerated populations as a serious domestic crisis in the United States, elected officials—both Democrats and Republicans—have manipulated the figures of "the criminal," "the welfare mother," and "the immigrant" to embody profound social fears. The "criminal," with its underlying racial implications, now serves as one of the major figures against which the nation imagines its identity. In the meantime, incarcerated people in the United States—disproportionately people of color—constitute what many prisoners refer to as a throw-away population, and there are continued calls nationwide for more severe sentencing. In the state of California, for example, "three-strikes-and-you're-out" legislation has taken a deep-rooted hold with the recent passage of Proposition 184, which precludes legislative interference with the "three-strikes" law. The "three-strikes-and-you're-out" law mandates a life sentence for any individual convicted of three felonies.

Although there is a substantial body of literature in criminology and related disciplines on the inefficacy of the prison as a site of rehabilitation, there is a relative paucity of literature examining the policy implications of research on women's imprisonment. There are notable exceptions,[3] but it is generally agreed that women have been marginalized in the development of prison policies.[4] For example, recent studies on prisons, prisoners, and prisoners' movements[5] focus exclusively on men. With the exception of William L. Selke in *Prisons in Crisis*, none of these authors even acknowledge the gendered character of their own analyses.

While we are sympathetic to Jeffrey Reiman's arguments in *The Rich Get Richer and the Poor Get Prison* that crime is produced by legislative policy—by policies that govern police and prosecutorial work—and by sentencing policies, his rather simplistic and mechanical class analysis ignores critical moments in the production of crime.[6] Specifically, it lacks insight into the ways gender, race, and sexuality act as crosscutting influences on the construction of criminal justice policies. While we would both classify ourselves as Marxist, we do also feel that Marxist accounts should not be reductive to class but, rather, should seek to understand and change the practices that reinforce the many forms of systematic oppression under capitalism.

Where work has been done with or on women prisoners,[7] these studies tend to emphasize the passivity of women prisoners. While women prisoners are systematically infantilized, this does not mean that they are entirely without agency. (See Judy Clark and Kathy Boudin's "Community of Women Organize Themselves to Cope with the AIDS Crisis" for an important exception involving the self-representation of imprisoned women as researchers, theorists, educators, and health practitioners.) In this sense, there are parallels between incarceration and the historical system of slavery in the United States. As slaves found ways to resist, while simultaneously camouflaging their acts of resistance, so women prisoners often develop creative ways to challenge the dehumanization of the prison system.[8] Yet, for the most part an implicit, but also often explicit, set of discourses organizes conceptions of women prisoners as incapable of interpreting, let alone exercising any control over, their situation.[9]

Women Prisoners: A Forgotten Population by Beverly Fletcher et al. is a recent compilation of studies edited by a group of self-described multiethnic social scientists who developed a Project for Recidivism Research and Female Inmate Training in Oklahoma. The researchers chose Oklahoma because it has the highest rate of incarceration for women in the United States, 3.8 per 1,000. Their study was comprised of a 142-question survey administered to more than 80 percent of all women incarcerated in Oklahoma jails in March 1991—557 women in all. In addition, the researchers surveyed 60 percent of the 163-person coed prison staff. The project's central aim was to study recidivism rates among women prisoners. We greatly appreciate the researchers' commitment to women prisoners, their willingness to address issues of race and its intersections with gender and class, and their scholarly efforts to seek liberatory strategies for incarcerated women. However, the articulation of "recidivism" as a problem emanating primarily from individual life histories diverts their analytical gaze from the institutional and structural forces that serve as a magnet, inevitably attracting former prisoners back into the system. In addition, while the central aim of the Oklahoma researchers was to present a comprehensive, triangulated study considering race as important as gender to the process of theorizing the women's prison population in Oklahoma, they manage to construct women prisoners mainly as social victims. A further reservation we have about this particular approach is that the editors rely on "A National Profile of the Woman Prisoner" produced in 1990 by the American Correctional Association. This profile provides a normative description of incarcerated women as single women of color in their late twenties who have been physically abused, have dropped out of high school, have had children, and have been arrested at least twice by the age of fifteen.[10] Without belaboring the point, such descriptions create stereotypical notions of incarcerated women, do not problematize discursive representations of criminalized women based on statistical averages, and thereby deny the women any agency.

However, there are exceptions to the type of work that leads to these narrow conclusions. Russell P. Dobash et al. aim to avoid constructing incarcerated women as passive human beings or mere victims of their social circumstances.[11] Instead, the authors rely upon a Foucauldian perspective, even as they are critical of Foucault's refusal to engage with gender as a category of inequality. Foucault's work is useful alongside Marxist accounts of crime and punishment under capitalism, but it is also necessary to be critical of it.[12] Dobash et al. examine official discourses on criminality and imprisonment of women and interrogate how such official discourses translate into government practices, both past and present. The authors also spent four months conducting intensive observation in a women's jail in Scotland in the mid-1980s; they interviewed a total of fifty-nine women prisoners.

The prison they worked in, Cornton Vale, was built specifically for women and is described officially as a therapeutic community.[13] The suggestion that women prisoners are more "difficult" than men prisoners descends from a nineteenth-century view of women in jail, an assumption that remains relatively unchanged in contemporary discourse. Dobash et al. also demonstrate that motherhood is a controlling ideological conception invoked in judgments about imprisoned women. The attitude common among senior sentencers is: "If a woman is a good mother then I don't want to put her in jail, and if she isn't, it doesn't matter."[14]

As is clear, we found their study to be very helpful in allowing us to develop our own work with incarcerated women. However, the authors do not discuss issues of race and racism for incarcerated women—which means that the racialized dynamics of women's incarceration are hidden from view. As a result, a key process in the incarceration of women is not analyzed in their work. At the same time, we do think it important to give serious consideration to the Dobash et al. study of women's imprisonment—and, indeed, their work has been extremely influential in settings such as official Scottish policy on jails. However, the authors' arguments are confined to ideas about prison reform, only rarely raising the possibility of the abolition of prisons. In light of our own interest in stimulating discussion about the prospects of strategies and institutions that do not rely foundationally upon imprisonment, this is indeed a significant silence.

One work that departs from this pattern is Pat Carlen's *Alternatives to Women's Imprisonment*.[15] Carlen highlights the difficulty of conceptualizing a penal system in which incarceration does not necessarily serve as the punishment of last resort. She also effectively argues for the recognition of women prisoners as autonomous human beings, i.e., not only as social victims. We are especially impressed by her dramatic proposal of an experimental five-year period in Britain in which only a small number of cells would be made available for women that judges wish to sentence to prison. Thus, rather than assuming that prisons constitute the ultimate site where social rehabilitation can occur, Carlen contextualizes her analyses and her calls for reform within an overarching strategy for the reduction and abolition of jails and prisons. Again, we found the arguments in Carlen's work to be of considerable value, but would, again, point to her silence on race and racism as an aspect about which we have reservations.

Our work has been conceptualized in light of the silence of and about women prisoners, and the silence on the ways in which race and racism are implicated in the process of incarceration for women. In addition, our work aims to depart from the current emphasis in existing academic literatures on women prisoners as victims and on prisons as institutions to be reformed rather than abolished. We will briefly describe our work in one prison to illustrate the ways these issues appear in practice, and to draw out some of the threads from a complex set of structures of oppression that are not reducible to either class nor to any other single category.

The Prison

Inmates at San Francisco County Jail #7 in San Bruno are misdemeanants sentenced to less than one year, or they are awaiting trial and/or possible transfer to one of the state prisons. At the time of our work there, the jail dormitories, separated according to gender and status, housed approximately 200 men and 100 women. This jail is a "program facility," which means that all the sentenced prisoners must participate in mandatory educational programs. In this sense, it is a jail-based alternative to traditional jails. It seeks to recruit racially diverse deputies who are sympathetic to the idea that jail should not only mean control and punishment, but should provide a wide range of multicultural educational opportunities for inmates.

The program facility is a "New Generation Jail," defined in corrections theory as a significant advance over the prevailing organization of jails. County Jail #7 thus incorporates the latest innovations in jail architecture and in inmate management practices, which are informed by a number of theoretical assumptions about the reasons jails have not worked in the past. While the new generation jail has discarded the model of cells along corridors and the use of multiple sets of bars, its open architecture, complemented by direct supervision practices on the part of the deputies, necessitates a more total form of surveillance.

County Jail #7 has six dormitories—two for women and four for men—each holding up to sixty people. The dorms are laid out in a circular arrangement around an elevated plexiglass control tower from which virtually every square inch of the dormitories can be monitored. Surveillance is also achieved via remote video cameras that are placed inside each dormitory, and recorded images are transmitted to a bank of video monitors in the control tower. Deputies are present in the control tower twenty-four hours a day and can turn to any camera for a closer view of any part of any dormitory. This system is a twentieth-century version of Jeremy Bentham's panopticon.

The dorms are shaped as wedges, with the broad part of the wedge having a passage out into a small yard at the back of the building, and the narrow part forming the main point of entry into the dorm. The ceilings are at least forty feet high. Bunk beds line the back walls, and there are single beds placed close to each other in the middle of the area bounded by the bunk beds. At the front of the dorm is the guard's desk, along with notice boards displaying jail rules, four telephones, and a whiteboard with the names of women who will perform the routine in-dorm tasks such as serving food and cleaning. In addition, at the front of the dorm near the guard's desk are five bench-style metal tables, each with twelve small stools around it. The dorm furniture is bolted to the floor. There is also some exercise equipment in one corner of the dorm, with the communal toilets and shower cubicles (with clear shower curtains) on the opposite side of the room. Many women referred to the dorms as "warehouses."

The inmate management practices of this jail call for a twenty-four-hour-per-day deputy presence inside the dormitory. This is a strategy of control that is very different from that of jails where inmates are locked up in cells containing four to eight women, where the guards look periodically through the bars to ensure that the women are not "misbehaving." Thus, the fundamental organizing principle of all new generation jails is pervasive surveillance. What is represented as "progressive" in this new process is the rendering obsolete of old-style inmate/guard relations that rely exclusively on bars and weapons. The new arrangement is meant to foster an educational rather than punitive environment. In fact, both of the women's dorms displayed a quote attributed to Malcolm X, printed in English and Spanish on a large poster reading: "A prisoner has time that she can put to good use. I'd put prison second to college as the best place for a woman to go if she needs to do some thinking. If she's motivated in prison, she's motivated to change her life."

Most of the women in the two dorms were women of color, with the majority being African American women. Despite the dramatic increase in incarceration rates for Latina women in the past decade, there was a relatively small population of Latinas. There was a very small number of women who could be identified as "Asian American," although in San Francisco's city jail at 850 Bryant Street, out of the forty women we saw on the sixth floor in late October 1993, there were at least six Asian women. One woman we interviewed told us that she was of Indigenous American origin. White women were few in number.

Women's uniforms consist of a T-shirt, a pair of sweatpants, and a sweatshirt. All three items were supposed to be monochromatic—blue, yellow, or orange. Blue clothing is worn by women who have been sentenced and are eligible for "outside clearance"—in other words, who are not a "flight risk." This group of women is able to work in the jail garden, as well as possibly attend computer classes, held in a small building next door (the old women's jail). Yellow clothing is worn by women who have been sentenced, and orange clothing worn by women who have not yet been sentenced. This last group, it was explained to us, is rarely allowed outside the building, as they are considered much more volatile than the rest of the population. However, because of the shortage of clothing of all colors at any one time, many women wear a combination of yellow and orange. Interestingly, some of the women interpreted the clothing colors as symbolizing a racial hierarchy.

There is yet another means by which each woman's classification can be identified. Each prisoner is required to wear a wristband bearing each woman's jail number. White wristbands are worn by women who have been sentenced, orange by unsentenced women, and blue by sentenced women who have outside clearance. Thus, the wristband is a visible and accurate way of identifying a woman's classification in the jail system. Again, interesting comments were ventured by many of the women regarding identity construction based on institutional classification.

Women's Bodies—Control, Surveillance, and Resistance

Many of the women with whom we spoke implicitly recognized the complex and contradictory character of imprisonment and, in particular, its purpose of simultaneously disciplining and rehabilitating the individuals who are thereby constructed as "criminals." A striking number of inmates made insightful remarks about persisting influences of racism even within the context of an institution explicitly dedicated to its elimination. We were especially interested in how the women at County Jail #7 discussed control and surveillance, and whether they found ways of resisting the power of imprisonment.

Many of the women were acutely aware of the structural emphasis on developing qualities of passivity and obedience in the educational and vocational programs as evidence of individual rehabilitation. Female correctional philosophy has, in fact, focused sharply on transforming the female "criminal" into a domesticated—i.e., passive and obedient—mother and wife. Jails aim to transform transgressive women—that is, to transform women so that they will acquire habits of passivity and obedience.[16] Considering the extent to which Black women are discursively represented as abnormally aggressive, this process often acquires racial implications. As Carol Smart notes in *Women, Crime and Criminology*, criminal behaviors are seen as masculine behaviors and, therefore, one of the objectives of women's incarceration is to make the women "more feminine" by instilling in them passivity and obedience.[17] However, as feminist criminologists have pointed out, passivity and obedience in the outside world are not qualities that assist women—and, we would add, especially women of color—to lead autonomous and productive lives once they have been released.

Women's bodies and minds are controlled via certain routines that are inherent to direct supervision jails. Women do resist such routines, though, and often successfully: laughter is an important weapon of resistance; devising collective means of protecting individual women from incursions of the guards and other expressions and acts of solidarity are another. Often individual strategies of respecting another woman's desire for privacy play an important role in affirming possibilities of resistance in this world where bodies, thoughts, and emotions are rendered public and subject to pervasive surveillance.

Although the prevailing academic and policy views deem custodialism and nurturance the two central organizing principles for women's jails,[18] these views differ from those of the women inmates we interviewed. The women rarely described or discussed nurturant principles as institutional practice. Moreover, the concept of nurturance is replete with contradictions, particularly in relation to women's incarceration. That is, many have argued that women's prisons are designed to provide a "pseudo-motherly" environment,[19] which results in women inmates being treated like children.

Sexuality

Sexuality has always played a pivotal role in ideologies of female transgression. The program facility presents itself as a progressive institution, and explicitly attempts to promote an antiracist, antisexist, and antihomophobic consciousness. All of the incoming women receive an orientation manual which states that: "Racism, sexism, anti-gay/lesbian remarks, or any other disrespect or devaluation of human beings are unacceptable in this facility."[20] Sanctions can be severe—one woman told us she had been transferred to a less desirable facility when allegations arose that she had made homophobic remarks about teachers and staff. In the education and counseling program, sexuality is invoked in a number of ways, both as a subject of study and as a locus of treatment. For example, there are workshops on sexual violence, AIDS, and nonheterosexual lifestyles. At the same time, sexuality—its expression and related behavior—is strictly policed by the jail authorities.

For example, heterosexual contact is prohibited. Until recently, there were coeducational classes for the horticultural program; now, however, the majority of the classes are segregated according to gender, and there are strict rules about women even looking at—let alone talking to—inmates from the men's dormitories when they cross paths in the corridors of the jail. In other words, relations between women and men are by definition seen as sexual ones. Women are also forbidden to kiss any visitors on the mouth, for the authorities argue that drug smuggling may occur in this way. The Rules and Regulations of the Director of Corrections state: "Inmates may not participate in illegal sexual acts. Inmates are specifically excluded in laws which remove legal restraints from acts between consenting adults. Inmates must avoid deliberately placing themselves in situations and behaving in a manner which is designed to encourage illegal sexual acts."[21]

Although the drug rehabilitation programs to which women are sometimes diverted as an alternative to jail or prison sentences are not under the jurisdiction of the Department of Corrections, these programs also require participants to refrain from sexual activity for long periods of time following their entry.

Many of the women pointed to the ideological legitimation of homosexuality—for example, that many of the deputies and teachers are openly lesbian or gay—and the simultaneous severe prohibition of homosexual expression on the part of inmates—"homosecting," as it is called in prison parlance. The women felt homosexuality led to more vigorous monitoring by jail authorities.

Clearly, the constant threat of surveillance is an effective psychological weapon in the enforcement of rules that prohibit any behavior that might be construed as sexual. If the prohibition of female-male physical contact tends to sexualize relations between women and men inmates, the rules against homosexuality have a similar effect on relationships between women. "Visiting" is prohibited in the bed areas, despite the fact that beds are separated by less than two feet and each bed is surrounded by three other beds. No two inmates are allowed to sit on one bed at the same time.

The only other available seating is on metal stools that are anchored to the concrete floor around the metal tables at the front of the dorm. These often are within earshot of the deputy, so there is no place in the dorm where women are able to have ordinary physical contact. Women are expected to remain in their own space, even though space in the dorms is extremely tight. Thus, in these enclosed dormitories, space itself is sexualized, and sexuality in turn is criminalized.

Conclusion

This preliminary outline of our work begins to map some of the structures of incarceration. It also suggests points of collision and intersection between the women's concerns and official/public debates about women's imprisonment. We have not included in this chapter some issues that we know are central to women's incarceration in Britain and the United States—such as the ways in which therapeutic communities are used to perpetuate a mentality of punishment, in spite of their often initially radical origins. We also have not dealt in any depth with the profound difficulty many people have imagining a society without jails and with very different notions of criminality that are not constructed along racial and class lines, a society in which there would be a strategic emphasis on education as opposed to incarceration. The quote over the door of the first purpose-built women's prison, opened in 1645 in Amsterdam, said:

"Fear not! I do not exact vengeance for evil, but compel you to be good. My hand is stern but my heart is kind."[22]

This rationale for women's imprisonment may seem coercive for current sensibilities. However, discourse on prisons and incarceration has changed surprisingly little since the nineteenth century, and we would argue that only anti-penalty and abolitionist approaches provide viable possibilities for challenging the current ideological trend of "Lock 'em up and throw away the key." A focus on the structures of regulation in prison should be a concern of Marxists in psychology. In order to understand and change this carceral world, it is necessary for Marxists to understand different varieties of oppression, and the ways these are policed in class society.

CHAPTER 12

Fighting for Her Future

Reflections on Human Rights and Women's Prisons in the Netherlands*

with Kum-Kum Bhavnani

Welfare, immigration, and crime are popular issues in US political discourse today. During the 1996 election campaigns, both Democrats and Republicans have drawn upon the symbiotic discourses of the welfare mother, the immigrant, and the "criminal" in constructing a retrograde racial politics that is a major threat to democratic possibilities for the future.[1] With a few notable exceptions, most elected officials—regardless of party affiliation—have identified an alleged crime wave as the newest threat to "national security," thus promoting long-term incarceration and expansion of an already mammoth prison system as the only imaginable response to crime. Political opposition to what is constructed as crime, associated with demands for longer prison sentences, more repressive conditions, and expanding prison space—reserved for an implicitly racialized "criminal"—is usually accompanied by a similar opposition to wel-

* First published in *Social Identities* 3, no. 1 (1997), 7–32. We wish to thank the women prisoners at Amerswiel Prison, whose names have been changed for purposes of this chapter, the Ministry of Justice in the Netherlands, Bernadette van Dam, director of Amerswiel, and Ria Wolleswinkel, who shared her research with us. We also thank Hoelje Lowenthal for translating from Spanish to English and Stefanie Kelly and Mary Jo Poole for their help with the transcriptions.

fare and to immigration from Third World countries. In this context, the proliferation of prisons and attendant ideological justifications for a rapidly swelling incarcerated population create the grounds for a kind of camouflaged racism that strengthens the repressive power of the state. Thus, it is somewhat ironic and deeply disturbing that few progressive organizations have integrated into their agendas an explicit opposition to a rapidly developing and highly racialized prison industrial complex.

As a prelude to our examination of gender, punishment, and human rights in the Netherlands, we suggest that the "crime" scare must be contested by a political strategy that works to reduce and ultimately abolish the use of imprisonment as a key means of (not) addressing social problems rooted in racism and poverty. Prisons have never accomplished their announced goal of ridding society of "crime."[2] Neither have prisons helped to eliminate the material conditions in poor communities and communities of color that can create trajectories leading members of these communities into the criminal justice system.[3] It is for these reasons that antiracist theories and practices must try to counter the widespread assumptions that prisons are here to stay and that we are powerless to affect their consumption of social resources that are better directed toward education, health, housing, and anti-poverty initiatives.

While we advocate the strategic reduction and eventual abolition of incarceration as the main response to the social problems that presently steer poor people of color toward the criminal justice system,[4] we recognize that all prison systems are not equally implicated in this process of racialized criminalization of poor people. That is, our politics of abolitionism involves a determination to examine systems that do not participate in the current patterns of ever-expanding jails and prisons that tend to reproduce the very problems incarceration presumes to solve. One such system, we argue, can be found in the Netherlands. This is not to dismiss critical analyses that have been proposed by Dutch writers, who point out that the prison system there has deteriorated over the last decade, especially as compared with other European countries.*[5] Moreover, in comparison with other European countries, the Netherlands has one of the lowest levels of women's participation in the labor force, and relatively few women are active in the political arena.† However, when women's prisons in the Netherlands are compared with the expanding network of women's jails and prisons in the US, it is clear that despite patterns of deterioration, the Dutch system still exhibits far fewer blatant human rights abuses.

Our study of women's incarceration in a transnational context focuses on the often unrecognized intersections of race and gender in the politics of imprisonment. The United States presently boasts the highest rate of incarceration in the world.[6] What is frequently ignored, however, even by those who acknowledge the dangers of committing vast numbers of youth from communities of color to jails and prisons, is that populations of women prisoners are growing at a rate that far surpasses the rate of increase in the population of imprisoned men. This gendered dimension of state-inflicted punishment is so frequently overlooked because of the comparatively small percentage of women behind bars. The approximately 87,000 incarcerated women in the US amounts to only 7.4 percent of the nation's total jail and prison population. But what has persuaded us of the contemporary importance of theoretical and practical work on women in prison is the fact that since 1980 the imprisoned female population has increased by 275 percent, while the male population has increased by 160 percent.[7] Moreover, during the decade of the 1980s, thirty-four new women's prisons were either constructed or created, as compared with seventeen in the 1970s and seven in the 1960s.[8]

One of the most revealing contradictions inherent in systems of punishment that rely primarily on incarceration is the degree to which

---

* For example, there was a 40 percent increase in custodial sentences for women between 1992 and 1994.

† We are grateful to Jan Nederveen Pieterse for emphasizing this fact.

they foster dependency and promote forms of institutionalization—both of which tend to ensure that once a prisoner is released, she more than likely will end up returning to prison. Within the context of the contemporary public debate on the role of prisons in US society, pervasive media representations of crime encourage a conflation of "violent career criminals" and those who have several convictions for nonviolent (often drug-related) crimes. These public discussions rarely link "recidivism" to the prison system's tendency to reproduce itself and, in the process, to promote conditions that lead to crime. Rather, what is referred to in criminological discourse as "recidivism" is typically explained by pathologies that are assigned to criminalized communities. The profusion of "three strikes" laws on the national and state levels indicates how swiftly ideologies of racial and class pathology have infected the legislative process.[9]

The fostering of dependency and institutionalization—a denial of agency—on which philosophies of imprisonment are based, is especially detrimental to women, whose agency is denied in patriarchal social systems that subordinate women's needs to those of men and children. Historically, women's prisons, even in their most progressive manifestations, have not merely denied agency to women inmates, but have infantilized them.[10] This ingrained pattern of infantilization creates the basis for a range of gendered human rights abuses. In their efforts to domesticate women prisoners, prisons have severely impeded women's efforts to empower themselves and thus to escape the revolving door that leads so many released prisoners right back into the criminal justice system.

In this paper, we focus specifically on a set of interviews we conducted (in English and with the aid of a Spanish translator) with thirty-nine women who were incarcerated in the spring of 1996 in Amerswiel Prison for Women, located in Heerhugowaard, the Netherlands. Having previously interviewed women incarcerated in the San Francisco County Jail, we chose to interview women in the Netherlands as a way of thinking critically about women's prisons in the US within a comparative, transnational context. In common with our findings about women incarcerated in California, we noted that there is a similarly disproportionate number of women of color (of Surinamese, South American, and Asian descent) who inhabit Dutch prisons—approximately half of all imprisoned women in the Netherlands are women of color. Moreover, similarly racialized notions of criminality construct the discursive landscape in the Netherlands. Nonetheless, after interviewing women prisoners as well as the director of Amerswiel and representatives of the Ministry of Justice, we reached the conclusion that Dutch prison practices are a vast improvement over US prison practices in many important respects. Yet, we do not so much propose the Dutch prison system as a model to be emulated by the US and other countries with repressive incarcerating regimes. Instead, we argue that precisely those aspects of the Dutch system that make it superior to the US system are those that attempt—sometimes successfully, sometimes not—to challenge from within the very limits of incarceration. The basis for this challenge is an announced respect for the human rights of those who are incarcerated.

Incarceration in the Netherlands

The criminal justice system in the Netherlands has been characterized by attempts to transform the nature and place of incarceration within the society and thus to adhere to a minimal notion of human rights for all prisoners. Some examples are: decriminalization of drug use and prostitution; relatively short sentences (although sentences in the past decade—especially for drug possession—have become significantly longer) and general suspension of one-third of the sentence; a report system that allows convicted people with a home address in the Netherlands to remain free until space is available, at which time they are required to report to the prison to serve their sentence; and a tiered system of closed, half-open, and open prisons available to many prisoners who have received long sentences as their punishment. There is also a system of day detention that permits prisoners to report to prison during the day—usually to receive training in areas such as social skills and assertiveness—and remain in their homes at night. Since 1995, a system of electronic monitoring has been in effect, although, as far as we are aware, no women have been included in this system. Thus, there are distinct moves toward institutionalizing alternatives to incarceration. What is interesting about the Dutch system is that even though it has not effectively arrested prison expansion, it has opened possibilities for imagining new ways of addressing behaviors that are socially constructed as crime. While consciousness of the structural linkage of racism to the criminal justice system in the Netherlands seems to be little more than embryonic, the measures they have taken to preclude the generation of a large-scale punishment industry may inhibit the development of the kind of sequestered racism that is so firmly anchored in the US prison industrial complex.[11]

As far as prison systems go, the Netherlands system is vastly different from the United States. What is perhaps most striking about the Dutch system is that it seriously attempts to follow the United Nations Standard Minimal Rules for the Treatment of Prisoners.* The Minis-

---

* Examples of the UN Standard Minimum Rules are:

- prisons shall be well-ordered communities, i.e. they shall be places where there is no danger to life, health and personal integrity;
- prisons shall be places in which no discrimination is shown in the treatment of prisoners;
- when a court sentences an offender to imprisonment, it imposes a punishment which is inherently extremely afflictive. Prison conditions shall not seek to aggravate this inherent affliction;
- prison activities shall focus as much as possible on helping prisoners to resettle in the community after the prison sentence has been served. For this reason prison rules and regimes should not limit prisoners' freedoms, external social contacts and possibilities for personal development more than is absolutely necessary. Prison rules and regimes should be conducive to adjustment and integration in normal community life.

Making Standards Work: An International Handbook on Good Prison Practice. (The Hague: Penal Reform International, 1995), 19.

try of Justice in the Netherlands recently assisted Penal Reform International in producing a document entitled *Making Standards Work: An International Handbook on Good Prison Practice.* The Handbook's perspective is one that derives the rights of prisoners from universal human rights as formulated in United Nations conventions, treaties, covenants, and rules. At a time when US politicians argue that prisoners have too many rights—and educational, vocational, and recreational programs in jails and prisons are being dismantled—it makes sense to consider those rights that can function as compelling principles in challenging repressive incarcerating regimes. Of the human rights enumerated in the Handbook, we are particularly concerned with the following:

> the right to life and integrity of the person
> the right to health
> the right to respect for human dignity
> the right to freedom from slavery
> the right to freedom from discrimination of any kind
> the right to freedom of conscience and of thought
> the right to respect for family life
> the right to self-development.[12]

While our ultimate goal is to help legitimize strategies of prison abolition based on arguments that punishment need not necessarily involve the loss of liberty, we realize that in examining prison conditions, we are looking at systems that assume that the right to liberty can be forfeited. Within this framework, the Handbook makes an extremely important point: "Many people in prison are serving sentences. They are in prison as punishment but not for punishment. The penalty consists in loss of liberty. The circumstances of imprisonment should not therefore be used as an additional punishment."[13] Therefore "living conditions in a prison," according to *Making Standards Work,*

> are among the chief factors determining a prisoner's sense of self-esteem and dignity. Where he or she sleeps, what he

> or she is allowed to wear, what and where he or she eats, whether he or she has a bed with sheets and blankets or sleeps on the floor, covered only with rags, whether or not he or she is allowed to wash and with what frequency, whether he or she has on-going access to a toilet or has to ask (or sometimes plead with) the guard each time, all this has tremendous influence on his or her physical and mental well-being.[14]

Amerswiel Prison for Women

Since there is no single standard governing physical conditions in US jails and prisons, prison architecture and material conditions vary according to and even within counties, states, and the federal system. As the network of jails and prisons has expanded throughout the country, specific facilities, constructed as a direct response to overcrowdedness, are often filled beyond capacity before they are actually opened. Doubling or even tripling the capacity of cells meant to house single inmates is not infrequent. Because of the lack of governing standards, even the worst material conditions may not be subject to improvement unless or until a lawsuit is successfully brought against the institution. The most frequent "solution" to overcrowdedness is the construction of new prisons.

In the Netherlands, there are strict rules governing prisoners' human rights to be housed under humane conditions that respect their privacy. In Amerswiel, where we conducted the majority of our interviews, each woman has her own private room as well as a private toilet and shower. Amerswiel is designated a closed prison: within the Dutch system, having served two-thirds of their sentence, inmates can be transferred from a closed prison to a half-open prison, which permits regular weekend home visits. During the six months prior to release, prisoners are eligible to move into an open prison where they work in surrounding communities during the week and spend weekends at home with their families.*

Amerswiel Prison is located in Heerhugowaard, a small town forty-five minutes outside Amsterdam. It is housed in a building that also houses a separate prison for men. At the time of our interviews, there were seventy-nine women inmates held in four units. The Short Term Unit housed twenty-six women serving less than one year as well as those awaiting trial. As there is no system of bail in the Netherlands, women considered to be at risk for reoffending or for flight (especially women from other countries who are charged with drug trafficking) are held in short term units along with sentenced women. The Long Term Unit housed twenty-seven women with sentences longer than one year. The longest sentence at the time of our interviews was twelve years. Of the other two units, one is called an Individual Guidance Unit, a special environment for women categorized as having mental illness, but not drug problems. The other is a Drug Rehabilitation Unit. Each of these facilities housed thirteen women and were organized around routines that were far more rigorous than those of the Long and Short Term Units. In the Drug Rehabilitation Unit, for example, women had regular, often daily group sessions with each other, during which they would discuss those factors that might keep them out of jail and away from drugs, as well as their own behaviors within the group. The announced goal of this unit was to motivate women to enter a drug rehabilitation clinic voluntarily upon their release from prison.

Having visited a number of jails and prisons within the United States, we were immediately impressed by the living conditions at Amerswiel. All the women at Amerswiel are housed in individual cells, which are eleven square meters, each of which has a (non-open-

* Transfer to a half-open or open prison operates on a case-by-case basis, depending on the fulfillment of certain criteria by the prisoner. She is required to have a home address in the Netherlands, she cannot be on drugs, she cannot be designated a "danger to society," and she must have demonstrated "good behavior" in the previous prison.

ing) window that looks out over the sports field or the exercise yard. Standard furniture in each cell consists of a bed, desk, a chest of drawers, closet, a movable chair and coffee table, a bulletin board, and shelving for books, food, and other belongings. Moreover, attached to each cell is a small alcove that houses a private bathroom containing not only a commode and sink but also a shower. Women with infant children are housed in slightly larger rooms, which have an extra area in which the child may be washed and fed.

The women are also able to rent from the prison authorities—and most women choose to do this—a television set with uncensored programming (including an abundance of hardcore erotic movies), a small refrigerator, a CD/cassette/radio, and a coffee machine, all at a cost of 11.5 guilder per week. Most cells bore the stamp of their occupants' individuality, decorated with photographs, postcards, and colorful bedspreads, curtains, and cushion covers. A number of the women kept birds—cockatiels, parakeets, or lovebirds—in their rooms. There is no jail uniform: all the women wore their own clothes.

In the Short and Long Term Units, in the middle of each corridor, along which the cells are situated, is an inmate lounge area containing couches, tables, and chairs. At the end of each corridor are two communal rooms, each equipped with cooking facilities, dining tables, a television, comfortable chairs, and coffee tables. Outside these rooms are two pay telephones.

Dayrooms (communal gathering points) are standard elements of the architecture of most US jails and prisons. The special significance of the communal rooms in Amerswiel resides in the role they play in promoting autonomous community building among the inmates. In most US women's prisons, there is a traditional culture of clandestine surrogate family structures,* which women create as a way of building worlds that appear to be untouched by prison regimes.[15] In Amerswiel,

* Often referred to as pseudo-families, these structures are often quite complicated, including mothers, fathers, sons, and daughters as well as grandparents, uncles, and aunts and cousins.

women constructed community among themselves by developing cooking and eating collectives. In the communal rooms, cooking and eating utensils are available to all the women in accordance with a schedule they create themselves. Moreover, the food sold in the prison store consists not only of canned and dry goods but also of fresh fruits, vegetables, and meat. It is true that necessity forces the women into these collective cooking/eating relationships—without exception, the prepared prison food was described as "awful" or like "dog food"—but it is also clear that these food collectives create space for unregulated and often lasting bonds among the women at Amerswiel.

Since many of the amenities of prison life—televisions, CD/cassette players, refrigerators, etc.—cost money, we immediately questioned whether such a situation did not privilege the inmates with access to outside financial resources. As it turned out, all inmates are required to work (or study), earning up to 27 guilder per week if they are unsentenced and up to 53 guilder per week if sentenced. The workday is four hours; they are able to devote the rest of the day to voluntary activities such as visits to the exercise yard, the gym (for volleyball, soccer, or aerobics), the fitness center (a room with free weights, weight machines, and aerobic machines), craft classes, computer classes, and the library. Their paid work was most often characterized as boring—they make car mats and small toys, and package cleaning supplies. Only those who were studying or whose work as janitors allowed them to move freely throughout the prison actually seemed to enjoy what they were doing.

That the most frequently borrowed book from the library was the *Handbook for Prisoners' Rights* (numerous copies of which were available) was a further indication of the extent to which prisoners were encouraged to assert and defend their rights. The library also has a number of large ring binders containing each month's newspaper articles on issues of justice, circulars from the Ministry of Justice regarding policies and procedures, and a third binder containing information on all recent complaints and grievances brought by prisoners in the Netherlands as well as the outcomes of these actions. In fact, we were consistently impressed by the depth of most of our interviewees' knowledge regarding their rights as prisoners. There is also a prisoners' commission that regularly brings grievances before the administration. It is also empowered to bring grievances before a civilian body designated for that purpose.

Compared to our work with women prisoners in California, these women amazed us with their sense of agency in circumstances inherently designed to rob them of their liberty. They seemed to be far more aware of their "human rights" as prisoners. Perhaps this is why they reported such low levels of tension among themselves, which was in contrast to the constant tension and frequent physical confrontations among the women prisoners in San Francisco. No woman we interviewed could recall a fight having broken out among the inmates there. On the contrary, a very pronounced culture of sharing seems to have developed in this prison. One woman from another European country arrested on charges of acting as a drug courier, who had no friends or relatives in the Netherlands, told us that other women in her unit had given her food, cigarettes, and comfort while she established a financial base and overcame her profound disorientation.

Incarcerated Women and Their Children

The most obvious configuration of problems facing many women prisoners emerges from the myriad ways their children suffer under the circumstances of their incarceration. In fact, this is often the only specifically gendered issue acknowledged by policymakers concerned with prison conditions. As important a document as the previously cited *Making Standards Work* may be, it is also weak in its tendency to conflate womanhood and motherhood, with the resulting implications that attention to gender in developing good prison practice is synonymous with attention to the needs of children of incarcerated women. For example: "The dilemma of whether or not to detain (babies with their mothers) is a real one. *The interests of the child are paramount.* Bonds with the mother are of great importance at this early stage. When small children are detained with their mothers, they are not prisoners in the ordinary sense, and their treatment must reflect that fact."[16]

Within the framework of a rights discourse, the abstract deployment of the rights of children can potentially justify the encroachment on the rights of the mother in ways that may resonate unfortunately with the contemporary construction of "fetal rights" in US political debates. In arguing against the uncritical prioritization of the child's interest, however, we do not mean to minimize the importance of contesting the ways imprisonment severs mother- (and father-) child relationships. In fact, our interviews revealed that this was a central concern—and not only among the women with young children. Rather, it is simply to suggest that the human rights prisoners possess should not be regarded as competing or hierarchal in nature. In other words, the right to respect for family life need not, for example, prevail over or compete with a woman's right to self-development.

Amerswiel Women's Prison is unique in that its director, Bernadette van Dam, is an internationally recognized feminist advocate of imprisoned mothers' and children's rights. Many of our interviewees expressed admiration for her public campaigns to render prison conditions less violative of family relations. While it still leaves much to be desired, the Dutch system is far more advanced than its counterpart in the US with respect to family life.* On the most basic level, women have the right to visit with their children. In closed prisons,

---

* Jan Nederveen Pieterse has pointed out that the "family orientation that makes for humane prison regimes [has] also served to keep women in the home." In this sense, the "right to family life," as a human rights principle, has been invoked in many contexts in such a way that perpetuates women's subordination. The development of the welfare state in Britain, for example, reveals such an ideological approach (see Fiona Williams, *Social Policy*). In our discussion of the right to family life, we therefore attempt to disarticulate women prisoners' concern for and about their children from the prevailing patriarchal and heterosexist family rhetoric.

such as Amerswiel, these visits take place in the formal visiting rooms, in the women's cells, in the rooms reserved for unsupervised visits (where sexual partners may also meet), and at children's parties held on Christian holidays (one of which we attended, since Easter fell during the middle of our interview period). Further, women prisoners who have an address acceptable to the authorities—and this usually excludes "foreign" women—by their request and at the discretion of the director, can go home and spend one weekend every two months with their children and families/friends during the last year of a long sentence.

We also visited a half-open prison located in Sevenum, in which children up to the age of four are permitted to live with their mothers. This is a recent development, occurring in the past three years. In an attempt to diminish the obvious effects of imprisonment on children, the child attends a day care center in the local community.* In addition to facilities where mothers may attend parenting classes and visit a playground, there was also a children's garden with goats and other small animals. Most of the women incarcerated at Sevenum are either classified as low flight risk or have served two-thirds of their sentences at institutions such as Amerswiel. If their addresses are acceptable to the authorities, the women are also able to spend weekends at home every four weeks.

The third form of incarceration in the Netherlands is the open prison in which inmates hold jobs in the surrounding community or participate in a training program during the day, spend weeknights in prison, and go home on weekends. In fact, open prisons close down every weekend. Sometimes women who have been in prison for a long time will move to an open institution in order to start reestablishing their relationships with their children. Thus the three main types of

---

* This choice is in line with the recommendation that "unless a baby or small child is taken out of the prison environment every week to see the outside world, learning and emotional development may be retarded and adaptation to society jeopardized." Penal Reform International, *Making Standards Work*, 130.

prisons—the closed prison, the half-open, and the open—all allow prisoners to continue or renew relationships with their children.

This is not to say that the process of creating livable prison environments for mothers and their children is unambiguous. Fleur, whose four-year-old daughter was being cared for by her seventy-year-old grandparents, argued that while the facilities at Sevenum were "nice," the routine was too demanding for both mother and child. "In the morning, they have the same routine like we have, so within one hour they have to dress up their children, they have to bathe, they have to eat, and bring the child downstairs to go there (the prison or community play group). You get crazy! They (the children) are not allowed to go around the building. They can sometimes go to the animals around here, but they are very tight."

That the routine need not be so rigorous was demonstrated by Rosa's description of her time at Breda, another closed prison, before she came to Amerswiel. "They put me in a double room, the baby comes first there. They give you flexible hours in order to give the opportunity to make the food and water. You can go out in the sunshine with the baby. Because there's no shower in the cell (unlike Amerswiel), when a woman goes to wash herself, the guards take care of the baby."

When her child was eight months old, however, she decided that she "was exhausted, I couldn't deal with it any more" and now her children are being cared for by her partner in Amsterdam, who is no longer incarcerated.

Anna had also decided that she did not want her child with her in the prison. "So I decided, well, there was a lady here, she's still here with her baby, and I notice, you know, you have so many mothers. . . . So I said I don't want that for [my child] either." In fact, another woman in Anna's unit remarked in a group meeting that this baby had twenty-seven mothers—and that there was no chance she would subject a child to such intense caregiving. This was not the main sentiment among the women we interviewed—it is hard to say if there was a main sentiment—but it is clear that the incarceration of children with their mothers is not without its complications.[17]

Among our interviewees, all the women who were mothers saw and/or talked with their children as often as possible. Those who consciously opted to forego visits with their children explained that they were reluctant to subject the children to the repressive conditions under which they lived, even for the relatively brief duration of a visit. When Claudia, whose family lives in Colombia, described her arrest, she expressed deep concern about its impact on her eight-year-old daughter, and recounted her own experience from the vantage point of the child, who was with her at the time.

> [M]y girl shouted to me "Mummy, Mummy I'm so afraid." And I said to my girl, "Calm down because nothing is happening." And then the police put his pistol in my side. And said "Shut Up," but I kept talking to the girl. I said "No, no, nothing is happening." And immediately the police put a Black cap over my head and handcuffed me. And then I heard my girl shouting "Mummy, mummy, this is not possible. What is happening?" . . . And I kept talking to my daughter and the police [put his] hand on my mouth to shut me up and then I bit him, his hand.

She continued by explaining how the police refused to let her speak with her daughter at the police station and the difficulties she encountered in seeking someone to care for her children (she also had a sixteen-month-old son).* A week or so later, Claudia's sister Victoria arrived from Colombia to look after her daughter. It was finally decided—"when my daughter saw that I was arrested she was very traumatized"—to send her daughter back to Colombia. The day her daughter was put on the plane, Claudia's sister, Victoria, was also arrested.

---

* Immediately after her arrest, her sixteen-month-old son came to be looked after by her parents-in-law, whose biological grandchild he was. They did not feel they could care for her older daughter from a previous marriage.

Relationships with children often occasion difficult engagements with issues of ethics. Women's concern for their children was apparent not only in the way their invocations of their daughters and sons evoked great warmth and love, but also in their difficult decisions regarding honesty with their children. For example, although all the women were aware, without exception, "that children... suffer discrimination, stigmatization and further hardship following the imprisonment of a parent,"[18] most of them had not kept their incarceration from their children. Dawn, a long-term prisoner, preferred Amerswiel (to which she had transferred only recently) because she could see her children twice a month for a two-hour visit. While she liked the afternoon parties that were held at Christian holiday times such as Christmas and Easter, she clearly preferred the "regular" visits with her children in her own cell.

> But here they may come, you can make something sweet... just like you are at home. And that I like. That's the only thing I like. . . . It's important. I care that my children can come inside, that they can see where their mother stays, you know, they can see where I sleep, they can see how my room looks, can see pictures of them[selves].

Maureen, who was in prison for killing her abusive husband (he had a history of physical violence toward her and her twelve-year-old son from a previous relationship), had two children living in separate foster homes. As a representative from her unit to the prisoner commission (CODEGO), she frequently acts as an advocate for the rights of her associates. She thus expressed concern "about their children. I see women who don't want to fight any more for their children, of course they feel too guilty, they've been in the wrong so long, because you have lots of people here who have been addicted to drugs outside and when they come inside and they don't use drugs anymore, the emotional side of their life is coming out. Most of the time they feel too guilty to try to fight for the children to visit them."

As she reflected on ways she encouraged other women to strengthen their ties with their children, Maureen also described her own predicament:

> One's called social leave, or a leave to see your children, and that's what I'm trying now to do. To go two days outside, to go one day to my daughter in the foster home, because I want to see where she is. And she wants to show me where she lives. Which school she's in, the things she's doing, her room, her teachers, everything. She wants to show me and it's very important in the first place for them, for me to go there and the second place it's important for me to see where they live.

Yet another theme emerging from the interviews was the way in which children often bear the burden of a process of criminalization that has more to do with the mere fact of their mother's imprisonment than with their guilt or innocence. Amina, whose trial had not yet taken place, made astute observations about the criminalizing impact of her arrest and its effects on her children:

> They gave me a paper—"criminal." I have on my back [the] name criminal now. . . . It's bad for my children. . . . For me it's not so [much of a] problem. But for the children. . . . When I will be back outside I will tell them what's happened. . . . Because maybe they hear it sometimes from other people.

Amina had not told her children she was in jail ("my children—they think I'm in a hospital, sick"). The day after this interview, she and her sister-in-law came up for trial along with other members of the family and, according to other women on their unit, the two were acquitted.

In light of prisoners' acknowledged human right to freedom from torture and other ill treatment, it might be productive to consider as more than a metaphor women's allegations that their concern for their children was used as a form of "torture." According to Victoria (Claudia's sister), "Like when you [are] arrested the police is torturing you with the problem of the children. . . . That one will not be able to see your children again. What will the children feel when they know that their mother is in prison? . . . And I said it was not their problem, it was my problem to resolve what I would tell my daughter when, how I would tell my daughter I had been in prison."

Rosa was four months pregnant when she was arrested in November 1994 and was held at Breda, the oldest prison in Holland.

> Breda is a very old prison. And so that I only saw a very small piece of the sky. But the guards are very warm hearted. When I came I was crying a lot and I asked them not to send me here. When I was pregnant they left the door (to my cell) open all the time. The guard helped me clean up the room in Breda. Because I was so, I had such a big belly I couldn't put on my pantyhose and the guard came and she dried my feet and put on my pantyhose.

Rosa then described her experience of giving birth in prison.[19]

> [W]hen I was due to give birth I said to the doctor "just give me an injection and I will have the child quick so I can go back to prison." [Labor began] at 9 o'clock in the morning, and at 12 o'clock, Angela was already born and at 1 o'clock I was back in the horrible hospital. Hungry, thirsty, "can you give me some lemonade" I asked the guard. He said "Drink water." They wouldn't give me a thing . . . I spent ten other days there. One day I got mad because Angela was crying, crying and her belly was aching and nobody came. So I took a chair and broke the window, and then everybody came. And I said "Nobody comes in. Just call a car and take me back to prison, or I'll break everything here." . . . The next day I went back to prison. But first there came a woman with papers threatening that Angela was going to be adopted. I wanted to kill her [the woman] . . . she was going to give the baby for adoption because I couldn't be spending many years with her in prison.

> "Just a moment," I said. I put the baby on the bed and took the flower . . . pot and hit her and the woman ran away.

This long quote allows us to see how racism (Rosa is Colombian), incarceration, and gender all converged in the event of Angela's birth. Rosa's breaking of the window and flowerpot, which had no serious repercussions on the length of her sentence or the conditions of her incarceration, demonstrated that even when the institutional imperatives of incarceration work against women prisoners, the women themselves, under conditions prevailing in the Dutch system, can creatively challenge those imperatives.

Thus, the Dutch system is one which permits, in a limited way, babies and small children to stay with their incarcerated mothers. However, as we have previously noted, it is also evident that there is a dilemma here. It is most often argued that the interests of the child are paramount. Yet, the interests of an incarcerated mother and those of her child cannot be tidily separated.[20] The women's obvious concern for their children does not translate into an unequivocal argument for keeping children in prison with their mothers. This is so not only because keeping a child in custody can disguise the fact that the child is not being punished by the state, but also because of the potential to control the mother's behavior through her children. We saw no evidence of such intimidation at Amerswiel, although we heard about alarming police behavior at the time of arrest.

At a moment when prisoners' human rights are systematically transgressed around the world, an uncomplicated argument that it is in the best interests of mothers and children to remain together even under the circumstances of imprisonment is tantamount to placing a moral obligation of imprisoned women to subject their children to the same forms of repression they experience. According to Fleur,

> If you talk about women, mothers with children in prison, you have to distinguish two things: the benefit of the mother and the benefit of the child. I mean, sometimes . . . they build up a

> relationship with the person who is raising him, you know? So if you take him away from the mother . . . at nine months, there can be some mental problems, because he is very much tied to the person he saw or she saw all the time. But on the other hand, a child also needs to experience, and if he has so little in his surroundings and if he has a mother who is so tense.

She continues:

> But I also have to be honest. There are also some women here where the child is better off here than outside. Because there are some women, they say they are not drug users, but there was one woman, who had her child in the car while she was getting [laid by a john] . . . and some women don't know how to take care of themselves. So how can they take care of the child?

There is thus another level of complexity that has often not been addressed in writings about the children of incarcerated mothers.[21] In our previous discussion of this issue, we pointed out that an uncritical focus on women's role as mothers promotes patriarchal notions that women's first duty and responsibility is to her children. Further, such arguments reinscribe biologistic and nuclear family frameworks for mothers and children rather than feminist frameworks that attend to human rights.[22] It is the latter framework that informs our work.

A human rights framework also permits us to define the discourse of infantilization that has been historically produced by gendered systems of incarceration as a basis for a whole range of human rights violations. In Cecilia's words, "You can't talk 'cause here, you can't do nothing, because they are the boss, you are the child. Just like a child they see you."

Nancy concurred: "I feel like a child . . . [T]hey send you to your room, they close the door, it's just like you don't have any rights, you know?" Being treated like children denies women any agency or, indeed, any humanity. While it should not be the case that children be defined only as dependent and, therefore, as less than human, it is also the case that the treatment of adults as if they were children reinforces the hierarchies inherent in prison regimes. Children are also, almost always, financially dependent on others, and this is often the case for women in prison.

> Kum-Kum: What do you hate most about being in jail?
>
> Carol: To be dependent financially—on my family. Before I was jailed, I had a house of my own.

Treating the women like children means that they are not viewed as independent agents. Dawn said that the "bad thing (about prison) is that all the people, all the guards, I mean justice, the judge, you are alone here and you are in dependence of other people. You can't do anything, nothing on your own." It is also the case, one woman argued, that in general, the guards can be narrow minded, particularly if they come from one region of Holland she associated with provincial attitudes.

> Fleur: They're not open. So if they deal with the Spanish women, they deal with them like they're not grown up people. Like they're dealing with children, you know? And I'm very irritated by that type of approach. I *hate* it.

This type of racism is also evident with respect to women whose official residence is outside the Netherlands as well as homeless women within the country. That women can only go for family visits if their address is acceptable to the authorities means that women who have no permanent address in Holland—frequently, but not exclusively, women from other countries—can never leave prison for a weekend trip, even if they are eligible for such leave. This imbalance, which is a consequence of a woman being a "foreigner" (and usually of color) means that despite the Netherlands' reputation of being one country with very low levels of racial tension due to progressive government policies, institutional racism is part of its system of imprisonment. Women who are not residents of the Netherlands are thus subject to the most obvious human rights violations.

Women's prisons, however, need not only induce dependency, domesticity, and obedience, and we found that the women we talked with in Amerswiel were almost all able to express feelings and hopes that we could hardly imagine being articulated by women incarcerated in California. Frances had just returned from an unsupervised visit with her boyfriend, who was being held in the men's prison located in the same building. "I want to have a child with him. That makes frustrating years, though, because I am already forty-four. So by getting pregnant, giving birth to a healthy baby, getting more problems and being here, it's all delayed for half a year. And I am late already. And that's what worries me. And sometimes it gives me a feeling that you can't breathe because I don't have time anymore."

We were also impressed when the women spoke with great admiration about Bernadette Van Dam, the director of the prison. For example, Anna, in discussing institutional support for women with children at Amerswiel, remarked, "I find she's (the director) very positive. Good woman. She really does a lot for the children." In the same vein, Myrna spoke about Van Dam: "I think she is a fighter. For women's rights and for a different sort of prison."

Agency and Empowerment

In interviewing incarcerated women in the Netherlands, we attempted to ascertain the extent to which prison practices there encouraged forward-looking personal strategies and the extent to which our interviewees felt empowered to make critical observations regarding their prison experiences as well as to exercise the right to choose how to fashion their own lives within and outside their prison experiences. Were they able to imagine meaningful and creative lives beyond their time in prison, and did conditions allow them to engage in significant efforts to acquire knowledge and develop skills that they would be able to draw upon once they are released? In posing these questions we are not entering into the age-old debate regarding the role of imprisonment as rehabilitation. Rather we are especially interested in ways in which the women we interviewed forged self-representations as empowered women with a sense of agency. We thus relate these questions to the right to self-development as formulated by Penal Reform International.

A number of women appeared to be very passionate about their efforts to acquire professional skills. Anna, whom we quoted above, is one of the members of CODEGO, the prisoners' commission that brings grievances to the administration and to the outside body concerned with complaints against the uniformed and nonuniformed staff. She indicated that she has been able to use her time in prison to strengthen herself and feels that she will want to continue her work to improve prison conditions for women once she is released. She is studying computer technology and is attempting to refine her language skills. Of Dutch Caribbean ancestry, she is fluent in Dutch, English, and Spanish. Given the significant number of Spanish- and English-speaking women in the prison, her knowledge of these languages probably played an important role in her election to the commission.

Anna's responses to our questions regarding the importance of her studies help us to complicate the charged issue of the way imprisonment breaks the bonds between mother and child. As previously indicated, one of the innovative prison practices being explored by the Dutch Ministry of Justice is the establishment of conditions permitting children to remain with their incarcerated mothers up to the age of four. Anna has been encouraged to transfer to Sevenum where she would be able to be with her youngest child. However, upon learning that conditions in Sevenum would not be as amenable to her studies as in Amerswiel, she decided against submitting a request to transfer. "[S]o then I refused to go, because studying here is very much better, the teachers really help you better, and . . . that is more important for me now, I realize. Because my children are all right, my parents are taking care of them, and what is important for me is to develop myself, you know. For when I get out, I could do something."

This decision was made even though Anna has most likely sustained criticism from those who feel that by placing her own interests to develop herself above those of her child, she is not a good mother. Perhaps her opposition to the arrangement in Sevenum—she claims that her child would have "too many mothers" there—is meant to counter such criticism.

An equally interesting example of a woman who criticized institutional opportunities was Linda's decision to forego the possibility of engaging in sexual relations with her husband during the monthly unsupervised visits permitted by the prison. She told us she could not tolerate the idea of having sex on the same bed as the other prisoners and their partners. While in actuality there are two rooms and two beds for the male and female population at Heerhugowaard, she said that "I don't like it. No, no. Everybody is in one bed. You have one, you don't have four or five. One. One room."

Instead of "real sex," she indicated that she prefers to watch the erotic movies, which are broadcast daily on the televisions virtually all the inmates have in their rooms. Moreover, she had instructed her husband to explore other sexual avenues, but to make sure he engages in safe sex. Upon her release, and before she resumes a sexual relationship with him, she will insist that he take an HIV test.

We were particularly struck by the way in which one prisoner's struggles to educate herself were praised by her peers. During the time we conducted interviews in April 1996, Andrea was preparing for her first day on an outside job. In fact, one day as we were waiting for the train to Amsterdam at the Heerhugowaard train station, we saw her disembarking from the train and preparing to bicycle back to the prison. Since she was the first woman in the history of the prison to have been allowed to take an outside job, her accomplishments became legendary among her peers as well as among the guards and administrative personnel. Myrna, who is sixty-four years old and said "I feel close to my end," insisted that "there should be more possibilities to study." "Do you remember

Andrea, a very beautiful colored girl? She has her first day of teaching today about computer things. I'm so proud of her. It's amazing, with the little time she could find, she got her diploma and now she's teaching."

When asked whether she felt it was possible to counter the widespread discrimination against ex-prisoners, Jean replied in the affirmative for those cases in which the prisoner is able to go to school and get a degree: "Andrea is doing that, for instance."

At twenty-seven, Andrea is the youngest of ten in her family, has no plans to get married, and made no reference to a desire for children. She has little contact with her own family, although she expressed a deep sense of responsibility for caring for her ailing mother. Rather than have her siblings visit her, she prefers that they send her the money they might use for train fare. Like Anna, she refused the opportunity to transfer to Sevenum, which not only houses mothers and their children but also is the only half-open prison for women in the country. While many of the women we spoke to anticipate the last period of their sentence during which they will be eligible to transfer to Sevenum, like Anna, Andrea has consciously chosen not to apply for entrance into the half-open prison because the facilities for studying are not as stable in Sevenum as in Amerswiel. In response to a question as to why she did not want to go to Sevenum, she said: "Because it's wicked there. The place is . . . people are different than here. And the study facilities are bad. And I don't want to work the whole day, from eight to five and don't do nothing. I just want to study and get some papers before I go outside. And their facility to do that is not as good as here. I don't have help, nobody to help me there, and here I have a lot of help from teachers."

Andrea also has a realistic sense of her own limitations and is afraid that if she did go to Sevenum, she might not return after a weekend at home. "If I go there and they let me go on parole, I will stay away. I won't come back. I won't finish my sentence, no. So that is one of the reasons I don't want to go." Yet, she is the first prisoner at Amerswiel to be allowed to leave the prison grounds to work at an office teaching people how to use computers.

Andrea's own self-representations complicate the notion that she is an extraordinary individual and point to her awareness of the serious material encumbrances she will no doubt encounter when her sentence is up. This is an important indication that her visions for the future are a lot more than fantasy. She refused, for example, to claim that she will never be arrested again—especially if she is unable to find a job. "And if I don't have a job, I have nothing to do. I would try to dance again. And if that don't work, I think I'm going back to the business. Because I have a house, I have to pay my rent. If my mother's still alive by that time I want to help her and my brother. I want to take one of my brothers in the house and help him. So I need money, yep."

Having already served almost three years of a five-year sentence, amazingly Andrea had managed to keep up payment of the rent on her apartment during the entire sentence time.

The most powerful characterization of Andrea's performance came from Maureen, who said, "I think that's great. She's fighting for her future." While she clearly was considered an exception within the prisoner population, both by her peers and by the prison staff, her pioneering accomplishments may very well open the way for a regular work furlough program at Amerswiel. In fighting for her future, Andrea and those who are conducting similar struggles demonstrate that if notions of human rights—and specifically the right to self-development—are allowed to prevail over rigid conceptions of incarceration, prisoners need not be treated as members of disposable populations.

Criticizing Imprisonment, Revisioning Punishment

As we have suggested throughout this article, we were consistently impressed by the myriad ways in which the women we interviewed in Amerswiel expressed their sense of personal agency. In fact, one of our transcribers (who had also worked on the California interviews) remarked to us that in comparison to the California women, whom she described as generally sounding depressed, the women in the Netherlands sounded much more engaging and self-confident. As we hope is apparent from the preceding sections, they made astute observations about the predicament of incarcerated mothers and their children and about their own self-development. They were also forthright in their criticisms of prison life and unhesitatingly presented ideas about alternatives to imprisonment.

Many of the women were aware of current debates about Dutch prisons, and specifically of the conservative opinion that the new prisons are places of quasi-luxury with a comfort level more akin to hotels or college dormitories than to prisons housing "criminals." Needless to say, such views resonate with contemporary conservative ideas about prison in the US. To recall one of the principles put forth in *Making Standards Work*, people "are in prison as punishment, but not for punishment. The penalty consists in loss of liberty. The circumstances of imprisonment should not therefore be used as an additional punishment."[23]

Despite the relatively comfortable circumstances of their incarceration—that is, if imprisonment can ever be described as comfortable—all the women save one strongly felt punished by this deprivation of liberty. Yvonne, who was the one exception, felt that doing time in Amerswiel was not "real punishment." "The way we live here in this prison, that's not a punishment. This is a hotel. I'm a dealer, you know, and I have several customers, maybe 40, maybe 50. When winter comes, they can steal some things, robbing shops and that sort of thing, to be arrested to come into prison while it's winter . . . It's not a punishment anymore to sit here. You can cook your own meal, you can have your own toilet, your own shower. . . . They spoil the prisoners."

Carol's remarks, on the other hand, reflected an awareness that no matter how well prisoners are treated, the loss of liberty itself is a severe punishment. "And I miss, I miss the clothes smelling after the fresh air, and the tiny little things: you appreciate them when you are in prison. Because you take them for granted when you are free."

Many of the women were nonetheless quite surprised to discover that prison life was quite different from the abundant representations in popular culture with which they were familiar. It should be pointed out that many of the women's ideas about incarceration were shaped largely by films produced in the US. Nona said that she had seen "a lot of movies and documentation about the American prison." Although Anna did not specifically refer to US movies, the first question she posed to a guard after her arrest—"The women here, are there many lesbians?"—was probably a consequence of the stereotypes present in US productions. Victoria told us that "you see prisons in the movies, and I've seen prisons, for example, in the United States where they lock people up, beat people and torture people. And I thought prison would be like that, but I think prisons there (in the US) are worse than in Holland; in Holland it's not like that. The only bad thing I see in Dutch prisons is that they close this door (pointing to the cell door)."

Considering how intransigent the very idea of prison has become as the only legitimate punishment (except perhaps the death penalty) for people who have apparently broken the social contract, we were especially interested in whether and how the women we interviewed would take the difficult step of questioning the necessity of imprisonment. When Frances was asked whether imprisonment was an effective form of punishment, she responded:

> I think it doesn't make people better. It makes them worse because they're bitter when they come out, they're very aggressive, they're very frustrated. I don't believe in . . . being put in prison, especially for a lot of the women here. OK, they did something they shouldn't have, but give them another way of punishment [which] doesn't make them bitter, doesn't separate them from normal life, from their families. It only creates bigger problems when you get out.

Although in the United States assumptions about the role of prison have gradually shifted from an emphasis on rehabilitation to an emphasis on punishment, Dutch prison discourse preserves the goal of rehabilitation. The ability of the inmates to think seriously about the failures of imprisonment reflects the central place of rehabilitation in prison discourse in the Netherlands. We might even go so far as to say that many of the women we interviewed sensed the inherently contradictory relationship between rehabilitation and incarceration as it was theorized by Foucault.*

The idea that imprisonment generates profound bitterness and other psychological dysfunctions was echoed by many of the women. They also discussed the difficulties they would necessarily encounter upon release, as a result of the sparse contact with their families and friends during the period of their incarceration. However, it was not only the debilitating psychological attitudes that can result from imprisonment that were pointed out. Many of the women identified structural contradictions that—as Foucault has pointed out—cause prison to produce the very conditions it presumes to eradicate. Anneke described her feelings about the revolving door leading out and back into prison:

> It (prison) doesn't work sometimes. It doesn't help. I see it myself. I'm in five times, and I'm back. So what is needed is how to survive after prison, when you finish . . . You can have wonderful ideas inside . . . but when you are nothing and nobody . . . you are going to need money . . . you make so much money on the street, you see other girls, men and women, and they use. And you take one time a sniff or something and you

---

* According to Foucault, "[i]n 1830 it was already understood that prisons, far from transforming criminals into honest citizens, serve only to manufacture new criminals and to drive existing criminals even deeper into criminality." See J. J. Brochier, "Prison Talk: An Interview with Michel Foucault," in *Power/Knowledge: Selected Interviews and Other Writings*, edited by Colin Gordon (New York: Pantheon, 1980), 40.

> start with that and there you go again. And then nothing interests you anymore, then you are back in jail. I think it's mad.

There is indeed a "madness" about the assumption that incarceration will rid society of crime, since it is rarely able to address the conditions that lead people into criminal justice systems. Because material conditions outside—such as poverty and unemployment and the resulting sex and drug economies—remain unchanged, and because prison itself constitutes a kind of abstract space with respect to real social conditions, prison increases the likelihood of an ex-inmate's return.

Although drug use has been decriminalized in the Netherlands, the increasing number of custodial sentences for women can be attributed to the rising drug economy and the involvement of women—especially from Third World countries—in drug trafficking. "I think prison should be there. There are criminals. I think that women should get less years, but these women with drugs, it's not good. It's better to set them free. . . . When it's true that the people have done something, when you are sure you have to punish them . . . but these poor women—you heard their stories, what their needs are—it is better to set them free and send them back to their own countries." This view was held by many, if not most of the women we interviewed. Victoria argued that incarceration was an appropriate sanction for murder ("I think there should be prison . . . these people that are doing criminal acts . . . to kill somebody"), and Rosa felt that sexual molestation of children should also be a cause for imprisonment: "When a person has committed a real, a very severe crime, like killing somebody or violating children, then you have to go to jail. But for drugs. . . . Why do they put people in prison for cocaine? . . . you should have that thing put around your ankle like in the United States. And for the foreigners, just send them back home."

Although there was a consensus regarding imprisonment for murder, a number of the women were sensitive to the fact that what is sometimes constructed by the court systems as murder—particularly in the case of women—is often self-defense, a more or less rational response to a male partner's abuse. According to Teresa, "People who are sitting for murder, you can't give them house arrest, that isn't possible. Unless, like some women here, it was more like self-defense. That's something else. Because I can't call it murder anymore. That's self-defense. I mean, like a girl over here, if a man should take my kid, put him with his head—'bang!'—in a plate, the plate breaks . . . the boy's face is all covered with blood, I'm sorry, I would have killed him also."

Teresa's critique of the imposition of imprisonment for acts that are understandable responses to domestic abuse reveals a sophistication on her part, which is also evident in her comments regarding social science research on the effects of incarceration in general:

> Especially for women, well, even some scientists said it, every punishment that is longer than two years doesn't do any good. It only makes it worse than before. And it's true, because I'm not even two years inside, and even I have something like—because if you asked me to do something illegal, with my own choice, then I would say "no way!" because I was a pretty good girl outside. But now . . . it depends on how much money I get for it . . . [and] how much here do I have to do for it. And if I see, well, it's enough money to sit for, maybe half a year, one year, no problem. I think I would do it now.

That alternatives are necessary because imprisonment is ineffective as rehabilitation—because it is inappropriate and harms children—was a theme present in Maureen's interview. However, she also put forward suggestions for changes within the existing prison system. She specifically called for improvements in the area of education and work, and argued that more women should opt for education:

> About the alternatives, I think it is very necessary to get the schooling better inside the prison and get some kind of space so you can work outside. Try to build up your freedom. Try to give us a chance to show them that punish[ment] is not good for so long, for such a long time. You've got to prepare to come back to the outside world so you can work again,

> you can take care of your children. When you are always doing nothing and then you suddenly go outside, you're a stranger . . . I think the only way inside is to go to school. Show them what you got inside. Show them that you're not . . . for the rest of your life a criminal. . . . So we need to show them that we can go outside, that the punish[ment] is not right for such a long time.

While most of the women readily agreed that there should be alternative ways of addressing the problems for which imprisonment is the most usual response, it was not as easy to come up with concrete ideas regarding different and more appropriate forms of punishment. However, there was frequent reference to the electronic bracelet currently being considered ("house arrest" as it was called by some) and employment in community services outside prison.

Kristen said that she would have preferred to have offered her services to a community organization in lieu of imprisonment:

> To clean something outside. There is a short[age of] working people in old people's homes. . . . Let's say I come out, I go to an old woman['s] house, or old people house, and I cook something special, that they give [me] a little bit of money for that food, and I do that free. You know how . . . how happy these old people will be? Then you have the animal houses, the kennels. To clean there. People who love animals, to clean there. . . . They don't have to pay salaries, so look. There are so many things outside to do.

The experience of imprisonment had persuaded some of the women whom we interviewed to make plans to work on issues related to women's imprisonment once they are released. Frances, for example, wanted to work in a program designed to warn young people "against criminal acts. I would like to work in a program like that to warn kids to think twice." Others wanted to work on issues related to formerly incarcerated women. Julia wanted to work in the

Tussenfasehuis project* in Amsterdam—a project that provided housing for women released from custody, but which, at the time of our interview, could only accommodate six to eight women. Lillian, who is from Central America, emphasized that women who have been imprisoned have a very low status in most, if not all, societies ("What are we? Nothing"). "When I get free," she said, "I want to work with women, with poor women, give them work in Mexico. That's my dream."

A similar dream was evident in Maureen's vision of her own future—and of the future of imprisonment:

> I don't think prison is good for anybody. . . . It's not doing anyone any good especially for the mothers with children . . . I don't think it's right to shut off people such a long time from their children. . . . When I go outside, I know for sure that I'm going to do something for the people who are still inside. . . . Somebody has got to show the government or the president or the queen, or anyone, that it's not right to shut off such a long time people from society outside. It's not good.

Conclusion

Certainly the historical tendency to formulate issues of women's prison reform within a bourgeois democratic "equal rights" framework has created as many problems as it has solved. The first contemporary female chain gang in the US, recently displayed in leg shackles on the streets of downtown Phoenix, Arizona, was justified

---

* She described the project as follows: "And when you go to the Tussenfasehuis you work in a program, you can work in a program, there are no difficult rules over there. The only thing they say, 'We don't want you addicted on drugs' and then you get out, they're gonna put you outside. 'But if you want to fight, we'll fight with you, we'll help you with going to social security, to get your money, your allowance, social service office and get your money every month, try to help you with finding an own home, a rented home.' So they start you up again."

by Sheriff Joe Arpaio, who said, "I don't believe in discrimination in my jail system."[24] In this sense a call for equal rights for women prisoners will only reinforce the US punishment industry. We therefore suggest a human rights perspective in the tradition of the 1951 Anti-Genocide Petition presented before the United Nations by Paul Robeson and W. L. Patterson on behalf of Black Americans.[25]

In order to develop radical oppositional strategies on behalf of imprisoned women within a human rights framework, it is necessary to acknowledge that a defense of prisoners' human rights cannot by itself contest the legitimacy of incarceration. Penal Reform International advocates that in responding to crime, "[w]herever possible sanctions and measures implemented in the community should be used before deprivation of liberty."[26] However the point of departure for their human rights agenda is precisely the loss of liberty under the custody of the state. For, "[w]hen deprivation of liberty is used, questions of human rights arise."

We are interested in encouraging further discussion on multiple levels—public policy, interdisciplinary research, grassroots organizing—on reductionist and abolitionist strategies with respect to incarcerated populations. Such interventions, we believe, are our only hope in halting the expansion of the US prison industrial complex. Therefore the question with which we have attempted to wrestle is how to frame a radical human rights approach that seeks not only to alleviate suffering among those who are imprisoned, but which also can be linked with prison abolitionism.

As Rose Johnston points out, while the ideas that underlie human rights can vary according to social contexts, there are still some basic "parameters necessary for human survival: maintaining bodily health, material security, social relations, and the opportunity for the development of a cultural and moral life—all those aspects of life which allow one to be human."[27]

While the prison system in the Netherlands cannot be proposed as a model—indeed, according to Dutch critics, it shows serious signs of deterioration under the pressure of the drug economy—it is far more consistent than the US in using human rights principles to structure conditions of custody. The most progressive aspects of the Dutch system—and especially those points where the prison system tends to contradict itself by moving beyond imprisonment—can provide leverage with which to criticize the US prison industrial complex. Perhaps Marguerite Bouvard's approach to the work of Mothers of the Plaza de Mayo can be extrapolated in such a way as to affirm the radical possibilities of human rights struggles with respect to prison work.[28] She suggests that the Mothers of the Plaza de Mayo constructed a new model for human rights activity—that is, one of openly working with democratic values in settings that are explicitly authoritarian. While her context is that of Argentina during the era of the junta, such an approach might help to radicalize prison work in the United States.

Notes

Preface

1. See, for example, Angela Y. Davis, Gina Dent, Erica R. Meiners, Beth E. Richie, *Abolition. Feminism. Now.* (Chicago: Haymarket Books, 2022).
2. This delegation was organized by Rabab Abdulhadi and Barbara Ransby and included Ayoka Chenzira, Gina Dent, G. Melissa Garcia, Anna Romina Guevarra, Beverly Guy-Sheftall, Premilla Nadasen, Chandra Talpade Mohanty, and Waziyatawin.
3. Nelson Mandela, "Address by President Nelson Mandela at the International Day of Solidarity with the Palestinian People," Pretoria, South Africa, December 4, 1997.

1. The Prisoner Exchange: The Underside of Civil Rights

1. Derrick A. Bell Jr., "The Space Traders," in *Faces at the Bottom of the Well: The Permanence of Racism* (New York: Basic Books, 1992), 159–60.
2. Bell, "Space Traders," 194.
3. Derrick A. Bell Jr., "After We're Gone: Prudent Speculations on America in a Post-Racial Epoch," in *Critical Race Theory: The Cutting Edge*, ed. Richard Delgado and Jean Stefanic (Philadelphia: Temple University Press, 1995), 3.
4. Michael A. Olivas, "The Chronicles, My Grandfather's Stories, and Immigration Law: The Slave Traders Chronicle as Racial History," in Delgado and Stefanic, *Critical Race Theory*, 11.
5. Olivas, "Chronicles, My Grandfather's Stories."
6. See Derrick A. Bell Jr., "Serving Two Masters: Integration Ideals and Client Interests in School Desegregation Litigation" and "*Brown v. Board of Education* and the Interest Convergence Dilemma," in *Critical Race Theory: The Key Writings that Formed the Movement*, edited by Kimberlé Crenshaw, Neil Gotanda, Gary Peller, and Kendall Thomas (New York: New Press, 1995).
7. Bell, "Space Traders," 192.
8. See Lani Guinier, *The Tyranny of the Majority: Fundamental Fairness in Representative Democracy* (New York: Free Press, 1994).
9. I have borrowed this term from David Theo Goldberg. See his article "Wedded to Dixie: Dinesh D'Souza and the New Segregationism," in *Racial Subjects: Writing on Race in America* (New York: Routledge, 1997).

10. Darrell K. Gilliard (BJS statistician), "Prison and Jail Inmates at Midyear 1998," March 1999, NCJ 173414.
11. According to the Sentencing Project, in 1996, 49 percent of state and federal prisoners were Black and 17 percent were Hispanic. See Sentencing Project, "Facts about Prisons and Prisoners," March 1999.
12. Jerome Miller, director of the National Center on Institutions and Alternatives, analyzed the March 1999 Justice Department statistics and concluded that by the year 2000, there would be 1 million African American adults behind bars. Approximately one in ten Black men will be in prison. See Miller, "Number of Blacks in Jail Rising Toward One Million," *San Francisco Chronicle*, March 8, 1999.
13. Bell, "After We're Gone," 307.
14. See Neil Gotanda's article, "A Critique of 'Our Constitution Is Color-Blind'" and other contributions of such scholars as Kimberlé Crenshaw, Gary Peller, Cheryl Harris, and Kendall Thomas in Crenshaw et al., *Critical Race Theory*.
15. Gilliard, "Prison and Jail Inmates at Midyear 1998."
16. This slogan appeared on CCRI literature and can be found on their website.
17. Lea McDermid, Kathleen Connolly, Dan Macallair, and Vincent Schiraldi, *From Classrooms to Cellblocks: How Prison Building Affects Higher Education and African American Enrollment in California* (Washington, DC: Justice Policy Institute, October 1996).
18. The California Civil Rights Initiative, a proposed statewide constitutional amendment by initiative (authors and principals: Glynn Custred and Thomas Wood), passed in 1996.
19. Albert G. Mosley and Nicholas Capaldi, *Affirmative Action: Social Justice or Unfair Preference*, (New York: Rowman and Littlefield, 1996), 65.
20. Mosley and Capaldi, *Affirmative Action*, 65–66.
21. *Ruffin v. Commonwealth*, 62 Va (21 Gratt.) 790, 796 (1871). Quoted in Leonard Orland, *Prisons: Houses of Darkness* (New York: Free Press, 1975), 81.
22. "Neither slavery nor involuntary servitude, except as a punishment for crime whereof the party shall have been duly convicted, shall exist within the United States, or any place subject to their jurisdiction" (Section 1 of the Thirteenth Amendment to the Constitution, ratified December 6, 1965).
23. See Angela Y. Davis, "From the Prison of Slavery to the Slavery of Prison: Frederick Douglass and the Convict Lease System," in *The Angela Y. Davis Reader*, ed. Joy James (Malden, MA: Blackwell, 1998).
24. Jamie Fellner and Marc Mauer, "Losing the Vote: The Impact of Felony Disenfranchisement Laws in the United States," Sentencing Project and Human Rights Watch, October 1998, 2.
25. Fellner and Mauer, "Losing the Vote," 8.
26. Gustave de Beaumont and Alexis de Tocqueville, *On the Penitentiary System in the United States and Its Application in France* (Carbondale and Edwardsville:

Southern Illinois University Press, 1964 [original edition, 1833]), 78.

27. Apparently Tocqueville contributed little to the writing of this tract. However, it did reflect the collaboration with Beaumont. See Thorsten Sellin's introduction to the 1964 edition.
28. Alexis de Tocqueville, *Democracy in America,* vol. 1 (New York: Vintage Books, 1954), 268. Here he is probably referring to the two prisons in Philadelphia: Eastern State Penitentiary at Cherry Hill and Walnut Street Jail.
29. Seymour Drescher, ed. *Tocqueville and Beaumont on Social Reform* (New York: Harper Torchbooks, 1968), 73.
30. "Consider a system in which the inmate is separated from those infamous but attractive pleasures that he finds in the company of other criminals, a system which leaves him alone with his remorse. Consider whether this system, after all, is not as repressive as what exists today. Consider, too, whether a system that absolutely separates the inmate from the gangrenous section of society and puts him completely in contact with its most honest portion, that perpetually opens the door toward hope and honesty and closes the door leading to crime and despair, whether . . . such a system must not be infinitely more moralizing than the one we now observe. In other words, let us ask whether the cellular system alone, among all others, necessarily leads to one great effect, the effect of absolutely preventing its inmates from ever being able to corrupt each other more than they were before, so that prison can never return men to the world more evil than those it received." Drescher, *Tocqueville and Beaumont,* 88–89.
31. Charles Dickens, *The Works of Charles Dickens,* vol. 27, *American Notes* (New York: Peter Fenelon Collier and Son, 1900), 119–20.
32. Dickens, *Works of Charles Dickens,* 131.
33. Sentencing Project, "Facts about Prisons and Prisoners," March 1999.
34. Angela Y. Davis, "Public Imprisonment and Private Violence: Reflections on the Hidden Punishment of Women," *New England Journal on Criminal and Civil Confinement* 24, no. 2, (Summer 1998).

2. Prison: A Sign of US Democracy?

1. Michael Tonry, ed. *The Future of Imprisonment* (New York, Oxford University Press, 2004), v.
2. Adam J. Hirsch, *The Rise of the Penitentiary: Prisons and Punishment in Early America* (New Haven and London: Yale University Press, 1992), 53.
3. Hirsch, *Rise of the Penitentiary,* 51.
4. James S. Campbell, "Revival of the Eighth Amendment: Development of Cruel-Punishment Doctrine by the Supreme Court," *Stanford Law Review* 16, no. 4 (July 1964): 996–1015.

5. Colin Dayan, *The Story of Cruel and Unusual* (Cambridge, MA: MIT Press, 2007), 7–8.
6. John J. Gibbons and Nicholas de B. Katzenbach, "Confronting Confinement: A Report of the Commission on Safety and Abuse in America's Prisons," Vera Institute of Justice, June 2006, https://www.vera.org/downloads/publications/Confronting_Confinement.pdf.
7. Elizabeth A. Hull, *The Disenfranchisement of Ex-Felons* (Philadelphia: Temple University Press, 2006), 17.
8. Hull, *Disenfranchisement of Ex-Felons,* 18.
9. Hull, *Disenfranchisement of Ex-Felons,* 19.
10. Jeff Manza and Christopher Uggen, *Locked Out: Felon Disenfranchisement and American Democracy* (New York: Oxford University Press, 2006), 68.
11. Hull, *Disenfranchisement of Ex-Felons,* ix.

3. From the Prison of Slavery to the Slavery of Prison: Frederick Douglass and the Convict Lease System

1. Frederick Douglass, "An Appeal to the British People," reception speech at Finsbury Chapel, Moorfields, England, May 12, 1846, in *Life and Writings of Frederick Douglass,* ed. Philip Foner, vol. 1 (New York: International Publishers, 1950), 155.
2. "Frederick Douglass Discusses Slavery," in *Documentary History of the Negro People,* edited by Herbert Aptheker (New York: Citadel Press, 1969), 310.
3. Frederick Douglass, "The Condition of the Freedman," *Harper's Weekly,* December 8, 1883, in *Life and Writings of Frederick Douglass,* ed. Philip Foner, vol. 4 (New York: International Publishers, 1955), 406.
4. In his speech on the occasion of the twenty-forth anniversary of emancipation in the District of Columbia, he said: "Look at these Black criminals, as they are brought into your police courts; view and study their faces, their forms, and their features, as I have done for years as Marshal of this District, and you will see that their antecedents are written all over them." Foner, *Life and Writings,* vol. 4, 435.
5. Foner, *Life and Writings,* vol. 4, 434.
6. Foner, *Life and Writings,* vol. 4, 406.
7. Marc Mauer and Tracy Huling, *Young Black Men and the Criminal Justice System: Five Years Later* (Washington, DC: The Sentencing Project, 1995).
8. Mauer and Huling, *Young Black Men,* 12.
9. John Hope Franklin, *From Slavery to Freedom* (New York: Vintage, 1969), 303.
10. Milfred Fierce, *Slavery Revisited: Blacks and the Southern Convict Lease System, 1865–1933* (New York: Brooklyn College, CUNY, Africana Studies Research Center, 1994), 85–86.
11. Foner, *Life and Writings,* vol. 4, 109.
12. Foner, *Life and Writings,* vol. 4, 110.
13. Fierce, *Slavery Revisited,* 230.

14. W. E. B. Du Bois, "The Spawn of Slavery: The Convict lease System of the South," *Missionary Review of the World* 24, no. 10 (New Series, October 1901).
15. Fierce, *Slavery Revisited,* 240.
16. Mary Church Terrell, "Peonage in the United States: The Convict Lease System and the Chain Gang," *The Nineteenth Century* 62, August 1907.
17. Fierce, *Slavery Revisited,* 229.
18. David Oshinsky, *Worse Than Slavery: Parchman Farm and the Ordeal of Jim Crow Justice* (New York: Free Press, 1996), 47.
19. Oshinsky, *Worse Than Slavery,* 56.
20. E. Stagg Whitin, *Penal Servitude* (New York: National Committee on Prison Labor, 1912), 1.
21. Fierce, *Slavery Revisited,* 88.
22. Foner, *Life and Writings,* vol. 4, 101.
23. Frederick Douglass, "The Need for Continuing Anti-Slavery Work," speech at thirty-second annual meeting of the American Anti-Slavery Society, May 9, 1865, in Foner, *Life and Writings,* vol. 4, 166.
24. Douglass was invited to present this paper along with Richard T. Greener, the first Black graduate of Harvard. Because he did not wish to engage in open debate around this controversial issue, he decided not to appear in person at the meeting but to send his paper to be read by someone else. Greener, who had taught at the University of South Carolina during Reconstruction, now taught at Howard and was a prominent organizer of support for the emigrants. See William S. McFeely, *Frederick Douglass* (New York: W. W. Norton, 1991), 301; Douglass, "The Negro Exodus from the Gulf States," address before convention of the American Social Science Association, Saratoga Springs, September 12, 1879, *Journal of Social Science* 11 (May 1880): 1–21. Reprinted in Foner, *Life and Writings,* vol. 4, 327.
25. Foner, *Life and Writings,* vol. 4, 325.
26. Foner, *Life and Writings,* vol. 4, 327.
27. "Certainly the control of Black labor was a leading motivation behind every significant effort to establish and maintain convict leasing for fifty years. Just as plain is the similarity between the brutal hardships of convict life and the oppression of slavery times. Finally, the racial character of convict leasing reinforced connections with the slavery regime." Matthew J. Mancini, *One Dies, Get Another: Convict Leasing in the American South, 1866–1928* (Columbia: University of South Carolina Press, 1996), 20.
28. D. E. Tobias, "A Negro on the Position of the Negro in America," *The Nineteenth Century* 46, no. 274 (December 1899): 960–61.
29. W. E. B. Du Bois, *Black Reconstruction* (New York: Russell and Russell, 1963), 506.
30. Du Bois, *Black Reconstruction,* 506.
31. Foner, *Life and Writings,* vol. 4, 332.

32. Foner, *Life and Writings,* vol. 4, 330.
33. Frederick Douglass, "The Color Line," *North American Review* 132 (June 1881), reprinted in Foner, *Life and Writings,* vol. 4, 344.
34. Foner, *Life and Writings,* vol. 4, 345.
35. Fierce, *Slavery Revisited,* 128–29n16. Matthew Mancini argues that while the Pig Law may have been in part responsible for an immediate increase in the number of convicts, in 1877 the penitentiary population began to drop—but in fact began to soar immediately after the repeal of this law in 1888. Mancini, *One Dies, Get Another,* 135–36.
36. Mancini, *One Dies, Get Another,* 120.
37. Mississippi Laws, 1876, c. 110, sec. 1, 3, 194–95. Cited in Oshinsky, *"Worse Than Slavery,"* 41.
38. Oshinsky, *Worse Than Slavery,* 28.
39. Fierce, *Slavery Revisited,* 89
40. J. C. Powell's *American Siberia* is quoted by Oshinsky, *Worse Than Slavery,* 71.
41. Frederick Douglass, "Address to the People of the United States," delivered at a Convention of Colored Men, Louisville, Kentucky, September 24, 1883, in Foner, *Life and Writings,* vol. 4, 379.
42. Frederick Douglass, "The United States Cannot Remain Half-Slave and Half-Free," speech on the occasion of the twenty-first anniversary of emancipation in the District of Columbia, April 1883, in Foner, *Life and Writings,* vol. 4, 357. Several months later at a Convention of Colored Men, he said, "Taking advantage of the general disposition in this country to impute crime to color, white men *color* their faces to commit crime and wash off the hated color to escape punishment." See "Address to the People of the United States," Louisville, Kentucky, September 24, 1883, in Foner, *Life and Writings,* vol. 4, 379.
43. Foner, *Life and Writings,* vol. 4, 359.
44. Frederick Douglass "Southern Barbarism," speech on the occasion of the twenty-fourth anniversary of emancipation in the District of Columbia, Washington, DC, 1886, in Foner, *Life and Writings,* vol. 4, 434.
45. Cheryl Harris, "Whiteness As Property," in *Critical Race Theory: The Key Writings That Formed the Movement,* ed. Kimberlé Crenshaw et al. (New York: New Press, 1995), 285.
46. Oshinsky, *Worse Than Slavery,* 41.
47. Mancini, *One Dies, Get Another,* 92.
48. Mancini, *One Dies, Get Another,* 93. Mancini quotes the 1886 NPA proceedings.
49. Fierce, *Slavery Revisited,* 89.
50. Frederick Douglass, "Why Is the Negro Lynched?" in Foner, *Life and Writings,* vol. 4, 492.
51. Oshinsky, *Worse Than Slavery,* 29.
52. Whitin, *Penal Servitude,* 1–2 (emphases added).
53. Foner, *Life and Writings,* vol. 4, 516.

54. Foner, *Life and Writings*, vol. 4, 516.
55. Fierce, *Slavery Revisited*, 43.
56. Foner, *Life and Writings*, vol. 4, 78.
57. Mancini, *One Dies, Get Another*, 99–100.
58. Mancini, *One Dies, Get Another*, 22.
59. Mancini, *One Dies, Get Another*, 23.
60. I obtained references for these three essays from Milfred Fierce's *Slavery Revisited.*
61. Fierce indicates that "not much is known about Tobias except that his parents were illiterate former slaves and that he was born in South Carolina around 1870. He described himself as "a member of the effete African race" and indicated that he was educated in the South and North, an education he financed by working with his hands." See *Slavery Revisited*, 243.
62. Tobias, "Negro on the Position of the Negro," 960.
63. Tobias, "Negro on the Position of the Negro," 959.
64. Tobias, "Negro on the Position of the Negro," 960.
65. Du Bois, "Spawn of Slavery," 743.
66. Du Bois, "Spawn of Slavery," 738.
67. Du Bois, "Spawn of Slavery," 738.
68. Du Bois, "Spawn of Slavery," 740.
69. Du Bois, "Spawn of Slavery," 741.
70. Du Bois, *Black Reconstruction*, 698.
71. Du Bois, *Black Reconstruction*, 744–45.
72. Terrell, "Peonage in the United States," 303.
73. Fierce, *Slavery Revisited*, 231.
74. Terrell, "Peonage in the United States," 306.
75. Terrell, "Peonage in the United States," 317.
76. Terrell, "Peonage in the United States," 311.
77. Terrell, "Peonage in the United States," 313.
78. Richard Barry, "Slavery in the South To-Day," *Cosmopolitan Magazine*, March 1907, reproduced in *Racism at the Turn of the Century: Documentary Perspectives, 1870–1910*, eds. Donald P. DeNevi and Doris A. Holmes (San Rafael, California: Leswing Press, 1973), 131.

4. From the Convict Lease System to the Super-Max Prison

1. Albert Wright Jr., "Young Inmates Need Help, From Inside and Out," *Emerge*, October 1997, 80.
2. See Jerome G. Miller, *Search and Destroy: African American Males in the Criminal Justice System* (Cambridge: Cambridge University Press, 1996).
3. Steve Donziger, ed., *The Real War on Crime: The Report of the National Criminal Justice Commission* (New York: Harper Perennial, 1996), 102.
4. Edgardo Rotman, *Beyond Punishment: A New View on the Rehabilitation of*

Criminal Offenders (New York: Greenwood Press, 1990), 115.

5. According to John Irwin and James Austin, "African-American women have experienced the greatest increase in correctional supervision, rising by 78 percent from 1989 through 1994." See: John Irwin and James Austin, *It's About Time: The Imprisonment Binge*, 2nd ed. (Belmont, CA: Wadsworth Publishing, 1997), 4.
6. Donziger, *Real War on Crime*, 99.
7. Richard Hawkins and Geoffrey Alpert point out: "Right now there is no uniformly accepted definition of recidivism. It generally refers to a return to crime, but in operation refers only to those detected in crime. Given that many crimes go undetected (some of which are committed by former offenders), virtually any official measure of recidivism is a *conservative estimate* of the failure rate among persons released from treatment. One reviewer of various recidivism definitions notes thirteen different indicators of 'failure,' ranging from a recorded police contact to being returned to prison." See Richard Hawkins and Geoffrey P. Alpert, *American Prison Systems: Punishment and Justice* (Englewood Cliffs, NJ: Prentice-Hall, 1989), 198–99.
8. David Theo Goldberg, *Racist Culture: Philosophy and the Politics of Meaning* (Malden, MA: Blackwell, 1993), 23.
9. Hawkins and Alpert, *American Prison Systems*, 30.
10. Angela Y. Davis, *Women, Race and Class* (New York: Random House, 1981), 9.
11. See James B. Jacobs, *Stateville: The Penitentiary in Mass Society* (Chicago: University of Chicago Press, 1977), 15–16.
12. Jacobs, *Stateville*, 58.
13. Michel Foucault, *Discipline and Punish: The Birth of the Prison*, trans. Alan Sheridan (New York: Vintage, 1979), 200.
14. Foucault, *Discipline and Punish*, 201.
15. Foucault, *Discipline and Punish*, 201.
16. Matthew Mancini, *One Dies, Get Another: Convict Leasing in the American South, 1866–1928* (Columbia: University of South Carolina Press, 1996), 25.
17. David Oshinsky, *Worse Than Slavery: Parchman Farm and the Ordeal of Jim Crow Justice* (New York: Free Press, 1996), 45.
18. Donziger, *Real War on Crime*, 87.
19. Kristin Bloomer, "Private Punishment," *San Francisco Chronicle*, May 10, 1997, A3.
20. Sue Anne Pressley, "Texas County Sued by Missouri Over Alleged Abuse of Inmates," *Washington Post*, August 26, 1997, A2.
21. Madeline Baro, "Video Prompts Prison Probe," *Philadelphia Daily News*, August 20, 1997.
22. Carl Manning, "Missouri Prisoners Say Beatings Worse Than Shown on Videotape," Associated Press, August 27, 1997, 7:40 P.M. EDT.
23. Human Rights Watch, *Cold Storage: Super-Maximum Security Confinement in*

Indiana (New York: Human Rights Watch, October 1997), 13.

24. Human Rights Watch, *Cold Storage.*
25. Human Rights Watch, *Cold Storage,* 14. Citation from Craig Haney, "Infamous Punishment: The Psychological Consequences of Isolation," *National Prison Project Journal* 8, no. 2 (ACLU) (Spring 1993): 3.
26. Miller, *Search and Destroy,* 227.
27. Miller, *Search and Destroy,* 227.
28. My usage of this term follows Terry Kuper's suggestion that entire populations are being "disappeared" from US society via the prison system.

5. Race and Criminalization: Black Americans and the Punishment Industry

1. See, for instance, the *Austin-American Statesman,* October 17, 1995.
2. Charles S. Clark, "Prison Overcrowding," *Congressional Quarterly Researcher* 4, no. 5 (February 4, 1994): 97–119.
3. Clark, "Prison Overcrowding."
4. Marc Mauer, *Young Black Men and the Criminal Justice System: A Growing National Problem* (Washington, DC: Sentencing Project, 1990).
5. Alexander Cockburn, *Philadelphia Inquirer,* August 29, 1994.
6. Marc Mauer and Tracy Huling, *Young Black Americans and the Criminal Justice System: Five Years Later* (Washington, DC: Sentencing Project, 1995).
7. Mauer and Huling, *Young Black Americans,* 18.
8. See Cockburn.
9. See Wahneema Lubiano, "Black Ladies, Welfare Queens, and State Minstrels: Ideological War by Narrative Means," *in Race-ing Justice, En-gendering Power: Essays on Anita Hill, Clarence Thomas, and the Construction of Social Reality,* edited by Toni Morrison (New York: Pantheon, 1992), 323–63.
10. Cornel West, *Race Matters* (Boston: Beacon Press, 1993).
11. Angela Y. Davis, "Modern Slavery American Style," (unpublished essay), 1995.
12. I wish to acknowledge Julie Brown, who acquired this brochure from the California Department of Corrections in the course of researching the role of convict labor.
13. Paulette Thomas, "Making Crime Pay," *Wall Street Journal,* May 12, 1994.
14. Lawrence A. Greenfield and Stephanie Minor-Harper, *Women in Prison* (Washington, DC: US Dept. of Justice, Office of Justice Programs, Bureau of Statistics, 1991).
15. Mauer and Huling, *Young Black Americans,* 19.
16. Michel Foucault, *Discipline and Punish: The Birth of the Prison,* trans. Alan Sheridan (New York: Vintage, 1979), 395.

7. Public Imprisonment and Private Violence: Reflections on the Hidden Punishment of Women

1. See Lucia Zedner, "Wayward Sisters: The Prison for Women," in *The Oxford History of the Prison*, ed. Norval Morris and David J. Rothman (New York and Oxford: Oxford University Press, 1998), 295.
2. Zedner, "Wayward Sisters."
3. See Russell P. Dobash et al., *The Imprisonment of Women* (Oxford: Basil Blackwell, 1986), 19–20.
4. Dobash et al., *Imprisonment of Women.*
5. See Joanne Belknap, *The Invisible Woman: Gender, Crime, and Justice* (Belmont, CA: Wadsworth Publishing, 1996).
6. See Belknap, *Invisible Woman.*
7. See generally Belknap, *Invisible Woman.*
8. Pat Carlen, *Women's Imprisonment: A Study in Social Control* (London: Routledge and Kegan Paul, 1983).
9. See Carlen, *Women's Imprisonment,* 18.
10. Carlen, *Women's Imprisonment.*
11. Carlen, *Women's Imprisonment,* 86.
12. Beth E. Richie, *Compelled to Crime: The Gender Entrapment of Battered Black Women* (New York: Routledge, 1996), 2.
13. Richie, *Compelled to Crime.*
14. "When applied to African American battered women who commit crimes, I used gender entrapment to describe the socially constructed process whereby African American women who are vulnerable to men's violence in their intimate relationship are penalized for behaviors they engage in even when the behaviors are logical extensions of their racialized gender identities, their culturally expected gender roles, and the violence in their intimate relationship. The model illustrates how gender, race/ethnicity, and violence can intersect to create a subtle, yet profoundly effective system of organizing women's behavior into patterns that leave women vulnerable to private and public subordination, to violence in their intimate relationships and, in turn, to participation in illegal activities. As such, the gender-entrapment theory helps to explain how some women who participate in illegal activities do so in response to violence, the threat of violence, or coercion by their male partners." Richie, *Compelled to Crime,* 4.
15. Belknap, *Invisible Woman,* 172.
16. Michel Foucault, *Discipline and Punish: The Birth of the Prison,* trans. Alan Sheridan (New York: Vintage, 1979).
17. Foucault, *Discipline and Punish.*
18. See Estelle B. Freedman, "Feminist of Feminine? The Establishment of Separate Women's Prisons, 1870–1900" and "The Women's Prison Environment," in *Their Sisters' Keepers: Women's Prison Reform in America, 1830–1930,* chaps.

3–4 (Ann Arbor: University of Michigan Press, 1981): 46–88.
19. See Belknap, *Invisible Woman*, 95.
20. Richie, *Compelled to Crime.*
21. Zedner, "Wayward Sisters," 318.
22. Zedner, "Wayward Sisters."
23. See Nicole Hahn Rafter, *Creating Born Criminals* (Urbana: University of Illinois Press, 1998), 50.
24. Elliott Currie, *Crime and Punishment in America* (New York: Metropolitan Books, 1998), 14.
25. Tekla Dennison Miller, *The Warden Wore Pink* (Brunswick, ME: Biddle Publishing, 1996), 97.
26. Miller, *Warden Wore Pink,* 97–98.
27. Miller, *Warden Wore Pink,* 100.
28. Miller, *Warden Wore Pink,* 100.
29. See Miller, *Warden Wore Pink,* 121.
30. See Miller, *Warden Wore Pink.*
31. See Curtis Wilkie, "Weak Links Threaten Chain Gangs: Revised Prison Work Program Facing Voter Disapproval, Inmates' Legal Action," *Boston Globe,* May 18, 1996.
32. See *48 Hours,* "Arizona Sheriff Initiates Equal Opportunity by Starting First Chain Gang for Women" (CBS television broadcast, September 19, 1996).
33. Human Rights Watch, *All Too Familiar: Sexual Abuse of Women in U.S. State Prisons* (New York: Human Rights Watch, 1996), visited May 31, 1998.
34. Human Rights Watch, *All Too Familiar,* 2.
35. See Human Rights Watch, *All Too Familiar.*
36. Linda Burnham, "Beijing and Beyond," *CrossRoads,* March 1996, 16.

9. Race, Gender, and the Prison Industrial Complex: California and Beyond

1. Elliott Currie, *Crime and Punishment in America* (New York: Metropolitan Books, 1998).
2. Joel Dyer, *The Perpetual Prisoner Machine: How America Profits from Crime* (Boulder, CO: Westview Press, 2000).
3. Dyer, *Perpetual Prisoner Machine.*
4. Julia Sudbury, "Transatlantic Visions: Resisting the Globalization of Mass Incarceration," *Social Justice* 27, no. 3 (2000): 133–49.
5. Amanda George, "The New Prison Culture: Making Millions from Misery," in *Harsh Punishment: International Experiences of Women's Imprisonment,* edited by Sandy Cook and Susanne Davies (Boston: Northeastern University Press, 1999), 190.
6. Dyer, *Perpetual Prisoner Machine,* 14.
7. Vivien Stern, *A Sin Against the Future: Imprisonment in the World* (Boston:

Northeastern University Press, 1998).

8. Lawrence A. Greenfield and Tracy L. Snell, *Women Offenders,* Bureau of Justice Statistics Special Report (Washington, DC: US Department of Justice, 1999).
9. Greenfield and Snell, *Women Offenders.*
10. Department of Corrections Services Division, Offender Information Services Branch, *Characteristics of Population in California State Prisons by Institution,* June 30, 2000, Estimates and Statistical Analysis Section Data Analysis Unit, Sacramento, CA.
11. Luana Ross, *Inventing the Savage: The Social Construction of Native American Criminality* (Austin: University of Texas Press, 1998).
12. Greenfield and Snell, *Women Offenders.*
13. Interview with Cynthia Chander, codirector, Justice Now, May 25, 2001; interview with Heidi Strupp, legal assistant, Legal Services for Prisoners with Children, June 1, 2001.
14. Melba Newsome, "Hard Time," *Essence Magazine* 31, no. 5 (2000): 146–50, 210–14.
15. Stephanie R. Bush-Baskette, "The 'War on Drugs': A War Against Women?" in *Harsh Punishment: International Experiences of Women's Imprisonment,* edited by Sandy Cook and Susanne Davies (Boston: Northeastern University Press, 1999) 211–29.
16. Bell Chevigny, *Doing Time: Twenty-Five Years of Prison Writing* (New York: Arcade Publishing, 1999).
17. *Making Standards Work: An International Handbook on Good Prison Practice* (The Hague: Penal Reform International, 1995), 95–96.
18. Terry Kupers, *Prison Madness: The Mental Health Crisis Behind Bars and What We Must Do About It* (San Francisco: Jossey-Bass, 2000).
19. Russell P. Dobash, R. Emerson Dobash, and Sue Gutteridge, *The Imprisonment of Women* (Oxford: Basil Blackwell, 1986).
20. *Truth to Power: Women Testify at Legislative Hearings,* excerpts from Legislative Hearings on Women in Prison at Valley State Prison for Women, October 11, 2000, and California Institution for Women, October 12, 2000, produced by Women in Prison Emergency Network, 2000. Videocassette, 40 min.
21. *Making Standards Work, 71.*
22. *Truth to Power.*
23. *Truth to Power.*
24. See the discussion of prisoners' complaints machinery in *Making Standards Work,* 37–40.
25. De Groot, A., T. Hammett, and K. Scheib, "Barriers to Care of HIV-Infected Inmates: A Public Health Concern," in *The AIDS Reader* (May/June 1996).
26. Susann Steinberg, Deputy Director of Health Care Services Division, California Department of Corrections, meeting with prisoner advocates (Sacramento: California Department of Corrections, October 10, 2000).

27. Amnesty International, *"Not Part of My Sentence": Violations of the Human Rights of Women in Custody* (New York: Amnesty International, 1999).
28. Unpublished interview with Davara Campbell, on file with Justice Now (Central California Women's Facility, July 16, 1999).
29. Joanne Belknap, *The Invisible Woman: Gender, Crime, and Justice* (Belmont, CA: Wadsworth Publishing, 1996).
30. UN Special Rapporteur on Violence Against Women, *Report of the Mission to the United States of American on the Issue of Violence against Women in State and Federal Prisons* (New York: United Nations Economic and Social Council, 1999), 12–14.
31. Human Rights Watch, *All Too Familiar: Sexual Abuse of Women in U.S. State Prisons* (New York: Human Rights Watch, 1996).
32. Nightline, *Crime & Punishment: Women in Prison: Medical Care*, November 2, 1999.
33. Legal interview with Regina Johnson, March 3, 1998, Valley State Prison for Women.
34. Live Jail-Cam, May 23, 2001, www.crime.com.
35. American Bar Association and National Bar Association, *Justice by Gender: The Lack of Appropriate Prevention, Diversion and Treatment Alternatives for Girls in the Juvenile Justice System* (Washington, DC: ABA and NBA, 2001).
36. American Bar Association and National Bar Association, *Justice by Gender.*
37. Legal interview with Maria Garcia and Gina Mendoza, October 20, 1998, Valley State Prison for Women.
38. Michael Welch, "The Role of Immigration and Naturalization Service in the Prison-Industrial Complex," *Social Justice* 27, no. 3 (2000): 73–88.
39. American Civil Liberties Union Immigrant Rights Project, *Justice Detained: Conditions at the Varick Street Immigration Detention Center* (New York: ACLU, 1993); Human Rights Watch, *Letter to INS Commissioner Doris Meisner* (New York: Human Rights Watch, 2000).
40. Welch, "Role of Immigration."
41. Federal Bureau of Prisons, "Quick Facts: April 2001," https://www.bop.gov/fact0598.html#Citizenship, accessed on June 1, 2001.

10. Women in Prison: Researching Race in Three National Contexts

1. See Kum-Kum Bhavnani, *Talking Politics: A Psychological Framing for Views from Youth in Britain* (Cambridge: Cambridge University Press, 1991). See especially chapter 3.
2. Elliott Currie, *Crime and Punishment in America* (New York: Metropolitan Books, 1998), 16.
3. Willem de Haan, *The Politics of Redress, Crime, Punishment and Penal Abolition* (London: Unwin Hyman, 1990), 37. See also Willem de Haan, "Abolitionism

and the Politics of 'Bad Conscience,'" in *Abolitionism: Toward a Non-Repressive Approach to Crime,* edited by Herman Bianchi and Rene van Swaaningen (Amsterdam: Free University Press, 1986), 158.

4. Vivien Stern, *A Sin Against the Future: Imprisonment in the World* (Boston: Northeastern University Press, 1998), 138.
5. See Angela Y. Davis, "Public Imprisonment and Private Violence: Reflections on the Hidden Punishment of Women," *New England Journal on Criminal and Civil Confinement* 24, no. 2 (Summer 1998): 339–49.
6. Since 1980, the US imprisoned female population has increased by 275 percent, while the male population has increased by 160 percent. Marc Mauer and Tracy Huling, *Young Black Men and the Criminal Justice System: Five Years Later* (Washington, DC: The Sentencing Project, 1995).
7. Mary Helen Washington, "Prison Studies as Part of American Studies," *American Studies Newsletter* 22, no. 1 (March 1999): 1.
8. See Katherine Beckett, *Making Crime Pay: Law and Order in Contemporary American Politics* (New York: Oxford University Press, 1997).
9. Mauer and Huling, *Young Black Men.*
10. "All around the world the same pattern can be seen. Prisons contain higher proportions than would be expected of people from groups that suffer from racism and discrimination. How does this disproportion happen? There are many reasons, often related to blatant discrimination in the wider society, and crude racism by the law enforcement agencies. Sometimes the disproportion arises from policies which concentrate minorities in poor areas and restrict their opportunities. Often the criminal justice processes tend to discriminate against minorities, sometimes in very subtle ways. . . .The cumulative effect of all this discrimination is the disproportionate number of minorities in the prisons of the world" (Stern, *Sin Against the Future,* 117).
11. Ruth Wilson Gilmore, "Globalization and U.S. Prison Growth: From Military Keynesianism to Post-Keynesian Militarism," *Race and Class* 40, nos. 2/3 (1998–99): 171–88. See also Michel Foucault, *Discipline and Punish: The Birth of the Prison,* trans. Alan Sheridan (New York: Vintage, 1979).
12. In Australia, for example, although Aboriginal people constitute only 1 to 2 percent of the general population, they comprise 30 percent of the imprisoned population. Stern, *Sin Against the Future.*
13. From the contract drawn up by the San Francisco Sheriff's Department.
14. See Kimberlé Crenshaw, Neil Gotanda, Gary Peller, and Kendall Thomas, eds. *Critical Race Theory: The Key Writings That Formed the Movement* (New York: New Press, 1995).
15. Interview at San Francisco County Jail, program facility, November 1993.
16. Interview at Amerswiel Prison for Women, April 1996.
17. Interview at Amerswiel Prison for Women, April 1996.
18. Interview at Amerswiel Prison for Women, April 1996.

19. Interview at Sevenum Prison, April 1996.
20. Interview at Sevenum Prison, April 1996.
21. Interview at Amerswiel Prison for Women, April 1996.
22. Interview at the Prison for Women in Havana, June 1997.

11. Incarcerated Women: Transformative Strategies

1. Kathleen McDermott and Roy King, "Mind Games: Where the Action Is in Prisons," *British Journal of Criminology* 28, no. 3 (1988): 357–77.
2. Barbara Bloom and David Steinhart, *Why Punish the Children?* (San Francisco: National Council on Crime and Delinquency, 1993).
3. Kathryn Burkhart, *Women in Prison* (New York: Doubleday, 1973); Pat Carlen, ed., *Criminal Women* (Cambridge: Polity Press, 1985); Pat Carlen, *Women, Crime and Poverty* (Philadelphia: Open University Press, 1988); Pat Carlen, *Alternatives to Women's Imprisonment* (Milton Keynes: Open University Press, 1990); Russell P. Dobash, R. Emerson Dobash, and Sue Gutteridge, *The Imprisonment of Women* (Oxford: Basil Blackwell, 1986); and Mary Eaton, *Women After Prison* (Buckingham: Open University Press, 1993).
4. Linda Hancock, "Economic Pragmatism and the Ideology of Sexism: Prison Policy and Women," *Women's Studies International Forum* 9, no. 1 (1986): 101–7.
5. Ronald Berkman, *Opening the Gates: The Rise of the Prisoner's Movement* (Toronto: D.C. Heath, 1979); William Wilbanks, *The Myth of a Racist Criminal Justice System* (Monterey, CA: Brooks Cole, 1987); John Braithwaite, *Crime, Shame and Reintegration* (Cambridge: Cambridge University Press, 1989); William L. Selke, *Prisons in Crisis* (Bloomington: Indiana University Press, 1993).
6. Jeffrey Reiman, *The Rich Get Richer and the Poor Get Prison: Ideology, Crime and Criminal Justice,* 3rd edition (New York: Macmillan, 1990).
7. Rose Giallombardo, *Society of Women: A Study of a Women's Prison* (New York: John Wiley, 1966).
8. Judy Clark and Kathy Boudin, "Community of Women Organize Themselves to Cope with the AIDS Crisis: A Case Study from Bedford Hills Correctional Facility," *Social Justice* 17, no. 2 (1990): 90–109.
9. See, for example, Thomas W. Foster, "Make-Believe Families: A Response of Women and Girls to the Deprivations of Imprisonment," *International Journal of Criminology and Penology* 3 no. 1 (1975): 71–8; Harriet Cookson, "A Survey of Self-Injury in a Closed Prison for Women," *British Journal of Criminology* 17, no. 4 (1977): 332–47; Candace Kruttschnitt, "Race Relations and the Female Inmate," *Crime and Delinquency 29, no. 4* (October 1983): 588–89; Christina Jose Kampfner, "Coming to Terms with Existential Death: An Analysis of Women's Adaptation to Life in Prison," *Social Justice* 17, no. 2 (1990): 11–125; and Beverly R. Fletcher, Linda Dixon Shaver, and Dreama G. Moon, *Women Prisoners: A Forgotten Population* (Westport, CT: Praeger, 1993).

10. Fletcher et al., *Women Prisoners.*
11. Dobash et al., *Imprisonment of Women.*
12. Michel Foucault, *Discipline and Punish: The Birth of the Prison,* trans. Alan Sheridan (New York: Vintage, 1979).
13. Dobash et al., *Imprisonment of Women.*
14. Dobash et al., *Imprisonment of Women,* 195.
15. Carlen, *Alternatives to Women's Imprisonment.*
16. Barbara Brenzel, *Daughters of the State: A Social Portrait of The First Reform School for Girls in North America* (Cambridge, MA: MIT Press, 1983).
17. Carol Smart, *Women, Crime and Criminology: A Feminist Critique* (London: Routledge and Kegan Paul, 1976).
18. Adrian Howe, "Prologue to a History of Women's Imprisonment: In Search for a Feminist Perspective," *Social Justice* 17, no. 2 (1990): 4–22.
19. Kim Jackson, "Patriarchal Justice and the Control of Women," *New Studies on the Left* (Spring 1989): 153–71.
20. *Orientation Manual,* 1.
21. Title 15, Crime Prevention and Corrections, Article i, Section 3007 (Sexual Behavior).
22. Cited in Dobash et al., *Imprisonment of Women,* 24.

12. Fighting for Her Future: Reflections on Human Rights and Women's Prisons in the Netherlands

1. See *New York Times,* September 17, 1996.
2. Foucault's observation with respect to the prison system in nineteenth-century France is equally applicable to the contemporary United States: "Prisons do not diminish the crime rate: they can be extended, multiplied or transformed, the quantity of crime and criminals remains stable or, worse, increases." Michel Foucault, *Discipline and Punish: The Birth of the Prison,* trans. Alan Sheridan (New York: Vintage 1979), 265.
3. Jeffrey Reiman, *The Rich Get Richer and the Poor Get Prison: Ideology, Crime and Criminal Justice,* 3rd ed. (New York: Macmillan, 1990).
4. See Pat Carlen's ideas regarding such a process with respect to women's prisons in Britain: Pat Carlen, *Alternatives to Women's Imprisonment* (Milton Keynes: Open University Press, 1990).
5. Rene Van Swaaningen and Gerard de Jonge, "The Dutch Prison System and Penal Policy in the 1990s: From Humanitarian Paternalism to Penal Business Management," in *Western European Penal Systems: A Critical Anatomy,* edited by Vincenzo Ruggiero, Mick Ryan, and Joe Sim (London: Sage Publications, 1995); Ria Wolleswinkel, personal communication, 1996.
6. Alexander C. Lichtenstein and Michael A. Kroll, "The Fortress Economy: The Economic Role of the US Prison System," in *Criminal Injustice: Confronting the Prison Crisis,* edited by Elihu Rosenblatt, (Boston: South End Press, 1996), 16.

7. Marc Mauer and Tracy Huling, *Young Black Men and the Criminal Justice System: Five Years Later* (Washington DC: The Sentencing Project, 1995).
8. Joanne Belknap, *The Invisible Woman: Gender, Crime, and Justice* (Belmont, CA: Wadsworth Publishing, 1996), 98.
9. Christopher Davis, Richard Estes, and Vincent Schiraldi, "Three Strikes: The New Apartheid" (San Francisco: Centre on Juvenile and Criminal Justice, 1996).
10. Russell P. Dobash, R. Emerson Dobash, and Sue Gutteridge, *The Imprisonment of Women* (Oxford: Basil Blackwell, 1986).
11. Mike Davis, "A Prison-Industrial Complex: Hell Factories in the Field," *The Nation* 260, no. 7 (1995): 229–33.
12. *Making Standards Work: An International Handbook on Good Prison Practice* (The Hague: Penal Reform International, 1995), 13.
13. *Making Standards Work*, 14.
14. *Making Standards Work*, 59.
15. Esther Heffernan, *Making It in Prison: The Square, the Cool, and the Life* (New York: Wiley-Interscience, 1972).
16. *Making Standards Work, 130*, our emphasis.
17. E. Lloyd, *Prisoners and Their Children* (London: Save the Children Fund, 1995).
18. Lloyd, *Prisoners and Their Children.*
19. See Ellen Barry's discussion of pregnant women in US prisons in "Pregnant Prisoners," *Harvard Women's Law Journal* 12 (1989).
20. Penal Reform International, *Making Standards Work*, 136.
21. See Kum-Kum Bhavnani and Angela Y. Davis, "Incarcerated Women: Transformative Strategies," in *Psychology and Society: Radical Theory and Practice*, ed. Ian Parker and Russell Spears (London: Pluto Press, 1996), 173–83.
22. Charlotte Bunch, "Transforming Human Rights from a Feminist Perspective," in *Women's Rights, Human Rights: International Feminist Perspectives*, edited by Julie Peters and Andrea Wolper (New York: Routledge, 1995).
23. *Making Standards Work*, 14.
24. "Sheriff in Arizona Uses Female Chain Gang," *Washington Post*, September 20, 1996.
25. See William L. Patterson, ed. *We Charge Genocide: The Crime of Government Against the Negro People* (New York: International Publishers, 1971).
26. *Making Standards Work*, 14.
27. Barbara Rose Johnston, "Environmental Degradation and Human Rights Abuse," in *Who Pays the Price? The Sociocultural Context of Environmental Crisis*, edited by Barbara Rose Johnston (Washington: Island Press, 1994).
28. Marguerite Guzman Bouvard, "A New Model in the Struggle for Human Rights," in *Revolutionizing Motherhood: The Mothers of the Plaza de Mayo* (Wilmington, DE: Scholarly Resources, 1994).

Bibliography

ACE Program. *Breaking the Walls of Silence: AIDS and Women in a New York State Maximum Security Prison*. Woodstock, NY: The Overlook Press, 1998.

American Bar Association and National Bar Association. *Justice by Gender: The Lack of Appropriate Prevention, Diversion and Treatment Alternatives for Girls in the Juvenile Justice System*. Washington, DC: ABA and NBA, 2001.

American Civil Liberties Union Immigrant Rights Project. *Justice Detained: Conditions at the Varick Street Immigration Detention Center*. New York: ACLU, 1993.

Amnesty International. *"Not Part of My Sentence": Violations of the Human Rights of Women in Custody*. New York: Amnesty International, 1999.

Aptheker, Herbert, ed. "Frederick Douglass Discusses Slavery." In *Documentary History of the Negro People*. New York: Citadel Press, 1969.

Arnold, Regina. "Processes of Victimization and Criminalization of Black Women." *Social Justice* 17, no. 2 (1990), 153–166.

Barry, Ellen. "Pregnant Prisoners." *Harvard Women's Law Journal 12* (1989), 184–188.

Barry, Richard. "Slavery in the South To-Day." *Cosmopolitan Magazine* 42, no. 5 (March 1907): 481. Reproduced in *Racism at the Turn of the Century: Documentary Perspectives, 1870–1910*, edited by Donald P. DeNevi and Doris A. Holmes. San Rafael, California: Leswing Press, 1973.

Beaumont, Gustave de., and Alexis de Tocqueville. *On the Penitentiary System in the United States and Its Application in France*. Carbondale and Edwardsville: Southern Illinois University Press, 1964 [original edition, 1833].

Beckett, Katherine. *Making Crime Pay: Law and Order in Contemporary American Politics*. New York: Oxford University Press, 1997.

Belknap, Joanne. *The Invisible Woman: Gender, Crime, and Justice*. Belmont, CA: Wadsworth Publishing, 1996.

Bell, Derrick A., Jr. "After We're Gone: Prudent Speculations on America in a Post-Racial Epoch." In *Critical Race Theory: The Cutting Edge*, edited by Richard Delgado and Jean Stefancic. Philadelphia: Temple University Press, 1995.

———. "Serving Two Masters: Integration Ideals and Client Interests in School Desegregation Litigation" and "*Brown v. Board of Education* and the Interest Convergence Dilemma." In *Critical Race Theory: The Key Writings that Formed the Movement*, edited by Kimberlé Crenshaw, Neil Gotanda, Gary Peller, and Kendall Thomas, 5–28. New York, New Press, 1995.

———. "The Space Traders." In *Faces at the Bottom of the Well: The Permanence of*

Racism, 158–94. New York: Basic Books, 1992.

Berkman, Ronald. *Opening the Gates: The Rise of the Prisoner's Movement.* Lexington, MA: Lexington Books, 1979.

Bhavnani, Kum-Kum. *Talking Politics: A Psychological Framing for Views from Youth in Britain.* Cambridge: Cambridge University Press, 1991.

Bhavnani, Kum-Kum, and Angela Y. Davis. "Incarcerated Women: Transformative Strategies." In *Psychology and Society: Radical Theory and Practice,* edited by Ian Parker and Russell Spears, 173–83. London: Pluto Press, 1996.

Bloom, Barbara, and David Steinhart. *Why Punish the Children?* San Francisco: National Council on Crime and Delinquency, 1993.

Bouvard, Marguerite Guzman. "A New Model in the Struggle for Human Rights." In *Revolutionizing Motherhood: The Mothers of the Plaza de Mayo,* 219–40. Wilmington, DE: Scholarly Resources, 1994.

Braithwaite, John. *Crime, Shame and Reintegration.* Cambridge: Cambridge University Press, 1989.

Brenzel, Barbara. *Daughters of the State: A Social Portrait of the First Reform School for Girls in North America.* Cambridge, MA: MIT Press, 1983.

Brochier, J. J. "Prison Talk: An Interview with Michel Foucault." In *Power/Knowledge: Selected Interviews and Other Writings,* edited by Colin Gordon. New York: Pantheon, 1980.

Bunch, Charlotte. "Transforming Human Rights from a Feminist Perspective." In *Women's Rights, Human Rights: International Feminist Perspectives,* edited by Julie Peters and Andrea Wolper, 11–17. New York: Routledge, 1995.

Burkhart, Kathryn. *Women in Prison.* New York: Doubleday, 1973.

Bush-Baskette, Stephanie R. "The 'War on Drugs': A War Against Women?" In *Harsh Punishment: International Experiences of Women's Imprisonment,* edited by Sandy Cook and Susanne Davies, 211–29. Boston: Northeastern University Press, 1999.

California Department of Corrections. *Monthly Ethnicity Population Report.* November 2000. www.cdc.state.ea.us/reports/montheth.htm.

Campbell, Davara. Unpublished interview on file with Justice Now. Central California Women's Facility. July 16, 1999.

Campbell, James. S. "Revival of the Eighth Amendment: Development of Cruel-Punishment Doctrine by the Supreme Court." *Stanford Law Review* 16, no. 4 (July 1964): 996–1015.

Carlen, Pat. *Alternatives to Women's Imprisonment.* Milton Keynes: Open University Press, 1990.

Carlen, Pat, ed. *Criminal Women.* Cambridge: Polity Press, 1985.

———. *Women, Crime and Poverty.* Philadelphia: Open University Press, 1988.

———. *Women's Imprisonment: A Study in Social Control.* London: Routledge and Kegan Paul, 1983.

Characteristics of Population in California State Prisons by Institution. June 30, 2000.

Department of Corrections Services Division. Offender Information Services Branch. Estimates and Statistical Analysis Section Data Analysis Unit. Sacramento, CA.

Chevigny, Bell, ed. *Doing Time: Twenty-Five Years of Prison Writing.* New York: Arcade Publishing, 1999.

Clark, Charles S. "Prison Overcrowding." *Congressional Quarterly Researcher* 4, no. 5 (February 4, 1994): 97–119.

Clark, Judy, and Kathy Boudin. "Community of Women Organize Themselves to Cope with the AIDS Crisis: A Case Study from Bedford Hills Correctional Facility." *Social Justice* 17, no. 2 (1990): 90–109.

Cook, Dee, and Barbara Hudson, eds. *Racism and Criminology.* London: Sage Publications, 1993.

Cook, Sandy, and Susanne Davies, eds. *Harsh Punishment: International Experiences of Women's Imprisonment.* Boston: Northeastern University Press, 1999.

Cookson, Harriet. "A Survey of Self-Injury in a Closed Prison for Women." *British Journal of Criminology* 17, no. 4 (1977): 332–47.

Churchill, Ward, and Vander Wall, J. J. eds. *Cages of Steel: The Politics of Imprisonment in the United States.* Washington, DC: Maisonneuve Press, 1992.

Crenshaw, Kimberlé. "Mapping the Margins: Intersectionality, Identity Politics, and Violence Against Women of Color." In *Critical Race Theory: The Key Writings that Formed the Movement,* edited by Kimberlé Crenshaw, Neil Gotanda, Gary Peller, and Kendall Thomas, 357–83. New York: New Press, 1995.

Crenshaw, Kimberlé, Neil Gotanda, Gary Peller, and Kendall Thomas, eds. *Critical Race Theory: The Key Writings That Formed the Movement.* New York: New Press, 1995.

Currie, Elliott. *Crime and Punishment in America.* New York: Metropolitan Books, 1998.

Davis, Angela Y. "From the Prison of Slavery to the Slavery of Prison: Frederick Douglass and the Convict Lease System." In *The Angela Y. Davis Reader,* edited by Joy James, 74–95. Malden, Mass.: Blackwell, 1998.

———. "Public Imprisonment and Private Violence: Reflections on the Hidden Punishment of Women." *New England Journal on Criminal and Civil Confinement* 24, no. 2 (Summer 1998).

———. *Women, Race and Class.* New York: Random House, 1981.

Davis, Christopher, Richard Estes, and Vincent Schiraldi. "Three Strikes: The New Apartheid." San Francisco: Centre on Juvenile and Criminal Justice, 1996.

Davis, Mike. "A Prison-Industrial Complex: Hell Factories in the Field," *Nation* 260, no. 7 (1995): 229–33.

Dayan, Colin. *The Story of Cruel and Unusual.* Cambridge, MA: MIT Press, 2007, 7–8.

De Groot, A., T. Hammett, and K. Scheib. "Barriers to Care of HIV-Infected Inmates: A Public Health Concern." In *The AIDS Reader* (May/June 1996).

de Haan, Willem. *The Politics of Redress: Crime, Punishment and Penal Abolition*. London: Unwin Hyman, 1990.

———. "Abolitionism and the Politics of 'Bad Conscience.'" In *Abolitionism: Toward a Non-Repressive Approach to Crime*, edited by Herman Bianchi and Rene van Swaaningen. Amsterdam: Free University Press, 1986.

Del Olmo, Rosa. "The Economic Crisis and the Criminalization of Latin American Women." *Social Justice* 17, no. 2 (Summer 1990): 40–53.

Dickens, Charles. *The Works of Charles Dickens*, Vol. 27 of *American Notes*. New York: Peter Fenelon Collier and Son, 1900.

Dobash, Russell P., R. Emerson Dobash, and Sue Gutteridge. *The Imprisonment of Women*. Oxford: Basil Blackwell, 1986.

Donziger, Steven R., ed. *The Real War on Crime: The Report of the National Criminal Justice Commission*. New York: Harper Perennial, 1996.

Douglass, Frederick. "Address to the People of the United States." Speech delivered at a Convention of Colored Men, Louisville, Kentucky, September 24, 1883. In *Life and Writings of Frederick Douglass*. Vol. 4. Edited by Philip Foner. New York: International Publishers, 1955.

———. "An Appeal to the British People." Reception speech at Finsbury Chapel, Moorfields, England, May 12, 1846. In *Life and Writings of Frederick Douglass*. Vol. 1. Edited by Philip Foner. New York: International Publishers, 1950.

———. "The Color Line." *North American Review* 132 (June 1881). Reprinted in *Life and Writings of Frederick Douglass*. Vol. 4. Edited by Philip Foner. New York: International Publishers, 1955.

———. "The Condition of the Freedman." *Harper's Weekly*. December 8, 1883. In *Life and Writings of Frederick Douglass*. Vol. 4. Edited by Philip Foner. New York: International Publishers, 1955.

———. "The Need for Continuing Anti-Slavery Work." Speech at 32nd Annual Meeting of the American Anti-Slavery Society, May 9, 1865. In *Life and Writings of Frederick Douglass*. Vol. 4. edited by Philip Foner. New York: International Publishers, 1955.

———. "The Negro Exodus from the Gulf States." Address before convention of the American Social Science Association, Saratoga Springs, September 12, 1879. *Journal of Social Science* 11 (May 1880): 1–21. Reprinted in *Life and Writings of Frederick Douglass*. Vol. 4. edited by Philip Foner. New York: International Publishers, 1955.

———. "Southern Barbarism." Speech on the occasion of the twenty-fourth anniversary of emancipation in the District of Columbia, Washington, DC, 1886. In *Life and Writings of Frederick Douglass*. Vol. 4. Edited by Philip Foner. New York: International Publishers, 1955.

———. "The United States Cannot Remain Half-Slave and Half-Free." Speech on the occasion of the twenty-first anniversary of emancipation in the District of Columbia, April 1883. In *Life and Writings of Frederick Douglass*. Vol. 4. Edited

by Philip Foner. New York: International Publishers, 1955.
———. "Why Is the Negro Lynched?" In *Life and Writings of Frederick Douglass*. Vol. 4. Edited by Philip Foner. New York: International Publishers, 1955.
Drescher, Seymour, ed. *Tocqueville and Beaumont on Social Reform*. New York: Harper Torchbooks, 1968.
Du Bois, W. E. B. *Black Reconstruction*. New York: Russell and Russell, 1963.
———. "The Spawn of Slavery: The Convict Lease System of the South." *Missionary Review of The World* 24, no. 10 (New Series, vol. xiv): 737–45.
Dyer, Joel. *The Perpetual Prisoner Machine: How America Profits from Crime*. Boulder, CO: Westview Press, 2000.
Eaton, Mary. *Women After Prison*. Buckingham: Open University Press, 1993.
Federal Bureau of Prisons. "Quick Facts: April 2001." accessed June 1, 2001. http://www.bop.gov/fact0598.html#Citizenship.
Fellner, Jamie, and Marc Mauer. "Losing the Vote: The Impact of Felony Disenfranchisement Laws in the United States." The Sentencing Project and Human Rights Watch, 1998.
Fierce, Milfred. *Slavery Revisited: Blacks and the Southern Convict Lease System, 1865–1933*. New York: Brooklyn College, CUNY, Africana Studies Research Center, 1994.
Fletcher, Beverly R., Lynda Dixon Shaver, and Dreama G. Moon. *Women Prisoners: A Forgotten Population*. Westport, CT: Praeger, 1993.
Foner, Philip, ed. *Life and Writings of Frederick Douglass*. Vol. 4. New York: International Publishers, 1955.
Foster, Thomas W. "Make-Believe Families: A Response of Women and Girls to the Deprivations of Imprisonment." *International Journal of Criminology and Penology* 3, no. 1 (1975): 71–8.
Foucault, Michel. *Discipline and Punish: The Birth of the Prison*. Translated Alan Sheridan. New York: Vintage, 1979.
Franklin, John Hope. *From Slavery to Freedom*. New York: Vintage, 1969.
Freedman, Estelle B. *Their Sisters' Keepers: Women's Prison Reform in America, 1830–1930*. Ann Arbor: University of Michigan Press, 1991.
Friedman, Lawrence M. *Crime and Punishment in American History*. New York: Basic Books, 1993.
Gaubatz, Kathryn Taylor. *Crime in the Public Mind*. Ann Arbor: University of Michigan Press, 1995.
Garcia, Maria, and Gina Mendoza. Legal interview. October 20, 1998. Valley State Prison for Women.
George, Amanda. "The New Prison Culture: Making Millions from Misery." In *Harsh Punishment: International Experiences of Women's Imprisonment*, edited by Sandy Cook and Susanne Davies, 189–210. Boston: Northeastern University Press, 1999.
Giallombardo, Rose. *Society of Women: A Study of a Women's Prison*. New York: John

Wiley, 1966.

Gibbons, John J., and Nicholas de B. Katzenbach. "Confronting Confinement: A Report of the Commission on Safety and Abuse in America's Prisons." New York: Vera Institute of Justice, 2006. https://www.vera.org/downloads/publications/Confronting_Confinement.pdf.

Gilliard, Darrell K. "Prison and Jail Inmates at Midyear 1998." Bureau of Justice Statistics. March 1999. NCJ 173414.

Gilmore, Ruth Wilson. "Globalization and U.S. Prison Growth: From Military Keynesianism to Post-Keynesian Militarism." *Race and Class* 40, nos. 2/3 (1998–99): 171–88.

Goldberg, David Theo. *Racist Culture: Philosophy and the Politics of Meaning*. Malden, Mass.: Blackwell, 1993.

Goldberg, David Theo. "Wedded to Dixie: Dinesh D'Souza and the New Segregationism." In *Racial Subjects: Writing on Race in America*. New York: Routledge, 1997.

Gotanda, Neil. "A Critique of 'Our Constitution Is Color-Blind.'" In *Critical Race Theory: The Key Writings that Formed the Movement*, edited by Kimberlé Crenshaw et al. New York: New Press, 1995.

Grace, Sharon, et al., ed. *Criminal Women: Gender Matters*. Bristol, UK: Bristol University Press, 2022. https://doi.org/10.56687/9781529208443

Greenfield, Lawrence, A., and Stephanie Minor-Harper. *Women in Prison*. Washington, DC: US Dept. of Justice, Office of Justice Programs, Bureau of Statistics, 1991.

Greenfield, Lawrence A., and Tracy L. Snell. *Women Offenders*. Bureau of Justice Statistics Special Report. Washington, DC: US Department of Justice, 1999.

Guinier, Lani. *The Tyranny of the Majority: Fundamental Fairness in Representative Democracy*. New York: Free Press, 1994.

Hall, Stuart, Chas Critcher, Tony Jefferson, John Clarke, and Brian Roberts, *Policing the Crisis: Mugging, the State and Law and Order*. New York: Holmes and Meier Publishers, 1978.

Hancock, Linda. "Economic Pragmatism and the Ideology of Sexism: Prison Policy and Women." *Women's Studies International Forum* 9, no. 1 (1986): 101–7.

Harris, Cheryl. "Whiteness As Property." In *Critical Race Theory: The Key Writings That Formed the Movement*, edited by Kimberlé Crenshaw et al. New York: New Press, 1995.

Hawkins, Richard and Geoffrey P. Alpert. *American Prison Systems: Punishment and Justice*. Englewood Cliffs, NJ: Prentice-Hall, 1989.

Heffernan, Esther. *Making It in Prison: The Square, the Cool, and the Life*. New York: Wiley-Interscience, 1972.

Hirsch, Adam J. *The Rise of the Penitentiary: Prisons and Punishment in Early America*. New Haven and London: Yale University Press, 1992.

Howe, Adrian. "Prologue to a History of Women's Imprisonment: In Search for a

Feminist Perspective." *Social Justice* 17, no. 2 (1990): 4–22.

———. *Punish and Critique: Toward a Feminist Analysis of Penality*. London: Routledge, 1994.

Hull, Elizabeth A. *The Disenfranchisement of Ex-Felons*. Philadelphia: Temple University Press, 2006, 17.

Human Rights Watch. *All Too Familiar: Sexual Abuse of Women in U.S. State Prisons*. New York: Human Rights Watch, 1996.

———. *Cold Storage: Super-Maximum Security Confinement in Indiana*. New York: Human Rights Watch, October 1997.

———. *Letter to INS Commissioner Doris Meisner*. New York: Human Rights Watch, 2000.

———. *Locked Away: Immigration Detainees in Jails in the United States*. New York: Human Rights Watch, 1998.

Irwin, John, and James Austin. *It's About Time: America's Imprisonment Binge*. 2nd ed. Belmont, CA: Wadsworth Publishing, 1997.

Jackson, Kim. "Patriarchal Justice and the Control of Women." *New Studies on the Left* (Spring 1989): 153–71.

Jacobs, James B. *Stateville: The Penitentiary in Mass Society*. Chicago: University of Chicago Press, 1977.

Johnston, Barbara Rose. "Environmental Degradation and Human Rights Abuse." In *Who Pays the Price? The Sociocultural Context of Environmental Crisis*, edited by Barbara Rose Johnston, 7–15. Washington: Island Press, 1994.

Johnson, Regina. Legal interview. March 3, 1998. Valley State Prison for Women.

Jose Kampfner, Christina. "Coming to Terms with Existential Death: An Analysis of Women's Adaptation to Life in Prison." *Social Justice* 17, no. 2 (1990): 11–125.

Kruttschnitt, Candace. "Race Relations and the Female Inmate." *Crime and Delinquency* 29, no. 4 (October 1983): 588–89.

Kupers, Terry. *Prison Madness: The Mental Health Crisis Behind Bars and What We Must Do About It*. San Francisco: Jossey-Bass, 2000.

Lichtenstein, Alexander C., and Michael A. Kroll. "The Fortress Economy: The Economic Role of the US Prison System." In *Criminal Injustice: Confronting the Prison Crisis*, edited by Elihu Rosenblatt, 16–39. Boston: South End Press, 1996.

Live Jail-Cam. May 23, 2001. www.crime.com.

Lloyd, E. *Prisoners and Their Children*. London: Save the Children Fund, 1995.

Lubiano, Wahneema. "Black Ladies, Welfare Queens, and State Minstrels: Ideological War by Narrative Means." In *Race-ing Justice, En-gendering Power: Essays on Anita Hill, Clarence Thomas, and the Construction of Social Reality*, edited by Toni Morrison, 323–63. New York: Pantheon, 1992.

Making Standards Work: An International Handbook on Good Prison Practice. The Hague: Penal Reform International, 1995.

Mancini, Matthew J. *One Dies, Get Another: Convict Leasing in the American South, 1866–1928*. Columbia: University of South Carolina Press, 1996.

Manza, Jeff, and Christopher Uggen. *Locked Out: Felon Disenfranchisement and American Democracy*. New York: Oxford University Press, 2006.

Mauer, Marc. *Young Black Men and the Criminal Justice System: A Growing National Problem*. Washington, DC: The Sentencing Project, 1990.

Mauer, Marc, and Tracy Huling. *Young Black Men and the Criminal Justice System: Five Years Later*. Washington, DC: The Sentencing Project, 1995.

McDermid, Lea, Kathleen Connolly, Dan Macallair, and Vincent Shiraldi. *From Classrooms to Cellblocks: How Prison Building Affects Higher Education and African American Enrollment in California*. Washington, DC: Justice Policy Institute, 1996.

McDermott, Kathleen, and Roy King. "Mind Games: Where the Action Is in Prisons." *British Journal of Criminology* 28, no. 3 (1988): 357–77.

McFeely, William S. *Frederick Douglass*. New York: W. W. Norton, 1991.

Miller, Tekla Dennison. *The Warden Wore Pink*. Brunswick, ME: Biddle Publishing, 1996.

Miller, Jerome G. *Search and Destroy: African-American Males and the Criminal Justice System*. Cambridge: Cambridge University Press, 1996.

Mosley, Albert G., and Nicholas Capaldi. *Affirmative Action: Social Justice or Unfair Preference*. New York: Rowman and Littlefield, 1996.

Newsome, Melba. "Hard Time." *Essence Magazine* 31, no. 5 (2000): 146–50, 210–14.

Nightline. *Crime & Punishment: Women in Prison: Medical Care*. November 2, 1999

Olivas, Michael A. "The Chronicles, My Grandfather's Stories, and Immigration Law: The Slave Traders Chronicle as Racial History." In *Critical Race Theory: The Cutting Edge*, edited by Richard Delgado, 15–24. Philadelphia: Temple University Press, 1995.

Orland, Leonard. *Prisons: Houses of Darkness*. New York: Free Press, 1975.

Oshinsky, David. *Worse Than Slavery: Parchman Farm and the Jim Crow Justice System*. New York: Free Press, 1996.

Rafter, Nicole Hahn. *Creating Born Criminals*. Urbana: University of Illinois Press, 1998.

Reiman, Jeffrey. *The Rich Get Richer and the Poor Get Prison: Ideology, Crime and Criminal Justice*. 3rd ed. New York: Macmillan, 1990.

Richie, Beth E. *Compelled to Crime: The Gender Entrapment of Battered Black Women*. New York: Routledge, 1996.

Rosenblatt, Elihu, ed. *Criminal Injustice: Confronting the Prison Crisis*. Boston: South End Press, 1996.

Ross, Luana. *Inventing the Savage: The Social Construction of Native American Criminality*. Austin: University of Texas Press, 1998.

Rotman, Edgardo. *Beyond Punishment: A New View on the Rehabilitation of Criminal Offenders*. New York: Greenwood Press, 1990.

Selke, William L. *Prisons in Crisis*. Bloomington: Indiana University Press, 1993.

Simmons, A. John, Marshall Cohen, Joshua Cohen, and Charles R. Beitz eds. *Punishment: A Philosophy and Public Affairs Reader*. Princeton: Princeton University Press, 1995.

Smart, Carol. *Women, Crime and Criminology: A Feminist Critique*. London: Routledge and Kegan Paul, 1976.

Steinberg, Susann. Deputy Director of Health Care Services Division, California Department of Corrections, meeting with prisoner advocates. Sacramento, CA: California Department of Corrections, October 10, 2000.

Stern, Vivien. *A Sin Against the Future: Imprisonment in the World*. Boston: Northeastern University Press, 1998.

Sudbury, Julia. "Transatlantic Visions: Resisting the Globalization of Mass Incarceration." *Social Justice* 27, no. 3 (2000): 133–49.

Terrell, Mary Church. "Peonage in the United States: The Convict Lease System and the Chain Gang." *The Nineteenth Century* 62 (August 1907): 306–22.

Tobias, D. E. "A Negro on the Position of the Negro in America." *The Nineteenth Century* 46, no. 274 (December 1899): 957–73.

Tocqueville, Alexis de. *Democracy in America*. Vol. 1. New York: Vintage Books, 1954.

Tonry, Michael, ed. *The Future of Imprisonment*. New York, Oxford University Press, 2004.

Truth to Power: Women Testify at Legislative Hearings. Excerpts from Legislative Hearings on Women in Prison at Valley State Prison for Women, October 11, 2000, and California Institution for Women, October 12, 2000. Produced by Women in Prison Emergency Network, 2000. Videocassette, 40 min.

UN Special Rapporteur on Violence Against Women. *Report of the Mission to the United States of American on the Issue of Violence against Women in State and Federal Prisons*. New York: United Nations Economic and Social Council, 1999.

Van Swaaningen, Ren[ac]e, and Gerard de Jonge. "The Dutch Prison System and Penal Policy in the 1990s: From Humanitarian Paternalism to Penal Business Management." In *Western European Penal Systems: A Critical Anatomy, edited by* Vincenzo Ruggiero, Mick Ryan, and Joe Sim. London: Sage Publications, 1995.

Walker, Samuel, Cassia Spohn, and Miriam DeLone. *The Color of Justice: Race, Ethnicity, and Crime in America*. Belmont, CA: Wadsworth Publishing, 1996.

Washington, Mary Helen. "Prison Studies as Part of American Studies." *American Studies Newsletter* 22, no. 1 (March 1999).

Welch, Michael. "The Role of Immigration and Naturalization Service in the Prison-Industrial Complex." *Social Justice* 27, no. 3 (2000): 73–88.

West, Cornel. *Race Matters*. Boston: Beacon Press, 1993.

Whitin, E. Stagg. *Penal Servitude*. New York: National Committee on Prison Labor, 1912.

Wilbanks, William. *The Myth of a Racist Criminal Justice System*. Monterey, CA: Brooks Cole, 1987.

Williams, Fiona. *Social Policy: A Critical Introduction*, Cambridge: Polity Press, 1989.

Wolleswinkel, R. personal communication, 1996.

Wright, Albert, Jr. "Young Inmates Need Help, From Inside and Out." *Emerge* (October 1997).

Zedner, Lucia. "Wayward Sisters: The Prison for Women." In *The Oxford History of the Prison*, edited by Norval Morris and David J. Rothman. New York and Oxford: Oxford University Press, 1998.

Index

"Passim" (literally "scattered") indicates intermittent discussion of a topic over a cluster of pages.

About Haymarket Books

Haymarket Books is a radical, independent, nonprofit book publisher based in Chicago. Our mission is to publish books that contribute to struggles for social and economic justice. We strive to make our books a vibrant and organic part of social movements and the education and development of a critical, engaged, and internationalist Left.

We take inspiration and courage from our namesakes, the Haymarket Martyrs, who gave their lives fighting for a better world. Their 1886 struggle for the eight-hour day—which gave us May Day, the international workers' holiday—reminds workers around the world that ordinary people can organize and struggle for their own liberation. These struggles—against oppression, exploitation, environmental devastation, and war—continue today across the globe.

Since our founding in 2001, Haymarket has published more than nine hundred titles. Radically independent, we seek to drive a wedge into the risk-averse world of corporate book publishing. Our authors include Angela Y. Davis, Arundhati Roy, Keeanga-Yamahtta Taylor, Eve L. Ewing, Aja Monet, Mariame Kaba, Naomi Klein, Rebecca Solnit, Olúfẹ́mi O. Táíwò, Mohammed El-Kurd, José Olivarez, Noam Chomsky, Winona LaDuke, Robyn Maynard, Leanne Betasamosake Simpson, Howard Zinn, Mike Davis, Marc Lamont Hill, Dave Zirin, Astra Taylor, and Amy Goodman, among many other leading writers of our time. We are also the trade publishers of the acclaimed Historical Materialism Book Series.

Haymarket also manages a vibrant community organizing and event space in Chicago, Haymarket House, the popular Haymarket Books Live event series and podcast, and the annual Socialism Conference.

Also Available from Haymarket Books

Abolition. Feminism. Now.
Angela Y. Davis, Gina Dent, Erica R. Meiners, and Beth E. Richie

Abolition for the People
The Movement for a Future without Policing and Prisons
Edited by Colin Kaepernick

Angela Davis: An Autobiography
Angela Y. Davis

Assata Taught Me
State Violence, Racial Capitalism, and the Movement for Black Lives
Donna Murch

Border and Rule
Global Migration, Capitalism, and the Rise of Racist Nationalism
Harsha Walia, afterword by Nick Estes, foreword by Robin D. G. Kelley

Clara Zetkin: Selected Writings
Clara Zetkin, edited by Philip S. Foner, foreword by Rosalyn Baxandall, introduction by Angela Y. Davis

From #BlackLivesMatter to Black Liberation
Keeanga-Yamahtta Taylor, foreword by Angela Y. Davis

Freedom Is a Constant Struggle:
Ferguson, Palestine, and the Foundations of a Movement
Angela Y. Davis, edited by Frank Barat, preface by Cornel West

Rehearsals for Living
Robyn Maynard and Leanne Betasamosake Simpson, afterword by Robin D. G. Kelley, foreword by Ruth Wilson Gilmore

About the Author

Angela Y. Davis is Professor Emerita of History of Consciousness and Feminist Studies at UC Santa Cruz. An activist, writer, and lecturer, her work focuses on prisons, police, abolition, and the related intersections of race, gender, and class. She is the author of many books, from *Angela Davis: An Autobiography* to *Freedom Is a Constant Struggle.*